KV-352-491

Children's Fiction

A HANDBOOK FOR LIBRARIANS

Sheila G. Ray B.A, F.L.A.

BROCKHAMPTON PRESS

54671

All rights reserved. No part of this publication
may be reproduced or transmitted in any form or
by any means, electronic or mechanical, including
photocopy, recording, or any information storage
and retrieval system, without permission in writing
from the publisher.

ISBN 0 340 10415 5

First edition 1970
Published by Brockhampton Press Ltd, Salisbury Road, Leicester
Printed in Great Britain by C. Tinling and Co. Ltd, Prescot
Text copyright © 1970 Sheila G. Ray

ST. MARY'S COLLEGE
LIBRARY
CHELTENHAM

CHILDREN'S FICTION

LIBRARIANS

This Book must be returned to
the Library on, or before, the
last date shown below.

Contents

Author's note

1 Introduction *page 7*
2 Traditional stories 11
3 Fantasy 23
4 Animal stories 33
5 Pony stories 38
6 Adventure stories 45
7 Science fiction 58
8 Family stories 66
9 School and career stories 78
10 Stories set in other countries 89
11 Historical fiction 101
12 Humour in fiction 113
13 Short stories 121
14 Classes of fiction 127
15 Fiction series 135
16 Paperback fiction 143
17 Fiction in translation 149
18 Prizewinning fiction 154
19 Illustration in fiction 161
20 Fiction for backward readers 166
21 Fiction for immigrants 173
22 Fiction for teenagers 177
23 Publishers of fiction 188
24 Read on from here 197
   Appendix—list of publishers 213
   Index 221

Author's note

THIS is not intended to be a guide to the best children's books; I have mentioned books which seemed to be good examples of the points I wished to make, but I have omitted many which are worthwhile and which children enjoy. For this reason, it seemed best not to include any lists of children's books. I have, therefore, tried to provide in the text sufficient information to identify a book, and where a paperback edition is available, this is usually indicated. In the case of classics where there are a number of editions I have indicated only one. Details of books in print published before the 1st January, 1969, can usually be found in *Children's Books in Print*, 1969. There is a full list of publishers with their addresses in the Appendix.

I should like to record my thanks to those children's librarians who have helped me to keep in touch, particularly Mr W. E. Yates and Mrs Judith Elkin of Birmingham Public Libraries, to Messrs Dunn and Wilson Ltd, to those publishers who so willingly answered my questions, to Antony Kamm of Brockhampton Press, who encouraged me to write this book, to my students of 1969–70 who first heard much of this material in the form of lectures and, above all, to my husband without whose patient assistance it would never have seen the light of day.

Introduction

IN recent years there has been a growing pre-occupation amongst publishers, booksellers, teachers, children's librarians and parents with the promotion of purposeful information books. Children have been stimulated to make increasing use of books to find things out for themselves, and in the campaign for self-improvement and the need to provide in school libraries and children's libraries tools geared to this need, there has been a tendency to overlook the equally important need to encourage children to read at least some of the wealth of imaginative literature which is intended for them. There is a danger that at the very moment when children's literature is receiving increased attention as a literature in its own right, when we have an increasing number of gifted writers producing books for children, this literature is likely to remain undiscovered by the majority of the public for whom it is intended—the children themselves.

This handbook to fiction is intended primarily for students preparing to become qualified librarians with a special interest in working with children and young people. It is also intended to help practising librarians who lack a specialist knowledge of children's books. Public library services to children are becoming increasingly important and there are few public librarians who do not come into contact with children at all during some part of their daily work, but not all of them, naturally, have the time to build up for themselves a body of specialized knowledge, through reading a wide range of books. I hope that this handbook will encourage the non-specialist librarian to explore at least a little among the books on the shelves in the children's library.

This material is arranged in the way which I feel will be most helpful to students preparing for the specialist papers in the Library Association Final Examination, the Registration Examination of the Library Association of Australia and the New Zealand Library Association Certificate. Many of the books mentioned fall into more than one conventional category under which they are discussed, while the second half of the book deals with areas which cover the whole range of categories but which are profitable subjects for discussion and further thought among students and colleagues. It is hoped that the index will compensate for any of the apparent discrepancies which arise from this arrangement.

Students in Colleges of Education, particularly those taking supplementary courses in children's literature and school librarianship, and practising teachers who want to acquire a basic knowledge of children's fiction will also find this outline relevant to their needs.

It does not set out to be a survey of 'best books', but a guide to those worthwhile books which children enjoy,—to introduce the adult to these and to help him identify other titles which can be used in the same way. It is no good expecting children always to read on the highest level; one must be realistic, and few children are going to be satisfied by a solid diet of Mayne and Sutcliffe. There is, however, a wealth of worthwhile children's books which are read and enjoyed by many children. I am very much concerned by the apparent gulf which exists between what critics admire and what children actually enjoy. I do not believe that this gulf is nearly as wide as it is sometimes thought to be, and I suspect that it could be narrowed considerably if adults took more trouble to find out what qualities in books appeal to children, and then looked for these qualities in those books which critics praise.

Children are very dependent on grown-ups—librarians, teachers and parents—for the books that they read, and the worst enemies of children's reading tastes may well be uninformed or misguided adults. Experience has shown that in libraries in some new towns which happen to lie in areas with high standards of library provision and an emphasis on quality in the selection of books, children acquire good reading tastes. In these new towns, the children have little home influence to affect their reading, and librarians and teachers, working together, have managed to implant a taste for quality. This is not to say that these children do not also enjoy comics and their book equivalents, but they do not expect to find them in the children's library. Children read on two levels, one of which is or should be catered for by librarians, teachers and parents; the other, as the need arises, by the children themselves with their own money.

The most popular books are those which children recommend to each other. Stories by authors who have written more than one book, and stories in series, are strong runners here. These books normally have a strong plot, clear characterization and a relatively unsophisticated style. They are the books which encourage the reading habit.

Books which are a little more difficult to read because of the way in which they are written can often move smoothly into this first group if they are introduced casually to children by some adult agency—teacher, librarian, parent, film or television. They can even be promoted through a reading programme or a very selective and imaginatively annotated booklist. These books of more apparent difficulty will widen children's horizons and enlarge their experience. Not all books which are featured in this way will become really popular, but there is little doubt that popularity can be stimulated and that children can be stirred from narrow and conservative tastes by the way in which a book is presented. The sincere enthusiasm of an adult can be very infectious.

A third group consists of those books which, having a good story and characters with whom the child reader can identify and sympathize easily, deter by a more complex style or contain difficult names (always a stumbling-block to some children). Reading aloud of part of the book will help a number of children over these stumbling-blocks when, unlike the most able readers, they may not be prepared to tackle them alone. The librarian will need to take particular care in the selection of such books since there is no point in making provision of material which will not be used unless he is prepared to take steps to promote it.

I have concerned myself mainly with fiction for children of nine to thirteen, since this is the age group for which most children's fiction is written. Nine is the age by which a high proportion of children are reading fluently; thirteen is the age by which many are moving on to adult books. But the fiction reading of the nine to thirteen year olds cannot be looked at completely in isolation, and I have therefore looked backwards to the picture book age and forwards to the adult novel, where this seemed appropriate, to round out the picture.

There is a need to promote and popularize modern authors of imaginative literature as well as to continue to provide good editions of the best of the old. Many books (quite rightly) continue to be read by succeeding generations of children. Books with outstanding qualities will usually stay in print, and be read and enjoyed for many years. Other books, perfectly good and valid for the generation for which they were written, can well be left behind, while some newer ones will need to be identified and rescued from the ever increasing output. What I hope will become very clear is the need for those adults who are in a position to influence children's reading to do so in an intelligent and imaginative but realistic way.

CHILDREN should have access to a wide range of traditional stories. These fairy tales, folk tales, hero tales, myths and legends, which have been handed down from one generation to the next, have their origins in the beginning of time; the story-teller was a much honoured member of the primitive tribe because he was the main source of popular entertainment. Although these stories have now been written down for people to read, their charm lies in the simple telling, the straightforward characterization, the simple plot and the element of repetition which bear witness to their oral origins. As anyone who has ever listened to a story knows, it is much easier to follow if it has a clear and uncomplicated plot and if the characters have striking qualities which differentiate them one from another, while the element of repetition both helped the story-teller and appealed to the listener.

These stories must have met the basic needs of the people who listened to them; they certainly meet the need which children and young people have, to hear and read stories about the youngest or the ill-treated child who, despite all the odds, succeeds and whose natural goodness is rewarded. Because these stories have developed out of an oral tradition, they provide a rich source of material for the teacher or librarian who wants a story to tell; because they were originally intended to appeal to an audience with a wide age-range and of mixed tastes, they are particularly suitable for the story-teller's audience, also likely to be of mixed ages and varied tastes.

In the case of some stories, there are many printed versions to choose from; the best are usually those which are most true to the spirit of the original, told in simple terms and simple language. Description, of course, is necessary when it is skilfully used to set the scene or to give atmosphere but it should not be allowed to spoil the essential simplicity of the original.

A number of traditional stories have been used very success-fully as the basis for picture books. The skilled artist, unable or unwilling to write his own original story, finds freedom in illustrating a traditional tale which he can adapt to his purposes, as opposed to matching his art to the text of another living person who has equal rights and a vested interest in the finished product. The simple style of the traditional story makes it suitable for picture book treatment in the hands of the creative artist. Victor Ambrus has used some traditional Hungarian stories such as *The three poor tailors* (O.U.P) and William Stobbs some English stories such as *Jack and the beanstalk* (Longmans Y.B) and *The story of the three little pigs* (Bodley Head). The charming story of *The tale of the turnip*, with its repetitive and cumulative patterns, is available in two attractive versions, one illustrated by Margery Gill, with the text by Anita Hewett (Bodley Head), another by Helen Oxenbury, as *The great big enormous turnip* (Heinemann). Brian Wildsmith has used several of La Fontaine's fables, for example *The rich man and the shoemaker* (O.U.P) which have the advantage of very little text but rather exotic human or animal characters, offering a rich inspiration to Wildsmith's style.

The teacher, librarian or parent looking for a story to tell will appreciate collections of stories chosen for this purpose, and anthologies which bring together, as do M. C. Carey's *Fairy tales of long ago* (Dent) or Kathleen Lines' *Jack and the beanstalk* (O.U.P), the best-known fairy stories are very useful.

One of the earliest collectors of fairy tales from many different sources was Andrew Lang who, between 1889 and 1910, published a series of 'colour' fairy books, starting with the *Blue fairy book* (Longmans Y.B). Many of his collections are still available in a modified form but Kathleen Lines has selected *Fifty favourite fairy tales* (Bodley Head), which provides a generous taste of the best.

Bodley Head have published a series of books geared to the needs of the story-teller. This series includes Ruth Sawyer's *The way of the story-teller* and Eileen Colwell's *A story-teller's choice*. Leila Berg's *Folk tales for reading and telling* (Brock-hampton) is another useful collection; all these include notes on how long the stories take to tell and helpful hints on how to tell them.

Hamish Hamilton and Methuen have both published collections of stories largely made up of traditional material, linked to a common theme. The Hamish Hamilton collections are edited by a number of distinguished writers including Alan Garner and William Mayne. Ruth Manning-Sanders, as well as editing *The Hamish Hamilton book of magical beasts*, is responsible for all the Methuen collections, the first of which, *A book of dragons*, was published in 1966.

Ruth Manning-Sanders is only one of a number of contemporary writers for children who have done outstanding work in retelling traditional stories in modern versions. Barbara Leonie Picard, Roger Lancelyn Green, James Reeves, Amabel Williams-Ellis, Rosemary Sutcliff, Ian Serraillier and, most recently, Kevin Crossley-Holland and Robert Nye have all produced versions of traditional stories which reflect some of the original spirit but at the same time are sufficiently modern in style to appeal to the children of today.

For each country or continent of the world there are traditional tales of all kinds. In some countries, the stories were originally brought together and written down by scholars whose names are now almost inseparably linked with the tales of their native countries—Jakob and Wilhelm Grimm with the German, Charles Perrault with the French and P. C. Asbjørnsen and J. Moe with the Norwegian stories.

The stories collected by the Grimm brothers were a by-product of their interest in the development of the German language. They were not written down for children and it is usually these stories of which adults are thinking when they complain of the unsuitability of fairy stories for children. One has only to compare the Grimm version of *Cinderella, Aschenputtel*, with Perrault's to see why. In the first, one step-sister cuts off her heel and the other, her toe, in order to try to make the glass slipper fit and, as they are taken in turn by the Prince on the back of his horse, the resulting blood drips down. Charles Perrault, on the other hand, wrote down his stories as they were told to his children by their nurse, and although they became popular and fashionable at the French

Court in the late seventeenth century, they are more suitable versions to use with younger children. At present, in this country, the most extensive Perrault collections are *Complete fairy tales* (Longmans Y.B) and *Fairy tales* (Cape). The best introduction to Grimm for children is through Wanda Gag's *Tales from Grimm* (Faber) and *More tales from Grimm* (Faber). There is an attractive version of Asbjørnsen and Moe's *Norwegian fairy tales* (Allen and Unwin).

The stories of Hans Christian Andersen, although inspired by the traditional folk-lore of Denmark, are really literary creations; they too, however, are available in a number of attractive editions, of which every library ought to include *Fairy tales and legends* (Bodley Head), which is beautifully illustrated by Rex Whistler.

Not nearly as well known as it should be is Arthur Ransome's *Old Peter's Russian tales* (Nelson), a collection of traditional stories which Ransome made during his Russian travels and which he set down as if they were being told by Old Peter to his grandchildren, Vanya and Maroosia.

There are several series which provide a representative coverage of the traditional stories of the world. Perhaps the most notable of these series is the 'Oxford myths and legends' (O.U.P), to which additions are still being made. More suitable for younger children are the collections of 'Favourite fairy tales told in . . .' (Bodley Head), made by Virginia Haviland, the Librarian of the Children's Services Division of the Library of Congress, and drawn from the vast resources of America's national library. Each volume contains up to half-a-dozen representative stories and is generously illustrated. There is also a 'Fairy tales of the world' series, from Muller; this systematically covers the countries of the world and there are some unusual selections. Some of the volumes are a little on the dull side in their choice of stories, but Roger Duvoisin's *Swiss fairy tales* (Muller) is a very good example of the best of the series. The most recent Muller volumes are in a new and more attractive format, with slightly larger pages, better margins, better paper and a second colour added to the original line illustrations.

Britain, it must be remembered, is made up of four separate countries, each with its own traditional tales. The English equivalent of the Grimms and Perrault was the much less well-known Joseph Jacobs and there is a fine collection of his *English fairy tales* (Bodley Head). James Reeves' *English fables and fairy stories* (O.U.P) provides a useful starting point and there are other 'Oxford myths and legends' volumes for Wales, Scotland and Ireland.

Beowulf, Havelok, King Arthur and his knights, and Robin Hood are folk heroes whose adventures have appeared in many versions from very early times and the writers of the '60s have added to these. Two good starting points are Barbara Leonie Picard's *Hero tales from the British Isles* (Kaye and Ward *and* Puffin) and *Tales of the British people* (Kaye and Ward). The latter includes the legend of Beowulf which can also be introduced to children in a number of other versions—Ian Serraillier's poetic retelling, *Beowulf the warrior* (O.U.P), Rosemary Sutcliff's prose *Beowulf* (Bodley Head, also available as Puffin under the title, *Dragon Slayer*) or Robert Nye's *Beehunter* (Faber) which many children will prefer for their own reading and which does not need to be introduced to them in quite the same way as the others. Robert Nye successfully recaptures the drama of the original, and the description of the emergence of Grendel from the black fen, for example, is only one of many particularly effective passages, but the conversation is contemporary in style and humour without being inappropriate to the dignity of the story.

Rosemary Sutcliff has woven the legends about Cuchulain, the great hero of Ireland, into a full-length story in *The hound of Ulster* (Bodley Head and Knight). Many children will need to be helped over the first few pages, which contain strange and difficult names, but once launched into the story of Cuchulain, his killing of the wolf-hound, and the story of how he came by his name, it can be read as a good, straightforward adventure story.

A knowledge of the Arthurian legends is useful for any child because later adult reading and experience will require at least a nodding acquaintance with them. These stories were first popularized through Sir Thomas Malory's version, printed by Caxton; the most enjoyable versions are Barbara Leonie Picard's *Stories of King Arthur and his knights* (O.U.P), Alice M. Hadfield's *King Arthur and his round table* (Dent) and Roger Lancelyn Green's *King Arthur and his knights of the round table* (Faber and Puffin). Roger Lancelyn Green has drawn on a number of sources in addition to Malory and has woven all the stories relating to the knights into a coherent whole. He includes the story of Sir Gawain and the Green Knight, taken from the old middle English poem, as part of the cycle and, without making too much use of poetic licence, has produced, while not spoiling the original spirit of the medieval romance, a fairly logical and understandable sequence of events.

One of Ian Serrailliers's most successful retellings is *The challenge of the Green Knight* (O.U.P), where he adapts the story of Sir Gawain as told in the poem. It is not a translation —Serraillier's version is much shorter than the original—but the use of the five-stress metre and the frequent alliteration, which reflect the spirit of the original style, together with Victor Ambrus' illustrations, genuinely stimulate the imagination of the child reader.

Another middle English poem, *Havelok the Dane*, has come in for a certain amount of attention in recent years and, for children, a choice can be made between the good retelling by Kevin Crossley-Holland, *Havelok the Dane* (Macmillan), and *The locked crowns* (World's Work) by M. Garthwaite, which many children may prefer since it is written as a straight adventure story, although some of the incidents do read rather strangely in this style of presentation. Kevin Crossley-Holland's version is full of vivid phrases and colour. The opening paragraph contrasts the blue dusk, the red silk counterpane, the yellow rushes and the sprigs of silver birch against the dun-colour of the stone walls. There is plenty of dialogue, with the occasional touch of humour, and the mention of familiar place-names helps to counterbalance the slightly strange names of the characters—Aethelwold, Goldborough and Godric.

Robin Hood has been dealt with as a straight historical character, a kind of early communist revolutionary, by Geoffrey Trease,* but Carola Oman's *Robin Hood* (Dent), while setting the stories firmly in the historical period of Edward II's time, recalls vividly the old ballads. Rosemary Sutcliff's

*see also page 103

Chronicles of Robin Hood (O.U.P), although it does not represent her best work, does provide a readable collection of stories. Ian Serraillier's version of the stories in *Robin in the greenwood* (O.U.P) uses the old medieval ballad form, and usually needs to be introduced to the children. Left to themselves, most children seem to prefer the prose versions by Rosemary Sutcliff and Carola Oman, together with Donald Suddaby's *New tales of Robin Hood* (Blackie).

Bodley Head have published a series of volumes covering the heroic sagas of many European countries. This includes *The treasure of Siegfried* (Bodley Head), in which E. M. Almedingen retells the story of the Nibelungenlied, the great German heroic saga, and another successful retelling by the same author is *The knights of the golden table* (Bodley Head); Prince Vladimir of Kiev and his knights have a family resemblance to King Arthur and his knights—they were sworn to fight against evil and to protect Kiev against the Tartars. *The ivory horn* by Ian Serraillier (O.U.P) provides a readable version of the story of Roland, the great French hero, one of Charlemagne's knights.

One of the finest and most imaginative versions of the Norse mythological stories is that by Barbara Leonie Picard, *Tales of the Norse gods and heroes* (O.U.P), in which some of her best work in this field can be seen. She has retold in simple but vivid language the stories about Odin, Thor and Loki, Sigurd of the Volsungs and Völund (or Wayland Smith). Without using an archaic or extraordinary vocabulary, she writes in a style which matches perfectly the heroic vigour of these stories. Roger Lancelyn Green tells the Norse legends as a continuous story in *Myths of the Norsemen* (Bodley Head), while Alan French provides an imaginative version of one of the Icelandic sagas in *Grettir the strong* (Bodley Head).

The Greek myths and legends, which Nathaniel Hawthorne, Charles Kingsley and Andrew Lang retold for children in the late nineteenth century, have survived well in their versions. It is interesting to compare them, where the stories overlap, but difficult to say whether one version is superior to another. This is largely a matter of personal taste and adults tend to be influenced or prejudiced in favour of the version which they themselves knew as children. The most old-fashioned element is the framework in which Hawthorne set his stories; he imagined a group of children gathered at Tanglewood House, hence the title of *Tanglewood tales* (Dent), with the stories being told by Eustace, the children's tutor. This framework can, however, be ignored and, in fact, is omitted from modern editions as a rule. Both *Tanglewood tales* and its sequel, *A wonder book* (Dent), are brought together in *Complete Greek stories* (Gollancz). Hawthorne's rather cosy style, and the fact that he introduced child characters into the stories—for example, Marigold into the story of King Midas—or converted heroines, such as Persephone, into small girls instead of young adults, seems to make his stories more suitable for younger children, while Kingsley's *The heroes* (Dent), even though he gives it the sub-title of 'fairy tales', has a ringing prose style which appeals to boys.

Both these versions and Lang's *Tales of Troy and Greece* (Faber) are available in modern editions. To complete the coverage of classical mythology, one should add Barbara Leonie Picard's *The Iliad* (O.U.P) and *The Odyssey* (O.U.P), which provide excellent introductions to these epic stories, N. B. Taylor's *The Aeneid* (O.U.P) and Ian Serraillier's modern versions of the stories of Jason, Perseus and Theseus, *The clashing rocks* (O.U.P), *The gorgon's head* (O.U.P) and *The way of danger* (O.U.P).

James Reeves has retold the *Fables from Aesop* (Blackie), providing a useful introduction to the proverbs and phrases which are a part of everyday life. While retaining the essential simplicity of the stories, he has told them in a way which appeals to modern children and has included sufficient detail to give interest to the stories. This is one book where illustrations in both black and white and colour throughout the text add immeasurably to the appeal of the book for children.

Fables, which are much less well known but which are extremely amusing, appear in Charles Downing's *Tales of the Hodja* (O.U.P). This edition is illustrated by Papas and provides an ideal introduction to these very short, humorous stories about the Hodja, a Turkish folk-lore character, who is wise and foolish in turn. Some of these stories can be used very successfully to provide an interlude between two longer stories in a story hour programme.

The stories about Aladdin and Ali Baba are as well known to English children, thanks to pantomime tradition, as those about Red Riding Hood and Cinderella. The Arabian nights stories, from which they come, were first introduced to English children in the version by Andrew Lang, published in 1898, but although this is still in print (Longmans Y.B), one of the most satisfactory modern editions is Amabel Williams-Ellis' *The Arabian nights* (Blackie), in which she presents the best known stories in a form which preserves the original framework, and Queen Shahrazad tells the stories for a thousand and one nights in order to save her life. This edition is illustrated by Pauline Baynes in a style appropriate to the setting of the stories and in a way which makes an immediate appeal to children.

In recent years, English children have been introduced to the folk tales of other continents. Indian, African and West Indian stories, in particular, are of growing importance in libraries and schools because they provide a rich source of material for the children with their origins in these cultures. In many stories from the Far East, Africa, America and Australasia, the reader can find plots, characters and themes very similar to those found in European and Middle Eastern stories. Animals tend to figure prominently, a fact which appeals to many children, and it can also be clearly seen that many traditional stories first developed from the desire of man to explain, in a way that he could comprehend, the natural mysteries of the earth. We take for granted the tales from Norse and Greek mythology which do this, and tend to overlook the fact that children read and enjoy Bible stories in much the same spirit as they enjoy folk tales. The English reader or listener tends to become much more conscious of this element in the stories drawn from Asian, American and Australasian countries.

The illustrations by Joan Kiddell-Monroe, who illustrates all the volumes in the 'Oxford myths and legends' series, seem particularly apt in Cyril Birch's *Chinese myths and fantasies* (O.U.P) and in Helen and William McAlpine's *Japanese tales and legends* (O.U.P). Each of these volumes opens with the myths originating in the story of creation, both including a selection of amusing folk tales; and the Japanese collection contains the legends of the Heiki, the great Japanese warriors, based on the twelfth century Japanese epic.

J. E. B. Gray's *Indian tales and legends* (O.U.P), another volume from the same series, contains fables, folk tales and adaptations from the two great epic poems of India, the Mahābhārata and the Ramayana. Barbara Leonie Picard has produced a more comprehensive version of the Mahābhārata in *The story of the Pāndavas* (Dobson), which retells the main theme of the epic, the rivalry between the two branches of the Kuru royal family. In *Indian tales* (Bell), R. Thapar provides a selection of the stories most likely to be familiar to Indian children, drawn from mythology, folk and fairy tales and historical legends. For younger children to read themselves there is a volume, *India*, in the well-produced, but short, 'Folk tales of the world' series, by A. W. Crown (E. J. Arnold). Taya Zinkin's *The faithful parrot and other Indian folk stories* (O.U.P) is a colourful collection in a format likely to appeal to the under nines.

Philip Sherlock's *West Indian folk tales* (O.U.P) includes stories told by the Caribs before the arrival of white men and the African negroes, but many of the stories are about the cunning Ananse, the spider man, who is a character found in both African and West Indian tales. He is clever, sometimes lazy, sometimes attracting the sympathy of the reader or listener as he manages to outwit someone stronger and more powerful than himself, sometimes coming off worst in a battle of wits and being paid out for his tricks. He appears in some of the stories in Peggy Appiah's *The pineapple child and other tales from Ashanti* (Deutsch), which are West African in origin, but in Sherlock's collection, the Ananse stories are set in a West Indian landscape.

Brer Rabbit, the hero of the American Uncle Remus stories, has the same sort of appeal as Ananse. Joel Chandler Harris collected these stories from the negroes on the cotton plantations and they were first published in 1880. Until recently, most of the versions published here were written in dialect and were difficult for children and many adults to read, but there is now a simplified paperback version (B.B.C. Publications) of five of the stories which were told on the *Jackanory* programme.

Stories of the American Indians are available in a number of volumes, most of which are restricted to tales told by a particular tribe. Each tribe had its own version of the story of the creation of the world. Many of the stories show great sympathy for and involvement with the animals of the North American continent, such as the coyote, and the same Great Spirit, Nanabozho, under slightly varying names, appears in stories from many tribes. Ruth Manning-Sanders' *Red Indian folk and fairy tales* (O.U.P) makes a good introduction and, for younger children, there is V. Hulpach's *American-Indian tales and legends* (Hamlyn), with unusual illustrations in colour.

The French influence in North America can be seen in Marcel Barbeau's *The golden phoenix* (O.U.P), a very fine collection of stories from French Canada. These stories were collected by Barbeau and rewritten in a very polished, literary style by Michael Hornyansky. They provide excellent material for the story-teller.

Finally, there are the traditional tales from Australasia. The Australian aborigines believe in a wonderful Dreamtime, during which everything was created and when animals could assume human form and humans animal form. Most of their stories are set during this Dreamtime, to which they believe they will return after death. For younger children, there is an attractive collection by R. Beckley, *Australia*, in the 'Folk tales of the world' series (E. J. Arnold). Older children can enjoy *The dreamtime: Australian aboriginal myths* by A. Roberts and C. P. Mountford (Angus and Robertson). For tales from New Zealand and the South Seas there is a collection by A. W. Reed, *Fairy tales from the Pacific Islands* (Muller), which begins with the story of the creation of the earth by Tane, the god of nature, as the Maoris tell it. Doris Rust has also produced two attractive collections of stories from this part of the world, *Tales from the Australian bush* (Faber) and *Tales from the Pacific* (Faber), and these are recommended for reading to or for being read by children under nine.

Many of these traditional stories, particularly the hero tales, contain difficult names and the best way of introducing them to children is through reading or telling them aloud. They can be a valuable source of inspiration for creative work in both schools and libraries, they can help to unite a group of children drawn from different cultures, but it is important that they should not be introduced to children at too early an age. The hero tales, for example, are very much enjoyed by children of eleven and twelve and it would be a pity to spoil their effect by encouraging children to read them too soon.

READ ON FROM HERE:

ALDERSON, B. W: Ian Serraillier and the golden world, *The Horn Book Magazine*, vol. 44, no. 3, June 1968.

COLWELL, E: Folk literature: oral tradition and oral art. *The Junior Bookshelf*, vol. 32, no. 3, June 1968.

COOK, E: The ordinary and the fabulous: an introduction to myths, legends and fairy tales for teachers and storytellers. C.U.P, 1969.

GREEN, R. L: Andrew Lang. Bodley Head, 1962. (Bodley Head Monograph.)

HUTTON, M: Writers for children : James Reeves. *The School Librarian*, vol. 14, no. 2, July 1966.

See also Reading list, *Chapter 11, for books and articles about Rosemary Sutcliff and* Read on from here, *Chapter 24, for the 'Bodley Head Monograph' about Ruth Sawyer.*

ENGLISH writers for children have always excelled at fantasy and there are many well-written examples of this genre among the best-known and most popular English children's books. There are, however, different approaches to the creation of fantasy although, to be successful, a fantasy must present a credible world with real and recognizable values. A kind of suburban fairyland, besprinkled with toadstools and inhabited by fairies with gauzy wings, is very much out of date.

Those fantasies which come nearest to folk-tale tradition share with folk tales the appeal to a very wide age group. Books like *The hobbit*, *The Borrowers* and *The piemakers* can be read to quite young children, long before they can read them for themselves, but they are also enjoyed and appreciated by adults. In each case, the author has created a self-contained and internally consistent world, Tolkien in an original mythology and the others in a simplified version of human life, scaled down to a size with which children can cope.

J. R. Tolkien's *The hobbit* (Allen and Unwin) was first published in 1937 but has only comparatively recently become widely known among children, due, in all probability, to the widespread interest among adults in *The lord of the rings* trilogy which continues the story. In a *Sunday Times* competition in 1968 Philip Neal, the seven year old winner, wrote 'The hobbit is staying on my shelf for ever'. Few seven year olds read *The hobbit* by themselves but it has the sort of humorous and adventurous elements which appeal to people of all ages. The beginning of the story, read aloud, immediately captures the attention.

In Helen Cresswell's *The piemakers* (Faber), the characters are human, but the England which they inhabit is so idyllic that the story can only be described as a fantasy. Here again there is a strong element of humour, and Jem and Arthy and Gravella, their daughter, have the same kind of appeal as Pod, Homily and Arrietty in *The Borrowers* (Dent), though the Borrowers are mini-sized people who live beneath the floorboards and live by 'borrowing' human belongings. Carol Kendall's *The Minnipins* (Dent), who also appear in *The whisper of Glocken* (Bodley Head), are much underrated characters who are nearly as popular as the Borrowers if only they are promoted among children. In *The whisper of Glocken*, each chapter is preceded by an excerpt from some Minnipin writings such as *Glorious True Facts in the History of the Minnipins from the Beginning to the Year of Gammage 880* by Walter the Earl, *Further maxims* by Muggles or *Gummy's Scribbles*. It is this attention to detail which appeals to a lot of children.

The English countryside of the folk tale is also used by B.B. in, for example, *The little grey men* (Methuen and Puffin). This uses the quest theme, for Sneezewort, Baldmoney and Dodder, the last gnomes in Britain, set off up a Warwickshire stream in search of their missing brother Cloudberry. The smallness of the main characters, in relation to the animals around them, appeals to children and the climax, I think, is particularly appealing—the three brothers take over the *Jeanie Deans*, the toy steamer which drifts ashore on the island in the lake where they are stranded. Dodder goes aboard and explores; there is a lot of fascinating detail and great excitement when he discovers the cargo of blackberries and peppermint creams. Some chapters later, safely back in their hollow-tree house at Oak Pool, they are still eating the peppermint creams.

Lloyd Alexander, an American writer, has actually drawn on Welsh folk lore for the background to his stories about Prydain. These are adventure stories with two central characters—Taran, the Assistant Pig-Keeper, and the tomboyish Princess Eilonwy—with whom children can identify. In *The black cauldron* (Heinemann) there is a quest to Annuvin to seize Arawn's cauldron, the source of the evil Cauldron-Born. For the last of the four stories, *The high king* (not yet published in the U.K.), Alexander was awarded the 1968 Newbery Medal. This series seems to have achieved much wider fame in America than it has here, yet the stories have much that should appeal to English children.

As children develop and begin to enjoy these books through reading them for themselves, they also begin to appreciate the type of fantasy which seems to be just around the corner from their own experience. One way of meeting this need is through the story in which human children move into a strange world in which the impossible can and does happen. Lewis Carroll's *Alice in wonderland* (Macmillan and Puffin), published in 1865, was one of the first successful fantasies of this kind; here the real world is seen only very briefly and Alice soon falls down the rabbit-hole into the distorted dream-world of the White Rabbit and the Mad Hatter. Charles Kingsley's *The water babies* (Gollancz), which had appeared earlier in 1863, used the same sort of pattern with Tom, the chimney sweep's boy, running away, climbing down the cliff face and going for a bathe in the river where he enters into a world in which creatures can speak. The first part of the story still appeals to children but the second part is overloaded with moralizing, and modern children either skip this or abandon the book at this stage.

Frank Baum's *The wonderful wizard of Oz* (Dent), published in America in 1900, has never, despite the Judy Garland film in 1939, enjoyed the same amount of popularity as it has had in the United States, perhaps because there had been no good library edition of it here until quite recently. This too starts off in the real world, but Dorothy is soon hurtled, by the hurricane, into the fantasy land of Oz, peopled by non-human creatures who can speak. J. M. Barrie's *Peter Pan* (Brockhampton) also starts with a short passage in the known world before the children are carried off to the Never-Never-Land.

Recently one of the most successful and popular fantasies of this kind has been C. S. Lewis's saga about the kingdom of Narnia, beginning with *The lion, the witch and the wardrobe* (Collins, Bles and Puffin) in which a similar framework is used. Four children go to stay in the country with an old professor. One day, while playing hide and seek, Lucy hides in an old wardrobe which proves to be one of the ways into Narnia. The later books do not develop or expand the adventures of the same four children though the reader's knowledge of Narnia is extended with each of the seven volumes. *The magician's nephew* (Bodley Head and Puffin), for example, describes the beginning of Narnia, the nephew being the old professor as a small boy, and the reader also learns the origin of the old lamp post which is the first thing that Lucy sees when she first ventures into Narnia.

The framework of human children in a fantasy world has tremendous advantages for the children's writer, and it is the one which children most readily accept. There is a child character with whom the reader can identify, there is a strong element of adventure and there is the security of knowing that just beyond the edge of the dream world, the real world is waiting to be returned to safely when the adventure is over.

In modern fantasies of this kind there is often an underlying note of seriousness. The Narnia stories, for example, can be read on two levels—either as enjoyable fantasy-cum-adventure stories, or as an allegory with Aslan, the lion, as the Christ figure in the battle between good and evil. Children undoubtedly enjoy them as fast-moving adventure stories and, although the Christian allegory element is there throughout, there are only one or two passages when an appreciation of this is necessary to make certain incidents acceptable to an adult. For example, in *The voyage of the Dawn Treader* (Bles and Puffin), Eustace is turned into a dragon and becomes a much pleasanter person as a result but some adults find Eustace's description of losing his dragon's skin and returning to human form distasteful and would find it even more so if it were not for the allegorical significance of this incident. Most children appreciate the under-lying conflict between good and evil, but do not appreciate the full significance of the story.

Alan Garner is also very much concerned with the conflict between good and evil. The inspiration for his first book, *The weirdstone of Brisingamen* (Collins and Puffin), was a traditional tale from Alderley Edge, the area where the story is set. The powerful Firefrost, the lost weirdstone, a small piece of crystal shaped like a raindrop, has been passed down to Susan in the form of a bracelet and this brings her and Colin, her brother, into involvement with the Wizard of Alderley, Cadellin. I think that far more successful, as far as many children are concerned, is *Elidor* (Collins and Puffin) where four children find their way into the kingdom of Elidor through an old church on a demolition site in Manchester. They are soon back in the normal world, with the four treasures which they are to guard; and these four treasures, which in Elidor were a spear, a sword, a stone and a cauldron, splendid with precious metal and jewels, become a length of iron railing, two splintered laths nailed together, a keystone and an old cracked cup. The rest of the story is taken up with the preservation of these treasures—a theme which very much appeals to children and which involves secrecy and excitement—until at the very end Elidor is saved and the treasures can be returned. Here the magic follows the children back into the real world; it is not something on which the door can be easily closed. *Elidor* is very much of the twentieth century and, at times, has overtones of science fiction.

At the same time as children are enjoying this kind of fantasy, they also enjoy stories in which magic is allowed to invade everyday life, often with humorous effect. Edith Nesbit set the pattern for these with *Five children and it* (Benn and Puffin), published in 1902, in which she introduced a new and original creature, a psammead or sand-fairy which has the power to grant wishes. The psammead's charm lies in the bad-tempered way in which it reluctantly grants the wishes. In Hilda Lewis's *The ship that flew* (O.U.P), the source of magic is a little Viking ship which on occasion grows big enough to carry the children on exciting adventures in time and space. Edward Eager, an American writer, acknowledges his debt to E. Nesbit by making his characters avid readers of the Nesbit books. In his *Half magic* (Macmillan and Puffin), there is a very logical sort of magic, for the children find just half of a magic charm which grants just half a wish, and this involves a lot of ingenious arithmetic in order to achieve the wishes they really want. In this kind of book, the magic always seems to go slightly wrong for the children who are on the receiving end, and they are frequently involved in awkward and amusing (for the reader) situations.

Mary Poppins, the magic nursemaid of the books by P. L. Travers (Collins and Puffin) and Hag Dowsabel in *The hag calls for help* by Lorna Wood (Dent) have a similar sort of effect upon the lives of the children they meet. These stories are entertaining to read, and the fact that the reader feels that he too might just be lucky enough to meet a psammead, or find a magic Viking ship, or even meet Hag Dowsabel at the bottom of his garden, make this type of fantasy one of the most popular.

In some of the oustanding fantasies of recent years, the whole story takes place in the everyday world and at the end the children in the story—and therefore the readers—are left to wonder if in fact the magic has ever happened. Pauline Clarke, in *The twelve and the genii* (Faber), hit on the happy idea of having Max, a small eight year old boy, find the twelve wooden soldiers which the Brontë children are supposed to have played with. The wooden soldiers come alive for Max and tell him of the adventures which the Brontës had invented for them. Max himself has no knowledge of the Brontës but the rest of the family, who have, become involved in preserving the wooden soldiers and escorting them to the museum at Haworth Parsonage. In William Mayne's *A grass rope* (O.U.P), the magic happenings are explained quite scientifically by Adam, a sixth former, but retain their magical quality for the youngest girl, Mary. These two books, both with Yorkshire settings, are beautifully written and are concerned with wider issues—in *The twelve and the genii*, for example, the fact that money is not the most important thing in the world; such books stretch the imagination and the experience of the ten year old child. *The twelve and the genii* can be returned to, with increased enjoyment, by older girls after they have heard more about the Brontë family from other sources.

Joan Aiken's fantasies stand out on their own. They are set in an England that never existed, with James III as king, wolves roaming the countryside, having crossed from Europe by the Channel Tunnel, snow lying thick on the ground and long train journeys at fifteen miles an hour. *The wolves of Willoughby Chase* (Cape and Puffin) is a splendid gothic novel, the sort of novel that a very imaginative child might try to write, but executed with consummate skill. There is the terrible school run by Mrs Brisket—the attraction of this episode in the book can be compared with the attraction which the early chapters of *Jane Eyre* and *Oliver Twist* have for eleven year olds—but the reader knows that in the end all will be well because Sylvia and Bonnie, the two central characters, are obviously destined to win through. There is the splendour of the six pairs of white kid skating boots—' " ... so Papa had several different pairs made and we thought one of them was certain to fit" '—offered to Sylvia who is suitably 'astonished at the lavishness of having six pairs made for one to be chosen'. The food, both good and bad, the justice meted out to the treacherous Miss Slighcarp, the dungeons and the secret passages all combine to make a splendid and romantic romp.

Time travel is a device sometimes used by writers of historical fiction, but it is also used with great success in books in which the fantasy element is uppermost. Hilda Lewis and E. Nesbit both exploited it in a humorous way. Lucy M. Boston, in her Green Knowe books, and Philippa Pearce, in *Tom's midnight garden* (O.U.P), use it to more serious purpose.

Lucy M. Boston's *The children of Green Knowe* (Faber) is a strange story which appeals to girls of about nine upwards, who presumably feel a motherly interest in Tolly, the seven year old boy sent to stay one Christmas with his great-grandmother. The world of Tolly is a nostalgic one, with a feeling of the continuity of history, and the children of the title are Linnet, Alexander and Toby, who lived at Green Knowe in the seventeenth century, and who remain as rather ghostly figures playing in the garden at Green Knowe, making Tolly aware of their presence, teasing him and finally revealing themselves to him, although at the end Tolly is playing with Percy Boggis, a boy of his own age and time, who is far from being a ghost. There are no concessions to childishness in this or the other four Green Knowe books, all of which hover on the dividing line between reality and fantasy.

In *Tom's midnight garden*, Tom is fascinated by the idea of time. He hears the old clock strike thirteen and he experiences 'time no longer', during which he can go out into the garden and meet Hatty, a little girl, who had lived in the house in Victorian times. His existence in this dream world soon becomes to him more real than his own, but although we only meet Tom for a few short weeks of his life, Hatty is growing up and, for her, Tom becomes thin like 'a piece of moonshine'. This is an immensely satisfying book, which appeals to children of eleven and twelve who themselves are fascinated by the passing of time. Girls of eleven and upwards who enjoy this also enjoy Penelope Farmer's *Charlotte sometimes* (Chatto), a time travel story set in 1918 and in the present; the exchanges in time of Charlotte who belongs to the '60s and Clare, who was at the same school and who slept in the same bed in 1918, are worked out with great restraint. This is a book for the thoughtful child, for Charlotte is very much concerned with the question of identity, just as Tom is concerned with the question of time.

Children of nine and upwards are immediately attracted by the word 'ghosts', and the title of Antonia Barber's *The ghosts* (Cape), which is also a time travel story, makes an immediate appeal to children looking along the library shelves. Some of them may be disappointed because what they really want are blood-curdling thrills, and the ghosts in this book are very gentle, two children, Sara and Georgie, badly treated by their guardian uncle, but saved by Jamie and Lucy who travel back in time to effect the rescue. The beginning of the story helps to create a mysterious atmosphere, and there is a happy ending. For children who ask for 'ghost stories' there are a number of good collections of short stories*, but to older ones with a taste for the supernatural one might suggest Ruth Arthur's *A candle in her room* (Gollancz) and William Mayne's *Earthfasts* (H. Hamilton and Puffin), which both have a strong supernatural element. The first, like most of Ruth Arthur's stories, has a romantic theme and is especially enjoyed by girls. *Earthfasts* has a Yorkshire setting, an old folk tale half-remembered, and the involvement of two boys with powers beyond human understanding. The two central figures are David and Keith, but the story is enjoyed by girls, and although there is a lot of typical Mayne description which sometimes slows down the action and hinders the less patient reader, one of the notable things about *Earthfasts* is the skill with which Mayne achieves a series of dramatic climaxes.

One of the charms of fantasy stories is the fact that animals and humans can meet together on equal terms. In the C. S.

*see also page 122

Lewis books about Narnia, for example, Lewis mixes human, animal and supernatural creatures quite happily, and children thoroughly enjoy this. The 'Dr Dolittle' books by Hugh Lofting (Cape) and the 'Uncle' books by J. P. Martin (Cape) are both series of fantasy stories, which mingle human or human-type figures with various animals. Dr. John Dolittle of the village of Puddleby reflects his creator's sympathy with animals, for he is hopeless at treating human beings but a great success at doctoring all kinds of animals. In the series of books about him, children can live out one of their favourite fantasies, that of being able to communicate with animals, for Dolittle is taught animal language by Polynesia the parrot, and from then on is a great success. There is plenty of action and a quiet touch of humour. These stories have taken on a new lease of life since the making of the film, which has introduced them to a new generation of children.

Uncle is an elephant who wears a purple dressing-gown and lives in a fabulous castle called Homeward, which is full of towers, lakes and gardens hidden away in unexpected places. Each of the five stories about Uncle consists of a sequence of incidents, linked loosely together. Uncle is perpetually at war with Beaver Hateman and the Badfort Crowd, who live at Badfort overlooking Homeward, and subject Uncle to a steady stream of insults and attacks. This warfare gives rise to the sort of slapstick humour which appeals to many children. Uncle, however, is rich and benevolent and invariably and inevitably comes out on top in his encounters with Beaver Hateman. There are certain other characters who appear in several, if not all, of the books, such as Old Monkey, Uncle's obsequious right-hand man, and A. B. Fox, the detective, but new characters are continually being introduced.

In his two books, *Winnie the Pooh* (Methuen) and *The house at Pooh Corner* (Methuen), A. A. Milne uses characters based on toys in Christopher Robin's nursery, who happen to be animals, but does not give them the characteristics which really belong to the animal in question, even though, by now, after forty years of conditioning, people may think that tigers are always bouncy, donkeys always gloomy and rabbits always organizing.

A. A. Milne's books, like those of Lofting and Martin, began as stories for a specific child and this is true of many success-ful fantasies. Parents or grandparents when making up stories to tell to children do so to a kind of story-specification, and where there is sufficient skill to write the stories down for other children to enjoy, it is not surprising that they have a wide audience.

In Kenneth Grahame's *The wind in the willows* (Methuen), also written for a specific child, we are moving nearer to the true animal story. Mole, Rat, Toad and Badger never really lose their essential animal qualities even though they are conceived in human terms and in fact become involved with human beings. Children themselves most enjoy the chapters about Toad and Toad Hall (which A. A. Milne transformed into a very suc-cessful stage play), but it is a book which can be read and enjoyed, for different reasons, by both children and adults.

READ ON FROM HERE:

ELLIS, A: Writers for children: Joan Aiken *The School Librarian*, vol 18, no. 2, June 1970.

FIELD, C: Writers for children: Mary Norton. *The School Librarian*, vol. 11, no. 5, July 1963.

GRAHAM, E: Kenneth Grahame. Bodley Head, 1963. (Bodley Head Monograph).

HUTTON, M: Writers for children: C. S. Lewis. *The School Librarian*, vol. 12, no. 2, July 1964.

LIVELY, P: The world of Green Knowe. *Books for your children*, vol. 5, no. 2, Winter 1969/1970.

LIVELY, P: The wrath of God: an opinion of the 'Narnia' books. *The Use of English*, vol. 20, no. 2, Winter 1968. Also in *Books for your children*, vol. 3, no. 4, Summer 1968.

MOULD, G. H: The weirdstone of Brisingamen: a four-way experience. *The School Librarian*, vol. 15, no, 2, July 1967.

ROSE, J: Lucy Boston. Bodley Head, 1965. (Bodley Head Monograph.)

TOLKIEN, J. R. R: Tree and Leaf. Allen & Unwin, 1964.

WATKINS, T: Alan Garner. *The Use of English*, vol. 21, no. 2, Winter 1969.

See also Reading list, *Chapter 4, for article on B. B.,* Reading list *Chapter 9, for article about William Mayne, and* Read on from here, *Chapter 24, for the 'Bodley Head Monographs' about J. M. Barrie, Lewis Carroll, C. S. Lewis, Hugh Lofting and E. Nesbit.*

Animal stories

MANY children grow up closely with animals and have a strong sympathy for them and, even if they do not have a pet of their own, to have one is their dearest ambition. From animal stories in which there is a strong fantasy element, children move on to stories which describe a close relationship between a human and an animal and then on to books in which the story centres on an animal living in its natural surroundings. One can distinguish here different uses of animals in fiction. In many cases, the animal is a substitute for a child character and here the story may relate closely to others outside this field, either as a variant of the adventure story or as a frame for the discussion of some problem of personal relationships; in others, the story, told from the animal's viewpoint, is effectively a fictionalized presentation of natural history.

Because of their sympathy with, and protective attitudes towards, animals, many children very much enjoy reading stories in which children are successful in their relationships with animals. This is one of the appeals of some of the Enid Blyton books; in *Mr Galliano's circus* (Merlin), for example, Jimmy Brown joins the circus and, in a very short space of time, manages to cure one of the performing dogs, when everyone else has failed to do so, recaptures an escaped chimpanzee and trains his own dog to perform in the circus ring. This is success with animals in its extreme form, but in other stories children are to be found rescuing and caring for animals who would otherwise have been killed or died.

In Bilberry summer (Collins), Maribel Edwin describes how a nine year old boy, who longs desperately for a puppy, finds a fox-cub and looks after it for a whole summer. This theme of care for wild creatures is a popular one, also used by D.

c

Faralla in *Swanhilda of the swans* (Blackie), in which two Danish children, with the help of sympathetic grandparents, look after an injured swan and its mate for the winter. Where children are involved with wild creatures in this way, there is always the inevitable parting at the end but both child and animal have benefited from their short relationship.

Helen Griffiths is a writer who is extremely successful at portraying the relationship which can exist between a young boy and an animal. *The wild horse of Santander* (Hutchinson) describes the friendship of a young, blind Spanish boy and an uncertain-tempered horse. In *The greyhound* (Hutchinson), which has a rather less exotic setting, Jamie, a London boy, manages to acquire a much-wanted dog but has to conceal his ownership of it until he has woven such a complicated web of deceit that matters come to a head and his secret has to be revealed. It is interesting to compare *The greyhound* with Philippa Pearce's *A dog so small* (Longmans Y.B. and Puffin), which seems to have the most appeal, for the widest range of children, of all her books. Here, another London boy, desperately longing for a real live dog, has to make do with an imaginary one for a long time. When his dearest wish is at last fulfilled, Ben wonders for a while if the imaginary dog, which always behaved exactly as he wished, was not really more satisfactory for a pet. As his grandmother very truly says, ' "People get their heart's desire . . . and then they have to begin to learn how to live with it." ' In the most worthwhile books, success with animals is something which has to be worked for and the need for a sense of responsibility on the part of the child is clearly shown.

Marguerite Henry's *King of the wind* (Longmans Y.B), awarded the Newbery Medal for 1948, is a story based on fact, woven around Sham, a beautiful Arabian horse, sent as a present by the Sultan of Morocco to Louis XV of France. Agba, a young mute Arab boy, is present when the colt is born, when its fate is in the balance because it bears the mark of the wheat ear, a sign of misfortune. Agba is chosen to travel with the horse on its journey to the Court of Versailles and, when the gift is rejected there, the boy and horse travel on to England where the horse becomes known as 'King of the wind' because of its speed of movement, and wins fame as founder of a breed of Arab horses.

Jean George's *My side of the mountain* (Bodley Head and Puffin) has much in common with early examples of the holiday adventure type of story such as Ernest Thompson Seton's *Two little savages* (Kaye and Ward) and Richard Jefferies' *Bevis* (Cape).* The story is told by the hero, Sam Gribley, who describes how, for a whole year, he lives off the countryside in the Catskill mountains on the rough farmland which his grandfather once owned. During the year he experiences winter snowstorms in his hollow tree house, as well as the pleasantly warm days of summer, and makes a special friend of Frightful, a young female hawk, whom he trains to hunt for him. This has all the charm of a Robinson Crusoe story, with plenty of hints on survival and how to cook wild plants and animals for food. There is excitement and adventure since Sam, from time to time, is hunted down or has to hide from the human beings who invade his hide-out. One of the book's special charms, from the librarian's point of view, is that Sam continuously emphasizes the value of books, from which he seems to have acquired most of the knowledge which helps him to survive. This is an excellent, well-written story to recommend to the practical child who is not very keen on reading.

Here, the scope of the animal story is beginning to widen and interest focuses more on the animal than on the human. This interest is even more clearly shown in René Guillot's books, in many of which he describes sympathetically the relationship which he believes can exist between animals and humans. In *Sirga* (O.U.P), he tells the story of the friendship between Ulé, a boy, and Sirga, a lioness, who are born on the same day in the African bush, and who, after a series of disasters, return together to the area in which they were born and spent their early lives. Guillot does not minimize the cruelty of the animal world, and there is matter-of-fact acceptance of brutality and the need to kill to live, but Guillot also has a tremendous love and respect for animals which he can communicate well, and he has also been fortunate in his translators, so that children whose tastes lie in this direction read his stories

*see also page 55

with great enjoyment. His stories mostly have unusual settings and this enhances their appeal for many children. Although he has written other types of story, it is his animal stories which are the most popular in the children's library.

Most children will enjoy at least some of these stories in which both humans and animals are involved, but stories concerned solely with the animals' point of view are, on the whole, rather less popular. Certain stories of this kind have established themselves as classics of children's literature, and many children or young people are introduced to Felix Salten's *Bambi* (Cape and Knight) and Henry Williamson's *Tarka the otter* (Bodley Head and Puffin), both of which were first published in the 1920s. Here the story is conceived in terms of the animal as hero, and the reader follows Bambi or Tarka from birth until they are full-grown animals and, in the case of Tarka, until his death. There is no sentimentalization of the animal world; it is seen as a society in which the only valid law is the survival of the strongest and the fittest. In *Bambi*, Salten comments on western civilization and the freedom and cruelty of man, and Bambi in his innocence wonders why man and animal cannot live peaceably together. Certainly, the child who reads both *My side of the mountain* and *Bambi* will realize that there are often two quite legitimate points of view in every situation. Sam, with all his love of wild animals, has to trap wild deer to feed and clothe himself and the child will sympathize with this need; but the child will also be concerned about the apparent cruelty with which Bambi and his fellow deer are hunted down.

Other writers who are concerned mainly with the animals are H. Mortimer Batten, Ernest Thompson Seton and A. Windsor-Richards; B.B. (the pseudonym of Denys Watkins-Pitchford), as well as writing fantasy stories in which animals feature prominently, has also produced stories of this kind, such as *Lepus: the brown hare* (Benn). Like Henry Williamson, these authors all have a great feeling for the countryside and for the creatures that live there, but children who are squeamish are unlikely to enjoy their books.

In recent years, there have been a number of adult best-sellers about animals; Gerald Durrell's *The overloaded ark* and *My family and other animals* (Hart-Davis), Joy Adamson's *Born free* (Collins) and Sheila Burnford's *The incredible journey* (Hodder and Stoughton) are good examples and all these, both in the special cadet editions where these have been published and in their original form, are extremely popular with children and young people. The books by Durrell and Joy Adamson are based on personal experience; Sheila Burnford's story is written as a documentary account of a successful journey made by three animals—two dogs and a cat—across Canada to their home.

The interest in and demand for these books amongst children ties up with their increasing demand for factual books about the animal world, and some of the animal stories which appeal to children are, in fact, found among the information books in many children's libraries. One book published for children in recent years is G. D. Griffiths' *Mattie* (World's Work), which tells the story of the one female hedgehog in a litter of three, from her birth until she crawls away to die nearly six years later. This book, too, is based on first hand observation, and straightforward factual information is inserted into the story at appropriate moments.

This is a field in which fact and fiction mingle happily, in which the barriers between adult and children's books tend to be broken down, and in which the standard of writing is usually high. A very useful collection which brings together examples of the best factual and fictional writing and which draws on both adults' and children's books for its material, is Margery Fisher's *A world of animals* (Brockhampton).

READ ON FROM HERE:

ELLIS, A: Man and beast. *The Junior Bookshelf*, vol. 32, no. 5, October 1968.

FISHER, M: B. B. as a writer for young people. *Bookbird*, vol. 5, no. 3, 1967.

PEARCE, P: Writing a book. *The Horn Book Magazine*, vol. 43, no. 3, June 1967. *This article is concerned largely with* A dog so small.

ST. MARY'S COLLEGE LIBRARY CHELTENHAM

THE pony story is closely related to other types of story; many of them take place during the holidays, are concerned with family relationships and some of the early ones had much in common with the animal story, but the popularity of the pony story in the last twenty years has been so phenomenal that it deserves special consideration.

Anna Sewell's *Black Beauty* (Dent and Puffin), published in 1877 and now firmly established as a children's classic, has been described as the first pony story. In fact, it is closer to being an animal story, since the typical pony story contains a certain amount of information about the art of riding. Anna Sewell wrote this book as a protest against the cruel treatment of London cabhorses, but she brought to her subject so much skill, affection and understanding that she created a story of real quality. It is not the message which has helped the book to survive, but the sincerity with which she wrote it. There is plenty of incident and a happy, fairy tale ending. In recent years, the fact that it is about a horse has almost certainly helped it to maintain its popularity.

Moorland Mousie by 'Golden Gorse', published in 1929, helps to bridge the time gap between *Black Beauty* and the post-war pony story. Mousie is an Exmoor pony who tells his story in a style very reminiscent of Black Beauty's. Mousie also comes face to face with adversity when, after proving too nervous and excitable a pony to be ridden by a child, he is sold to a butcher and then to a greengrocer, who treats him badly. At the end, however, Mousie is reunited with Patience, his first mistress, and all ends happily when he proves to be a suitable ride for her little brother. In *Moorland Mousie*, although the story is told by the pony, there is more emphasis on riding techniques and on the schooling of horses.

The plot of Enid Bagnold's *National Velvet* (Peacock), published in 1935, was described as the 'super-daydream' by Raymond Mortimer. Velvet Brown, the fourteen year old heroine,
sharing a pony with her three sisters and a small brother,
suddenly inherits five horses and then wins a piebald in a
raffle. It is the piebald which she and her butcher father's
assistant decide to run in the Grand National, with Velvet as
the jockey. This, and the fact that it wins, make a splendid
fantasy, the impossibility of which is explained in an author's
note, and it would seem to be the perfect answer to every pony-
tailed, pony-mad girl's demand for a good book. It was not
intended as a children's book and some of the dialogue and
incidents may make children's librarians pause before shelving
it in the children's library. This would be a pity as it is the kind
of book which, introduced to the right twelve year old, might
well develop her reading tastes and encourage her to read at a
more sophisticated level. The style and characterization are
immeasurably superior to the average pony book; at the same
time, its plot makes it supremely readable.

By the middle of the 1930s the holiday adventure story
launched by Arthur Ransome was well and truly afloat and, in
1937, Katharine Hull and Pamela Whitlock introduced ponies
into an Arthur Ransome type of story, *The far-distant Oxus*,
but although ponies are important and very much part of the
action, it is taken for granted that the six children are competent riders and, although pony races on the beach are described, the competition is only among the children themselves
and the rosettes are homemade.

Ponies were used in much the same way in Mary Treadgold's
We couldn't leave Dinah (Cape and Puffin), published in 1941.
This adventure story, set on an imaginary Channel Island, opens
on the day of a Pony Club meeting when Caroline Templeton
is greeted by her young brother, Thomas, with the news that
'Ole Hitler's goin' to take this island!' When many of their
friends, their father and Thomas are evacuated, Caroline and
Mick, her other brother, are left behind by accident and it is
some time before they can be rescued. Ponies come in at every
important point in the story. Treachery during a Pony Club
fancy dress Carnival enables the Germans to take the Tower

stronghold which might have held out for a while against invasion. Mick and Caroline hide in the cave which is the Pony Club headquarters, and it is due to a pony throwing Nannerl, the small grand-daughter of the German commander, that Mick manages to get hold of a vital piece of information which can be passed on to the British Secret Service. Here, again, the children are competent riders, and there is no pre-occupation with learning to ride or winning rosettes.

The typical pony story developed after the war and its basic plot has changed very little in the twenty years since. Girl acquires pony, learns to ride and jump and, together, pony and girl succeed. Sometimes it is the girl who has got to learn most, sometimes the pony. The child characters do include boys, but this type of story is read almost solely by girls and for many of them the pony story must be the forerunner of the light romance, with pony substituting for handsome hero. Frequently, the story is told in the first person by the heroine who usually writes in a chatty, amusing style which helps to fill out a rather thin plot.

A good example of the basic pony story, in which the girl reader can live out her own fantasy-life, is Ruby Ferguson's *Jill's gymkhana* (Brockhampton and Knight). This is the first title in a series and was published in 1949; the rather naïve heroine who tells the story makes a passing reference to the family cheese ration, but otherwise the story has not dated. Jill's mummy is widowed, a writer and short of money. Jill nevertheless goes to a private school, attended by girls who own ponies and win rosettes. Jill eventually does the same, over-coming financial problems by a combination of persistence and good luck. Jill panders to the reader's fantasy by assuming that the reader knows all about grooming and the finer points of riding and by assuming that she, Jill, is the one who doesn't know. Jill is a typical pony story heroine in that she can bring in references to *Adam Bede* quite naturally but is totally un-aware of the fact that Bring and Buy sales are run for charity and not for oneself. 'And I have written this book to show what a quite ordinary person can do with a quite ordinary pony, if he or she really cares about riding' says Jill on the day when she wins three firsts, three seconds and a third at a gymkhana. It is little wonder that this series is extremely popular and that all the titles in the series are currently in print.

However, there have been some changes in the pony story, and this can be seen by comparing the now out of print *The Mandrake: a pony* by Kathleen Herald, published in 1949, with *Fly-by-night* (O.U.P), written by the same author under her better-known name of K. M. Peyton in 1968. Admittedly Lesley has to borrow money to buy the Mandrake, but the background is distinctly middle-class whereas in the later book Ruth uses her National Savings for the same purpose, her family have just moved to a new estate and mother is rather 'towny', wearing frilled aprons, and takes in foster children. In *Fly-by-night*, there is much more emphasis on personal relationships and the human characters are more interesting. The reader is concerned about what happens to Peter McNair, the strange boy whom Ruth befriends, Ron, the brother's mate, Elizabeth, the small foster child, and Pearl, the girl who has everything. These minor characters are all clearly drawn. Finally, Ruth's achievement, during the year covered by the story's action, consists of successfully schooling her horse so that she finishes sixth in a cross-country event.

At its worst, the pony story can be rather trite. Characters are oversimplified and children who are unable to ride fearlessly and well are regarded as outcasts who can only join the magic circle by becoming both fearless and skilled winners of rosettes. In Judith M. Berrisford's *Jackie's pony camp summer* (Brockhampton), Jackie and her cousin, Babs, appear to be a couple of irresponsible teenagers who have somehow managed to get themselves jobs as pony camp helpers. They prove in some ways to be more of a hindrance than a help, and although Jackie eventually triumphs by solving the problem of Paul, the mysterious twin, and indirectly helps him to regain his lost confidence, she is involved in some far-fetched incidents and coincidences to this end, including the near-drowning of her own pony when she rides it into the sea. Pony books such as this are shallow in terms of characterization and plot and the style is usually peppered with exclamation marks and slang. There is no careful building up of background, character and atmosphere, with the result that the plot seems wildly improbable and the resulting book makes little demand upon the child reader.

What worthwhile pony books are there to meet the request for 'a pony story, please'? Interest in ponies starts at an early age. Barbara Willard's *The penny pony* (H. Hamilton and Puffin), an Antelope book, is a charming story of two small children who dream of owning a pony and who, for a penny, acquire an almost lifesize model of one. For months they get many hours of pleasure from it but eventually it is sent to a jumble sale and sold to a museum. Cathy and Roger are heartbroken but cheer up considerably when they are allowed to call a real, live pony their own and have the promise of learning to ride.

For older girls, apart from the titles already praised, Mary Treadgold's *The Heron ride* (Cape and Knight) and *Return to the Heron* (Cape) both contain plenty of horsey detail in a well-written story. In the first of these, Adam and Sandra, orphan brother and sister, are staying with Miss Vaughan during the long summer holidays. Sandra is keen to ride well and looks enviously at the children who are staying at the local riding-school-cum-holiday-home from the back of Toby, the Vicar's odd-job pony which he has lent her to ride. But trouble and mystery surround the new owner of the riding school, and his purchase of the house called 'The Heron', and gradually the two children are drawn into this. Although, by the end of the book, Sandra is on her way to riding well, the reader is also far more aware of the other sides of her character than is usual in this type of story.

Patricia Leitch, Primrose Cumming and the Pullein-Thompson sisters, Christine and Diana, all write stories which contain the essential elements of the popular pony story and much of their work is marked out by better-than-average characterization and rather more unusual plots. *The flying horseman* (Dent) and *Four rode home* (Dent and Knight), both by Primrose Cumming, are good examples of what can be done by a competent author in this field. Kitty Barne's *Rosina Copper* (Evans) and its sequel, *Rosina and son* (Evans), although a little dated, are also worth recommendation to the girl of ten and upwards who is keen on pony stories.

In Monica Edwards' stories about Punchbowl Farm and Romney Marsh, ponies frequently appear although there are other interests in life and riding and tack-cleaning are things which the children do alongside their other activities. In these books, the child characters develop into convincing teenagers and young adults as the series progresses, and so help the readers to develop too.

Older girls should certainly be introduced to Vian Smith, one of the most outstanding writers of horse stories to emerge in recent years. His first, *Martin rides the moor* (Longmans Y.B) was published in 1964. More recently there has been *The Lord Mayor's show* (Longmans Y.B), which tells the story of Jennifer and Graham, the two older teenage children of Danny Duncan, an ex-steeplechase jockey who seems always to have suffered ill-luck. Graham has managed to break away from the world of horses, but when his father is badly injured, he returns to the dust-covered, rather run-down stables to run them and to try to make them pay. As in all Vian Smith's books, there is very sensitive characterization, with a sympathetic picture of Andrew, the younger brother, who finally rides the Lord Mayor to victory on the racecourse.

K. M. Peyton's first book in the trilogy about Christina of Flambards (O.U.P) is also useful for the older pony-story enthusiast as it widens the scope of the pony story quite considerably and shows that there are other things in life.*

A good corrective to too many pony stories is C. Northcote Parkinson's *Ponies plot* (Murray and Puffin), a hilarious satire, with ponies looking for girls, instead of girls looking for ponies. In the stables the ponies discuss the sort of girl they would like to have ' " ... about nine, standing about fifteen hooves and weighing not more than four stone twelve pounds" '. Daisy Dundreary, the owner of the riding school, gets engaged and the school is to be closed down. The ponies have to find new homes and each of their stories is told in turn. The hero, however, is Skylark who, as the story becomes more and more fantastic, becomes the world's first Astrohorse, goes to Pegasus where he meets a winged horse and goes to the flying college called (naturally) Cramwell, because so much has

*see also page 185

to be learnt. His space ship ruined, he flies back to earth on his own, is interviewed on 'Tonight' by Cliff Michelmore, allows Kellogg's to name their new breakfast food after him and declines a life peerage. These few examples will show that the humour and satire are fairly sophisticated and the book therefore best introduced to the child when she is beginning to move on to less horsey pastures.

The reading of pony stories is a phase through which many girls pass, but there are some titles which will encourage them to read more adventurously and prevent them from settling too comfortably into a rather narrow rut of stories about success in the showring and elsewhere.

READ ON FROM HERE:

See Reading list, *Chapter 22, for article about K. M. Peyton.*

Adventure stories

CHILDREN, when asked what sort of stories they like, frequently reply 'adventure' but further questioning usually fails to obtain a qualification of this, and it is apparent that this term covers a wide range of books even to the same child. Of course, children like a story which is adventurous and, in fact, there must be an element of adventure in every successful children's book.

What makes a good adventure story? Within the general category of adventure, it is possible to distinguish a number of sub-divisions, but all adventure stories have certain features in common. The emphasis is on plot; the characters have an object which is clearly stated in the opening chapters and the story ends when this object has been successfully achieved. There must be plenty of movement and incident in the unfolding of the story and there must be an element of suspense —is the object going to be successfully achieved or not?

The earliest adventure stories were written for a wide audience and the same books appealed to both children and adults. During the early twentieth century, it became customary to write either for children or for adults and a note of unreality crept into those books intended for children. When the main characters were children, adults had to become rather shadowy background figures. Parents were smartly disposed of on the first page so that the children could get on with the adventure unimpeded by adult advice or interference.

During the late 1960s, one can see a change in the better children's books. Home background and even parents are in evidence and the reader usually has some idea of the kind of schools to which the children go and what they think of them. This is a very different situation from that found earlier, particularly in the holiday adventure stories of Ransome and his successors, where the children appear to have no existence between the beginning of term and the end of it, unless, of course, they have mumps or, better still, are in quarantine and can therefore be away from school with a clear conscience.

One of the earliest books is Defoe's *Robinson Crusoe* (Dent), originally published for adults in 1719 but now read almost solely by children in a variety of abridged editions. This set the pattern for desert island stories, in which the immediate object is survival and the ultimate one, rescue. Many adventure stories written since have borrowed elements from the Robinson Crusoe type of story, particularly the efforts involved in personal survival and living off the land. Contemporary authors tend to prefer a group of young people rather than a solitary character and are also concerned with the effects of the circumstances on the characters of the castaways. There is, however, usually a harking-back to Crusoe or to the Swiss Family Robinson. One story very much in the Crusoe tradition is Scott O'Dell's *Island of the blue dolphins* (Longmans Y.B. and Puffin) which, like *Robinson Crusoe*, has basis in fact. On an island off the Californian coast, Karana, a young Indian girl, is left behind with her younger brother when the rest of the women and children are taken off after the men of the tribe have been slain by white hunters. The young brother is killed and, after this, Karana lives on her own, contriving to exist and absorbed in the life of the wild creatures until she is finally rescued. This fine story was awarded the Newbery Medal in 1961.

William Golding's *Lord of the flies*, although a novel for adults, is enjoyed by many young people and this idea of exploring the effects of desert island living on a group of young people is one which has been used by a number of contemporary children's writers. Ivan Southall, in *To the wild sky* (Angus and Robertson), and Richard Armstrong, in *The mutineers* (Dent), both pursue this theme with such frightening effect that it would be unfortunate if these books were read by a less than strong-minded or less than sophisticated child. *The mutineers* is a horrifying book where the effect of power on the leader of a gang of delinquents, combined with the fact that there is no one who is both strong enough and interested enough to make any attempt to oppose him, leads to terrifying disaster.

Sometimes the desert island situation is due to freak weather conditions as in Ivan Southall's *Hills End* (Angus and Robertson *and* Puffin) or to an accident as in M. P. de Ladebat's *The village that slept* (Bodley Head). In the latter, although the setting is a deserted village in the Pyrenees, two young children and a baby are the sole survivors of an air crash and they manage to live on their own for eighteen months until they are rescued and the Crusoe influence is very strong. Ivan Southall, in *Hills End*, set in Australia, is very much concerned with the effect of isolation on the group of children, cut off from their parents after a freak storm.

In less exotic surroundings, and therefore more closely related to the holiday adventure story, but with equal emphasis on the difficulties of survival and the importance of compassion, are Hester Burton's *The great gale* (O.U.P), set at the time of the East Coast floods of 1953, and Margaret Baker's *Castaway Christmas* (Methuen and Puffin). During the few days in which children have to cope with flood water, rescues and clearing up against the background of the ever constant worry of what is happening to their parents from whom they are separated, both the Vaughan children in the first book and the Ridleys in the second develop sides of their characters which have hitherto been hidden and prove to be brave and resourceful in a time of crisis. The time of the floods proves to be a turning point in their lives; as Hester Burton says of Mark and Mary, '. . . it was just that they were the last days, the very last days, that she and Mark were ever quite like that!'

An avalanche leads to a similar sort of situation in *Avalanche!* (Brockhampton and Puffin). Werner, a young Swiss boy in this book by A. Rutgers Van Der Loeff, develops through the book as a result of the series of avalanches which bring disaster and hardship to his village. He has to face up to the loss of his parents, although they are eventually dug out safely, he strikes up a friendship with Paolo, an Italian orphan from the Pestalozzi village, and, through his experiences, learns compassion for other people. This is a story of courage in the face of hardship—not only of Werner's but of a number of other boys and of the aged Aunt Auguste who realizes that she must give up her heart's desire, the girl she has adopted, for the child's own sake.

One of the greatest of all adventure stories is *Treasure Island*

(O.U.P. and Puffin) by Robert Louis Stevenson, published in 1883, and here buried treasure is linked to the island theme. The historical setting of the eighteenth century enabled Stevenson to provide a boy hero with whom the young reader can identify. Jim Hawkins tells most of the story, which contains all the elements of romantic adventure—pirates, treasure and islands; the heroes have to face tremendous odds but, in the end, are triumphant. Many of these elements of adventure are reflected in later books.

True descendants of *Treasure Island* are either historical fiction, where the same sort of situations, events and characters can be given credibility, or sea or exploration stories. One story of this kind, with lost treasure and smugglers, is J. Meade Falkner's *Moonfleet*, first published in 1898. Like *Treasure Island*, it is told by a young boy and has a convenient historical setting at the end of the eighteenth century. *Moonfleet* is a good story, racily told, and has become very popular with children in recent years since an attractive new hardback edition (Arnold), a paperback edition (Puffin) and a successful television presentation helped it to emerge from undeserved obscurity.

With a roughly contemporary setting, the author has the problem of introducing young characters and it is almost preferable when the author quite frankly and unhesitatingly suspends disbelief as Willard Price does in his series of stories about Hal and Roger Hunt. In *Underwater adventure* (Cape and Knight) the two brothers, still in their teens, have been given a year off school to make expeditions for their father, 'the famous animal collector', and their father's reason for arranging this is because he wishes to give them a practical education in natural history. The Willard Price series can make no claims to be great literature but the books are full of factual information and are written in a competent and business-like way. Though there is a strong vein of violence and the evil characters tend to be thoroughly evil, Price's attitudes to the natives who accompany the expeditions are more acceptable than in the majority of this type of story. Even the best of them tend to perpetuate some of the attitudes which critics find so disturbing in W. E. Johns' books about Biggles. Arthur Catherall's sea stories are found in many children's libraries but in *Jackals of the sea* (Dent and Dragon), for instance, one finds the typical, rather objectionable, imperialist attitude implicit in such clichés as 'white master' and 'young Britisher'.

Rider Haggard wrote *King Solomon's mines* (Dent and Puffin) as a result of a bet that he could not write a book as exciting as *Treasure Island* and thus set off a new stream of adventure stories. It represents a type of story which is not written nowadays, successfully at any rate, for children. Haggard did not saddle himself with child characters—Sir Henry Curtis, Allan Quatermain and Captain Good are all fully grown men, although they are young in spirit. The adventure is related in an almost documentary style as if it actually happened and for the space of time that one is reading the book, one can believe that it is a true account of events which actually happened. In this sort of context it is possible to accept the happy coincidences such as the use of the moon's eclipse to get the heroes out of a tight spot. This book is frequently found in children's libraries and can be read with enjoyment by children of nine and ten upwards. Because it has become a classic, the blood-thirsty element seems to be acceptable and, after reading this kind of full-blooded story, it is not surprising that the more able readers move straight on to adult novels at around the age of twelve or thirteen. Writers such as Nevil Shute and John Wyndham have Haggard's gift of unfolding a good adventurous plot in a readable way. Having encouraged children to read *King Solomon's mines*, there seems little point in trying to cater specially for this particular market at a relatively unsophisticated level. The level to which this type of story can sink when it is aimed solely at children can be seen very clearly in Enid Blyton's *The secret mountain* (Blackwell and Armada).

The same considerations apply to a book like *The prisoner of Zenda* by Anthony Hope (Dent and Armada), which is a supreme example of romantic adventure and which set a fashion for stories set in Ruritanian-type countries. English children substituting for Ruritanian kings and queens and stories set in Ruritanian countries, in which children are involved, were frequently found in books published in the period

D

up to 1960 but, with Communist power firmly established in the area usually associated with Ruritania, the fashion for this type of story now seems to have died out.

A number of adventure stories are set within the framework of a journey. Ian Serraillier's *The silver sword* (Cape and Puffin), first published in 1956 and based on fact is one of the outstanding adventure stories of the post-war period and is recommended to each other by boys and girls of about nine to eleven. Some of its popularity may be due to the fact that it translated very successfully to the television screen as a serial and this brought it to the attention of children who might not otherwise have seen the book. It does, however, possess the essential qualities of good story-telling—a fast-moving story, not held up by diversions, with plenty of suspense, good characterization and a range of central characters with whom the readers can sympathize, from the motherly Ruth to the lovable and resourceful scoundrel, Jan. The author also satisfies the demand for 'what happened afterwards?' The most skilful touch, however, lies in the use of the paper-knife made like a sword, which is the talisman carried across war-torn Europe by the four children and which is finally the means of reuniting them with the parents of three of them. Above all, there are the spirit of hope and message of peace which pervade the book.

The journey culminating in a happy ending also provides the framework for *I am David* by Anne Holm (Methuen and Puffin), translated from the Danish in 1965, although here the emphasis is on character as much as journey and some children find the fact that the difficulties of the last part of his journey are glossed over rather irritating. David is twelve years old; he escapes from a rather vaguely depicted concentration camp in Eastern Europe and makes his way across to Italy and up through Europe to be reunited with his mother. Although the story is not told by David, all the events are seen through his eyes—hence the rather shadowy quality of the camp which is the only 'home' he can recall. David dominates the action completely, succeeds in his object against overwhelming odds and there is a spirit of hope and belief in the importance of freedom which carries the journey to a successful conclusion.

In both *The silver sword* and *I am David*, the children benefit from an element of luck and coincidence but in stories of this quality, this element falls naturally into place. It is interesting to compare with these, Hanna Stephan's *The long way home* (Heinemann), also based on fact. Peter is a small German boy, taken from his home in East Prussia in 1941, who travels home again by way of Russia, China, Tibet, India and Egypt. The author does not seem to have made up her mind whether she is writing an adventure story, a documentary or a travel book and consequently fails to produce a really satisfactory book of any kind.

On the run by Nina Bawden (Gollancz and Puffin) is set in England and has an eminently topical theme. Ben, bored during his stay in a London flat, makes friends with a strangely assorted couple—Thomas, the son of an exiled political figure, and Lil, a deprived child whose mum is away in hospital. Ben finds himself, willy-nilly and almost against his better judgment, involved in helping these two to run away. The discomforts of being on the run, of camping out in a cave, are not glossed over. A first-class story about running away is Ruth Morris's *The runaway* (Puffin). Here the setting is Australia and when Joanne Mitchell, who tells the story, runs away because it seems to her that she is an unwanted orphan, it is three months before she is missed. Bruce Carter's *Target island* (H. Hamilton) combines running away with the Crusoe theme. Two brothers, who are frankly bored, and Matty, an ill-treated orphan, run away from their London homes and set sail in a yacht belonging to Matty's rich uncle. Instead of arriving in America, as they confidently expect to do, they arrive on a deserted island in the Outer Hebrides, which is being used for target practice. There is even a Man Friday, in the shape of Mr Bull, the church verger, who has remained behind in protest after the rest of the population has been forcibly evacuated.

In this 'journey' type of story, the adventure element must arise from the circumstances of the journey. No false note should be struck by the introduction of a mystery or excitement in the shape of spies or crooks as happens in a book by Showell Styles, *Journey with a secret* (Gollancz). Here a journey across North Wales has to be enlivened by the advent of a young Hungarian refugee girl in rather dubious circumstances. Despite the excellent descriptions of the countryside in which the adventure takes place, the plot has an air of complete unreality for which the excellence of the regional setting is quite unable to compensate.

What many children undoubtedly visualize when they specify 'adventure story' is a story in which the main characters, preferably children of their own age, outwit a gang of criminals after some successful detective work. Many children like to feel they are part of a gang or group, and some of the best achievements in this type of story are set in an urban area with a gang fully engaged in its own activities and only accidentally getting involved in the solving of some crime.

Paul Berna's *A hundred million francs* (Bodley Head and Puffin) is set in an industrial suburb of Paris where a gang of children have evolved their own particular form of entertainment, which is riding a wooden horse down a steep hill. One day the horse is stolen and, in chasing the thieves, the children also find the men responsible for a mail-van robbery. In C. Day Lewis's *The Otterbury incident* (Bodley Head and Puffin), a gang of children spends a half-term holiday earning money to pay for a broken window; the money is stolen and, tracking down the thieves, these boys too, quite by chance, get involved in capturing much more dangerous criminals. In Roy Brown's *A Saturday in Pudney* (Abelard-Schuman), a gang spends a day looking for the younger brother of one of their members, three year old William Buntley, who mysteriously disappears early one morning. In finding William, they also solve the mystery of some missing jewels.

In these three stories the children are not looking for adventure; they are immersed in their own pursuits and happen to get involved with chasing criminals, as a result of their everyday doings. This seems a much more valid way of writing a crime detection story for children than having a set of children who are deliberately looking for mystery and adventure (and inevitably finding it) or having a schoolboy or schoolgirl detective, who is looked upon with respect by adults in the same line of business. Both these approaches are used by numerous authors writing on a more mediocre level.

Much of the quality of the stories by Berna, Day Lewis and Brown lies in the speed at which they move and the way in which the police are involved as helpful characters at just the right moment. Thrills arise from the fact that in *The Otterbury incident*, the boys don't fetch the police until it is nearly too late (and are severely reprimanded for this), while in *A hundred million francs* and *A Saturday in Pudney*, the children seek the help of the police right at the outset to track down the missing wooden horse and the missing William Buntley respectively but the police are concerned with more serious crime, not realizing that these missing objects are, in fact, important clues to the criminals they are seeking. This type of adventure story is not new. Erich Kästner's *Emil and the detectives* (Cape and Puffin) was first published in English in 1931. Emil is on his way to Berlin to stay with his grandmother with his money pinned inside his jacket when it is stolen. In chasing the thief, with the help of a gang of boys, he also manages to win a £50 award.

Writers are frequently criticised for an unrealistic approach to adventure stories, but unfolding the story of a group of quite ordinary children outwitting the adult crooks can be done with considerable style. In Desmond Skirrow's *The case of the silver egg* (Bodley Head and Puffin), the Queen Street gang, led by Mini Morris, the young but enterprising son of an egg-head professor, manage to trace the missing professor who has been kidnapped together with his latest invention. There is considerable quality in the style of writing, the original ideas (' "I can't see why they don't all use trampolines, like us" ' says Fatty Sharp after Mini had trampolined his way into the government laboratories) and the element of farce. This makes the unfavourable light in which almost all the adults are portrayed quite acceptable since they become a background of caricatures for the boys who are themselves clearly distinguished by physical characteristics—Fatty Sharp, Flinty Stone, Sniffer, Speedy Murray and so on.

Paul Buddee's *The unwilling adventurers* (Brockhampton) is a book where the unlikely situation is carried along by the racy style in which it is written. For example, it begins 'You wouldn't think that a kid like me, who is only twelve, would have a mate with a real bullet hole in him, would you?' Another factor which helps this book is the Australian setting which is established on the second page and which enables the young English reader to settle down comfortably to the hair-raising adventures. This is an ideal book to offer to the eight to ten year old who asks for 'a James Bond, miss?' and it is a pity that there are not more of the same quality.

One modern adventure story for boys which comes close to the standard of R. L. Stevenson is Allan Campbell McLean's The hill of the Red Fox (Collins and Puffin), in which twelve year old Alastair Cameron travels up to Skye to stay in the croft which is his but which he does not remember. On the train journey from Glasgow to Mallaig, he sees two mysterious strangers, one of whom thrusts a message into his hand as they go through a tunnel. Innocently, he becomes involved with MI5. There is violence and excitement but the story makes an appeal to the emotions as well and the author builds up the background which is a perfect setting for this tale of adventure. He shows that it is possible to produce a story which satisfies the demand for adventure and mystery but which is also well worth reading.

There are still to be found in the pages of children's books some clean-limbed, Richard Hannay types, attractive young men who represent the British Secret Service in thrilling adventure stories which will appeal to boys in particular. Henry Treece departed from his usual historical themes to write three very successful stories about Gordon Stewart, beginning with Ask for King Billy (Faber) and Howard Jones's Beware the hunter and The web of Caesar (Cape) are excellent stories in the same style. Also having young men rather than children as heroes are Leif Hamre's books about the Norwegian air force, beginning with Otter three two calling (Brockhampton) and John Wingate's stories about Peter Sinclair of the Royal Navy, of which Full fathom five (Heinemann) is a good example. These books are likely to appeal to boys who like their excitement mixed with a background of technical detail.

Sometimes adventure stories are of a less hair-raising kind and the gang gets its thrills by being involved in a matter of social importance. Eric Allen's The latchkey children (O.U.P) fight to save the tree in their playground. The decrepit Georgian houses, converted into flats, in *Songberd's Grove* by Anne Barrett (Collins) are transformed as a result of the activities of Martin and his friends while in *The battle of St George Without* by Janet McNeill (Faber), a gang of children in a run-down corner of a city find their way into a closed-up church and set out to protect it when it is threatened with demolition.

The best gang stories have plenty of humour along with the thrills and sometimes this peculiarly small-boy type of humour is the strongest characteristic—for example in E. W. Hildick's books about Lemon Kelly and Jim Starling, both of whom hark back to that most humorous gangster of all, William.

The fashion for holiday adventure stories was set by Arthur Ransome in 1930 when he first sent the Swallows and Amazons sailing on Lake Windermere. Two earlier books, Richard Jefferies' *Bevis* (Cape), published in 1882, and Ernest Thompson Seton's *Two little savages* (Kaye and Ward), published in 1903, had both described boys living an open-air life, the one in Wiltshire, the other in the Canadian backwoods, but these had been isolated instances of this type of story. With the arrival of the 1930s, this kind of holiday came within the bounds of possibility for a greater number of children and the Swallows and the Amazons also included girls. In fact, Nancy Blackett, Captain of the Amazons, is clearly the dominant character in all the books in which she appears. Ransome's books, which hark back to *Treasure Island* in the character of Captain Flint and in the naming of places around the lake, although long by today's standards, are still popular with a minority of children and they do demonstrate the main characteristics of the best stories of their kind. They have a strong sense of region—be it Lake District, Norfolk Broads or elsewhere—and the children have to rely for survival on their own abilities and initiative; the children are also useful members of society. The adults hover comfortably in the background, except for Captain Flint who counts almost as one of the children. The adventure arises naturally from the situation. In *Winter holiday* (Cape and Puffin), through a misunderstanding, Dick and Dorothea set off for the North Pole before the main expedition and are in danger when a blizzard sweeps across the frozen lake; in *Great Northern?* (Cape), the children are in conflict with the adult egg-collector, Mr Jemmerling, who threatens to destroy the rare bird which Dick has spotted. To give added interest to the basic solution, Ransome brings in sailing, astronomy, signalling and bird-watching, hobbies which are realistically related to the children's ages and abilities.

Other authors, less knowledgeable, have been obliged to fall back on less convincing pastimes, such as chasing crooks, trapping smugglers, finding treasure and other unlikely achievements. An account of the day to day doings of a holiday would pall and some kind of excitement has to be added. There are various alternatives to treasure-hunting and spy-catching. In some stories, the excitement is provided, as in gang stories, by campaigning for some good cause. The children in Joan Ballantyne's *Holiday trench* are concerned in preventing adults from driving their cars on to the beach; in Lois Lamplugh's *Rockets in the dunes* (Cape), the children living near a seaside town mount a campaign to prevent the taking over of a stretch of sand-dunes by the War Department. These themes have considerable relevance to children today.

The growing interest in archaeology provides another theme. In *The stolen seasons* by David Divine (Macdonald), set on the Roman Wall, three children who, challenged by their father, set out to prove that it would have been possible for a group of barbarians to cross the wall unseen by the Romans, are involved in saving a valuable piece of silver which is unearthed in an archaeological dig. In Walter Macken's *Island of the great yellow ox* (Macmillan), four boys cross swords with a pair of adult archaeologists on the west coast of Ireland. In both these books, the characterization and the style of writing compensate for the rather unlikely plots. Joy Bagshaw, in *The hobstones* (Chatto), places so much emphasis on the element of treasure hunt in the archaeological dig itself that it does not appeal to the child in search of a readable adventure story and only finds favour with the more thoughtful and archaeology-minded child.

Philip Turner shows something of Ransome's skill in applying his own technical knowledge in *The Grange at High Force* (O.U.P). In this and in the other books about Arthur, Peter and

David, one finds the same sort of attention to detail that is so characteristic of Ransome. Restoration work on a church, the firing of a ballista and many other pursuits, all described in considerable detail, occupy these boys in the time spent away from school. Perhaps the selectors of the Carnegie Medal winner were looking back nostalgically to Ransome, the first winner of the Medal for his *Pigeon Post* (Cape), when they awarded the Medal to Philip Turner in 1965.

In all the books mentioned so far, action and incident are paramount but in Turner's books, one can see a change, a growing concern with home background and school. In *Nordy Bank* (O.U.P), also a Carnegie Medal winner, and *The summer in between* (O.U.P), Sheena Porter and Eleanor Spence respectively use the framework of a holiday adventure story as a background to the development of character. The main interest of these books lies in watching the development of Bron in *Nordy Bank* and of Faith in *The summer in between* and for this reason, they appeal mainly, if not only, to girls.

Here, in these two books, the movement towards producing an integrated picture of life, with adventure set firmly in a realistic background of home and school, can be seen quite clearly and, because there is an element of adventure in most children's books, it is becoming increasingly difficult to draw a firm line between adventure and family stories.

READ ON FROM HERE:

BAYFIELD, J : From Simon Black to Ash Road and beyond. *Bookbird*, vol. 6, no. 4, 1968.

BOTT, G : Writers for children : Arthur Ransome. *The School Librarian*, vol. 10, no. 3, December 1960.

LOMAS, D : Arthur Ransome : a birthday appreciation. *The Junior Bookshelf*, vol. 28, no. 1, January 1964.

PORTER, S : Nordy Bank. *The Junior Bookshelf*, vol. 29, no. 5, October 1965.

WARD, R : Adventures on the Isle of Skye : notes on the novels of Allan Campbell McLean. *The School Librarian*, vol. 15, no. 1, March 1967.

See also Read on from here, *Chapter 24, for 'Bodley Head Monographs' about R. L. Stevenson and Arthur Ransome.*

THE science fiction stories written by Jules Verne, H. G. Wells and Sir Arthur Conan Doyle in the late nineteenth and early twentieth centuries still have a place in the children's library and are read and enjoyed, especially by boys, from the age of ten or eleven upwards. These three writers were real masters of story-telling, and their tales have a credibility not shared by many of the later writers who tried to popularize this type of story for children by including youthful characters, and who felt that the scientific awareness of children did not make too many demands on their own knowledge or research ability in this field.

In *From the earth to the moon* (Dover) and its sequel, Verne not only showed remarkable prescience in setting the site for the firing of the moon missile in Florida, and on nearly the same latitude as Cape Kennedy, but also set the pattern for telling science fiction in a documentary style. This, or the use of the first person narrative as in H. G. Wells' *The first men in the moon* (Collins) and some of Doyle's *The Professor Challenger stories* (Murray), helps to make a fantastic story convincing to the reader, and gives it a sense of excitement and urgency.

One of the most popular series with younger boys is that by Hugh Walters, whose stories about Chris Godfrey, the young astronaut, and his friends clearly demonstrate some of the problems facing authors who write science fiction for children. The heroes, it is felt, must be young men with whom the boy reader of nine to twelve can identify and yet must, from a practical point of view, be at least in their twenties. This produces a curious breed of heroes who have the technical knowledge and ability of twenty-five year olds but the attitudes to life and maturity of children. So in Walters' *Terror by satellite*

(Faber), there are the young technician, Tony Hale, in the satellite observatory and his earthbound friend, Sid Stafford, communicating by transmitters which they have made themselves, and thereby saving the whole earth from destruction by a power-mad commander, but at the same time talking and reacting like rather immature ten year olds.

Two other popular science fiction writers with this age group are Angus MacVicar and Patrick Moore. MacVicar's early science fiction stories, published by Burke, are now out of print, but it is possible to see the reasons for his popularity in *Super Nova and the rogue satellite* (Brockhampton and Knight). There is plenty of action and excitement, simple but impressive technical detail, and straightforward characterization. Patrick Moore is known to many children through his television programmes. His early science fiction stories also have gone out of print but the most recent, *Planet of fire* (World's Work), is reminiscent of a Buchan adventure story, although the plot is far from convincing. Barry Nolan, a young orphan, is motorcycling through Ireland when, suddenly, in a quiet, remote corner, he meets a group of Buchan-type heroes, is invited to join their team and sets off in their rocket on a trip to Venus to rescue the stranded crew of a Russian space-ship. Walters, Moore and MacVicar all have praiseworthy attitudes towards international rivalry in space and the villains are never 'foreigners'. The colonists in MacVicar's Port Imbrium are internationally representative, while Chris Godfrey's chief friends are an American and a Russian. The sometimes ludicrous effect of the skilled but immature heroes is presumably unnoticed by younger readers, but possibly explains why boys rapidly move on to adult science fiction if they are really interested.

For slightly older boys a convincing documentary style is essential. By writing in this way James Blish manages to carry off a most improbable plot in *Welcome to Mars* (Faber). Reference is made to the American Apollo project which is described as having consumed billions of dollars and as being 'still utterly bogged down'. (The moon has not yet been reached, although the story is set well in the future.) Dolph Haertel, seventeen years old, discovers the secret of anti-gravity, which

serves the same purpose as Wells' Cavorite, and takes off for
Mars, where he makes a successful landing, in a spaceship
made from an old crate. He is followed by his girl-friend,
Nanette, and together they live a Robinson-Crusoe-like existence, made possible by Dolph's technical skill and his discovery
of the uses of tumble-lichen which provide an unending supply
of food and water. The fantastic plot is backed up by scientific
detail and unfolded with humour, and the introduction of a
girl character and the detailed account of house-keeping on
Mars give the story a special appeal for girl readers.

Robert A. Heinlein, an extremely competent writer of science
fiction, is also popular with young people. His heroes are con-
vincingly involved in adventure; there is enough scientific
jargon and enough strangeness in the space world as Heinlein
visualizes it to please the critical reader. In *Between planets*
(Gollancz), young Don Harvey is suddenly recalled to his
parents who are scientists on Mars; he is chosen to carry an
important message from Earth to Mars, but war breaks out
between Venus, newly declared a Republic, and the Federation
of Earth, and he finds himself on Venus instead. The story is
told in a convincing way; the hero is clearly young enough
for the reader to identify with, and he is not expected to carry
out jobs beyond his capabilities. There are strange creatures—
the Venusian dragon, the gregarians or move-overs and the
Martian aborigines, all of whom are vividly described; and
there is mystery and excitement. Although the universe has
obviously advanced in time, all the conceptions are clearly
understandable to the reader. There is a successful conclusion
when Don eventually arrives on Mars to deliver the message-
carrying ring to his father. Another book by Heinlein, *Tunnel
in the sky* (Gollancz), harks back to the Crusoe theme; a group
of young people undergo a survival test in which they are
accidentally cut off from base. As well as the problem of
physical survival, they also have to face the problems of living
together as a community.

In John Christopher's *The lotus caves* (H. Hamilton), Marty
and Steve are two boys who have never known earth except at
second hand through their parents' stories and through radio
and television. They are both Lunarites, born and brought up in

the artificial environment of the Bubble which has been constructed to protect the human community in the rarefied conditions of the moon. Bored to distraction after a schoolboy prank has cut them off temporarily from the pleasures of the recreation centre, they find a 'crawler', a kind of tank used to cross the moon's surface outside the Bubble, in which the previous user has carelessly left the key. The boys venture out to First Station, long ago abandoned by early pioneers on the moon, find a log-book and are led to look for a mysterious flower-like growth described in it. They find the flower, and the huge net-work of caves which enables it to survive on the arid wastes of the moon—and also Andrew Thurgood, believed to have died seventy years before, but looking very little different from the way he must have looked when he disappeared, nurtured in the Shangri-la of the lotus caves; Thurgood is strangely uninterested in the things which must have happened since his disappearance and he finds it difficult to communicate—' "He probably needs to get used to not being by himself. It's a long time to be a Robinson Crusoe" '. But the boys are not satisfied to be unrescued Robinson Crusoes, and struggle against the plant's determination not to let them escape. John Christopher conveys the boredom of life in an artificial atmosphere, whether it be in the Bubble or in the lotus caves; he gets over the fact that family ties are too precious to be ignored and he uses the science fiction story to put over these facts which have validity in any world.

In *The universe between* (Faber), Alan Nourse makes an appeal to the young by having first a seventeen year old girl and then, a generation later, her teenage son as the key to making contact with another universe, that of the Thresholders, which appears to exist alongside the known universe. There is nothing childish about Gail, nor about her son Robert. Gail happens to possess a high degree of adaptability; she realizes that a human trained from birth to adjust to the second, apparently incompatible, universe would be an even better contact, and she sets about training her son from the moment he is born. This is all documented in a very convincing way, and on the last page there is a clever but satisfying twist to bring the story to a conclusion.

Blish, Heinlein, Christopher and Nourse all write science fiction for adults as well as children and although in the books which I have mentioned they do make some concessions to the young reader there is nothing childish about their approach. The situations which they describe are treated in much more depth than those described by the first group of authors, Moore, MacVicar and Walters, and therefore their stories appeal to a slightly older age group, who want something more than 'cowboys and Indians in space'.

André Norton is undoubtedly one of the most outstanding writers of junior science fiction, and she makes her young heroes into credible beings—for example Troy Horan in *Catseye* (Gollancz and Puffin)—but her style of writing also makes considerable demands on the reader, for she invents a whole range of new and unfamiliar vocabulary in order to conjure up her own version of the future.

Science fiction is popular with both boys and girls, although girls show a preference for books with a sociological bias and their interest lies in the effect of technology on human beings rather than in the details of the technology itself. However science fiction conditions arising in our own world, although explored in novels for adults, are scarcely used by writers for children. An early example, Donald Suddaby's *Death of metal*, published in 1952, is now out of print and although the plot is worked out in an interesting way, its style and attitudes have dated it badly. Richard Parker's *The Hendon fungus* (Gollancz) starts off well. England is being destroyed by a creeping fungus which undermines the foundations of buildings, and the effects of this are vividly described. But a number of children find the end of the story disturbing on account of the rather casual attitude taken by the Hendon family who are responsible, albeit unwittingly, for introducing the alien plant into England. For, at the end, they fly off to Australia, leaving the situation, admittedly somewhat ameliorated by this time, comfortably behind them.

Science fiction can be used as a framework to explore social questions in the contemporary world and it is used in this way by Nicholas Fisk in *Space hostages* (H. Hamilton). In the pleasant village of Little Mowlesbury, a space-ship lands and the whole of the child population is persuaded aboard. The world is tottering on the brink of the Third World War, and the children are hostages to fortune, hovering in space while the crisis is resolved. When the mad Flight Lieutenant responsible for their situation dies from an excess dose of radiation and the children are on their own, there is a struggle for leadership between Brylo, the clever, adopted, coloured boy, and Tony, hitherto the acknowledged leader but corrupted by the power he suddenly wields. It is under Brylo's command that the space-ship finally returns to earth, when the political crisis is solved, and the end presents a return to normality.

Ursula Moray Williams's *The moonball* (H. Hamilton), a 'Big Reindeer Book', is a good example of science fiction for younger children. Like *Space hostages*, the story begins with a cricket match on the village green. This opening on a nostalgically typical English scene has the effect of making what follows seem even more strange than it would otherwise do. The moonball is found lying on the cricket pitch after a storm, and spends about six months among the children of the village; it has the power to change its shape and nature, and although it has no mouth or teeth or visible means of support, it manages to polish off bacon and eggs and coffee when no one is looking. The moonball soon establishes itself as a very real personality and without communicating in any normal way, makes acute observations on the ways of adults. There is interesting characterization of the children from William and Vicky who, out of a sense of responsibility for the moonball, follow it to London to watch over it when it is taken to the Natural History Museum, to Freddie, the Nipper, who ends up in the Juvenile Court for housebreaking in order to rescue the moonball. Before the moonball takes off, it indirectly teaches the children something and makes a difference to them and the lives they lead.

A different approach to science fiction, and the one perhaps most suitable for the under elevens, is the story in which a child from another planet arrives in our own recognizable, roughly contemporary world. Patricia Wrightson uses this approach in *Down to earth* (Hutchinson), where a small group of oddly assorted Sydney children unite to protect a boy whom they know as Martin the Martian. One of the children is con-

scious of the difficulties which are likely to arise if Martin
falls into the hands of the authorities, and senses some of the
problems. These problems are more clearly seen in Alexander
Key's *The forgotten door* (Faber) when the alien child, although
protected by the family into which he falls by chance, is the
object of a witch-hunt by the less thinking members of the
community. This is a much more frightening book, painting a
picture of intolerance arising from ignorance which the adult
knows is only too possible.

For adults, science fiction represents a possible way of escape
to a better world. Older children too may look nostalgically at
the pre-technological age, and it is these children who will most
enjoy John Christopher's trilogy, one of the most interesting
science fiction series of recent years. In *The white mountains*,
The city of gold and lead and *The pool of fire* (H. Hamilton),
the heroes are young men; the world has been devastated by a
nuclear war and has reverted to a medieval way of life, now
dominated by mechanical robots known as tripods. At the end
of the third book, the tripods have been defeated, but it looks
as if the pattern of international strife, temporarily ended by
the need to defeat an alien race, is about to begin all over
again.

In two books by Peter Dickinson, *The weathermonger* and
Heartsease (Gollancz), England in reaction has returned to
medieval times; witchcraft is feared and machines are banned.
The nostalgic element is very clear here; there is an emphasis
on the lack of petrol fumes, and the English climate is successfully controlled by town 'weathermongers' who produce
weather to order—and perfect summers, snow for Christmas,
rain showers as required. The reason for this state of affairs
proves to be linked to Merlin and in *The weathermonger* the
elements of science fiction and fantasy are very closely inter-
linked.

There is much in science fiction that is akin to fantasy. André
Norton, for instance, writes both types of story very successfully. The two elements are perhaps most skilfully interwoven
in Madeleine L'Engle's *A wrinkle in time* (Longmans Y.B. and
Puffin). The two Murry children and Calvin O'Keefe are children
of above-average intellect, Charles Wallace Murry so much so

that he is commonly regarded as sub-normal in the community in which they live. The Murry parents are scientists, and father has disappeared; in a series of almost fantasy-like adventures, the children 'tesser' in time and space in order to rescue him from an evil planet. The struggle between good and evil in this book is akin to the struggle found in Narnia and Elidor, and some of the characters—Mrs Whatsit, Mrs Who and Mrs Which, for example—have a quality of fantasy about them.

In *The iron man* (Faber), Ted Hughes has tried to create a modern myth in terms of science fiction. Hogarth, the farmer's son, who is the first person to see the Iron Man, might have stepped straight out of the pages of a traditional story. The Iron Man is diverted from his practice of eating essential farm machinery by being given the run of a scrap-metal yard where, in a modern civilization, he serves a very useful purpose; even better, he saves the earth from the ravages of a monster from outer space. This is an unusual story, but it is ideal for reading aloud to children of seven and upwards.

At quite an early age, around eleven and twelve, children who enjoy science fiction will move on to reading adult stories, and authors such as John Wyndham are widely read and enjoyed by many young people. It is not surprising that the series of volumes, *Out of this world*, edited by Amabel Williams-Ellis and Mably Owen (Blackie), have been so successful in the children's library; each of the seven volumes contains a selection of stories originally intended for adults, but chosen for these collections because they seem particularly suitable for young people. These, seen as 'sampler' collections, may well lead them on to full-length novels by the same authors.

READ ON FROM HERE:

FISHER, M: Writers for children: André Norton. *The School Librarian*, vol. 15, no. 2, July 1967.

See also Reading list, Chapter 8, for article about Patricia Wrightson.

E

Family stories

IN family stories, the emphasis is on developing personal relationships rather than on adventure, but everyday life has to be recreated in a way that is both convincing and sufficiently interesting to hold the reader's attention. The central characters are shown coming to terms with the people around them, adults as well as other children, and may well be looking for substitutes for non-existent or unsatisfactory parents. The family story provides a useful framework for dealing with problems caused by social and economic conditions, but these problems must be dealt with as an essential part of the story, and the result should not be a documentary-story-with-a-purpose. A good plot with a satisfactory ending is still essential if it is to retain the interest of the reader. Well-written stories of this kind can be helpful in enabling children to sort out their own personal relationships and attitudes to society at large.

These stories, even where most of the central characters are boys, appeal almost solely to girls, who tend to be much more interested in people around them. Some boys read the occasional story which falls into this category, but it is the girls who read them persistently.

The family story is a field in which American writers have made a special contribution, perhaps because there has been a longer tradition of understanding between parent and child than elsewhere. Certainly the American nineteenth-century family stories have worn better than their English counterparts written by Mrs Molesworth, Mrs Ewing and Charlotte Yonge. Louisa M. Alcott's *Little women* (Blackie and Puffin), published in 1868, contains the essential qualities of the good family story. Father admittedly is away at the Civil War (this provides a convenient framework for the story), but mother is very much in evidence and the author shows the relationship between the four sisters, their mother, and the friends and relations around them as a developing one. This book, with Susan Coolidge's *What Katy did* (Blackie) and the Canadian L. M. Montgomery's *Anne of Green Gables* (Harrap and Puffin), forms a trio of the books which girls 'are most likely to have read'. The two latter books, although Katy has no mother and Anne is an orphan, also have a strong sense of family and community which appeals to girls and leads them on to read the rest of the series. Unfortunately none of the later books by Louisa M. Alcott, Susan Coolidge nor L. M. Montgomery seems to come up to the standards of their first.

The trans-Atlantic setting seems to play little part in the popularity of these three authors, although it undoubtedly adds interest to Laura Ingalls Wilder's series which begins with *The little house in the big woods* (Methuen and Puffin) and in which a high standard is maintained throughout. Mrs Wilder based these stories on her own childhood experiences, though they are told in the third person. Laura's father was full of pioneering spirit and, as the North American continent opened up towards the end of the nineteenth century, he took his family westward, to face considerable difficulties as they made a series of homes in newly established communities. In the last of the seven books, *These happy golden years* (Lutterworth), Laura is old enough to teach in a school, twelve miles away from home, and every Friday Almanzo Wilder comes to take her home for the weekend. At the end of the book, when Laura is eighteen, she and Almanzo marry. Mrs Wilder afterwards wrote *Farmer's boy* (Lutterworth) which tells Almanzo's story before he meets Laura. In these books everyday life is recreated to the extent that it is sometimes exciting but always interesting, and reading them will help a girl to mature emotionally as Laura herself does through the books. There are also detailed accounts, which a lot of children enjoy, of the food prepared by Mrs Ingalls, and *The long winter* (Lutterworth and Puffin), the story of a particularly hard time, provides an opportunity of entering vicariously into a vivid experience.

Sidney Taylor's *All of a kind family* (Blackie) and its sequel are given additional interest by their setting on New York's Lower East side at the turn of the century, and by the fact that the family is Jewish, so that there are plenty of background details about Jewish festivals and customs. Also American, but with rather more conventional settings, are the stories about Lucinda, *Roller skates* (Bodley Head) and *Lucinda's year of Jubilo* (Bodley Head), by Ruth Sawyer, and the stories about the Moffats and the Pyes by Eleanor Estes. These are set in the early part of the twentieth century and tend to reflect the greater freedom and easier relationship with adults which American children, living in a less class-stratified and more informal society, enjoyed at this time as compared with their English counterparts. Both Ruth Sawyer's sympathetic portrait of Lucinda and Eleanor Estes' of Rachel Pye and Jane Moffat (whose problems of being the 'middle' child are sympathetically treated in *The middle Moffat* (Bodley Head)) will strike a chord in many girls of ten and eleven. Finally there are the stories about the four Melendy children who in Elizabeth Enright's *The Saturdays* (Heinemann) decide to pool their weekly pocket money and take it in turns to spend the full amount on a really satisfying Saturday expedition. The number of family stories which are included among the Newbery Medal winners is a tribute to the American contribution in this field.

The early English family stories tend to reflect the prosperous middle-class tradition of the period, according to which children led their own lives in the nursery, looked after by nanny, and only met their parents once a day, cleaned up for the occasion and on their best behaviour. This can be seen in E. Nesbit's *The story of the treasure seekers* (Benn and Puffin) where, doubtless because of the family's reduced fortunes, there is no nanny but the children are left very much to their own devices. E. Nesbit also set a pattern for humorous family stories, much of the humour arising from the would-be anonymous style in which Oswald relates the attempts of the Bastable children to restore the family fortunes. Another of her family stories, *The railway children* (Benn and Puffin), is a good example of a book which gained popularity through a successful television presentation.

A shortage of money is common in family stories (although

family fortunes are frequently restored during the course of the book) but there is usually a comfortable feeling of security about the family relationship which compensates for the lack of money. Noel Streatfeild frequently writes about families who are short of money, but the children are nevertheless comfortably blanketed from the realities of life, often by a sort of unpaid nanny or family-governess figure. Her stories also contain a strong sense of family relationships, loyalty to one's brothers and sisters and a firm belief in the rightness of one's parents, even though they may temporarily seem irritating or obstructive. In *The painted garden* (Collins and Puffin), she uses her favourite theme of children succeeding in the entertainment world, but it is Jane, the difficult middle child of the family, on whom the main interest centres and who succeeds in the most splendid way of all, as a star in a film of Frances Hodgson Burnett's *The secret garden*. *The secret garden* (Heinemann and Puffin) is itself a good example of the genre, with Mary, the unwanted and disagreeable orphan, learning to come to terms with her new surroundings.

There is still an atmosphere of gracious living in many contemporary family stories, but on the whole the picture painted is rather less lavish and more in keeping with common experience than it was ten years ago. Antonia Forest's *The Thursday kidnapping* (Faber) describes one day in the life of a Hampstead family, but the Ramsays share their house with a Hungarian couple and their baby, Bart. Ellen, the eldest Ramsay girl, does a newspaper round, and the story starts early in the morning with this newspaper round and finishes late in the evening when the family is reunited again after a worrying and anxious day. The children are left to look after Bart while their mother and Bart's go to the January Sales, but he disappears in his pram when they leave him outside the library. The rest of the day is spent in tracking him down. The security of the Ramsay household, despite its passing anxieties,—'it was lovely coming home'—contrasts with the home background of the insecure Kathy, alternately spoiled and disliked by her parents, and makes the homecoming all the more satisfying for the children. The story is full of acute observation of characters, events, places and dialogue.

William Mayne is also good at suggesting the relationship between children and their parents, and his families are usually comfortable working-class. For girls, in particular, a good introduction to Mayne is *A parcel of trees* (H. Hamilton and Puffin). Many girls sympathize with Susan and her desire for somewhere private where she can escape from her younger sister Rosemary. Like a number of Mayne's books, this has a treasure hunt theme, and Susan's search for a place of her own leads her, with the help of a friendly solicitor, to prove her claim to a piece of waste land. During her quest, her developing relationships with her family and with the people in the village are shown.

Delia Huddy, Jenifer Wayne and Richard Parker are all notable for the way in which they can build up a picture of the normal give and take of family life, particularly through their dialogue. There is excitement—floods in Delia Huddy's *No place like Trickett's Green* (Longmans Y.B) and Jenifer Wayne's *The night the rain came in* (Heinemann and Puffin) and the discovery of a Jutish boat in Richard Parker's *Private beach* (Harrap)—but the real appeal of these stories lies in the style in which they are written and the way they show the relationship between the children and between them and their parents. These books have above average characterization, and the sort of zany family humour which transmutes quite ordinary incidents into something worth reading about. Even the minor characters, who appear only briefly, are brought to life in their comments and attitudes. Nothing is exaggerated beyond the bounds of possibility, but everything and everyone is seen through the eyes of a kindly humorist.

Margaret Macpherson has written a number of family stories set in Skye. In *The new tenants* (Collins), the Shearers move from Glasgow to a little croft, left to Mr Shearer by his uncle. Liz, the eldest daughter, who is the focus of the story, is concerned about the apparent friendliness of Danny, a local ne'er do well, who is always hanging around, appearing to help but laughing at Mr Shearer behind his back. Danny proves to be the villain of the piece, and his downfall provides the framework of the story, but the real enjoyment lies in the picture of Liz's relationship with her parents—to her father of whom she wants to be proud, to her mother who wants nothing better than to go back to Glasgow, to her three young sisters and to the boys at the village school.

In recent years, apart from the move to show society as it really is, there has been a trend towards the portrayal of working-class families from the inside, though there are still complaints, surely unjustified, about the lack of such books. Eve Garnett's *The family from One End Street* (Muller and Puffin), awarded the Carnegie Medal for 1937, was for many years held up as one of the few examples of a successful story with a working-class background. To the adult reader it now seems very dated, but to the children themselves it has something of the appeal of *Little women* because of the sincerity with which it portrays family life and the simple enjoyment they get from minor pleasures. In Elizabeth Stucley's *Magnolia Buildings* (Bodley Head and Puffin), published twenty-three years later, life in the raw is seen very much more clearly, although the pattern is the same—an account of a year in the life of the Berners family, starting with Gloria (known as Ally, short for Glory Alleluia) determined to find glamour in the New Year. Val, the younger brother, is potentially a bad lot, rather than mischievous like the boys in the Garnett books, and it is only Mum's firmness which makes him, under her escort, take a purse which he has stolen to the police station. The portrait of the mouse-like Aunt Glad is almost cruel, although in the end she emerges as a triumphant, if unexpected, bride. There is, nevertheless, a cosy background of grandparents leading a rather idyllic life in the country.

It seems to be difficult for children's authors, who tend to have middle-class backgrounds themselves, to capture the atmosphere in just the right way. In *Gumble's Yard* and *Widdershins Crescent* (Hutchinson and Puffin), John Rowe Townsend describes the Thompson family which consists of Walter and his girlfriend, Doris, Walter's two children and his niece and nephew. In the first book the children are left to cope as best they can when Doris and Walter disappear on their own activities; in *Widdershins Crescent* the family, reunited, is moved out from the slums to a new Council house estate, a new start in life which provides new problems to be overcome. Kevin, the nephew, tells the stories and one sometimes feels that he is really a middle-class observer, not wholly integrated into the milieu of the book. Perhaps the writer who comes nearest to capturing the flavour of life among disadvantaged English children without condescension is Sylvia Sherry in *A pair of Jesus-boots* (Cape); it is interesting that she is also one of the comparatively few English writers to write successfully and objectively about children in other countries where she has lived. Rocky O'Rourke is a gang leader in the Liverpool slums; his greatest hero is his brother, Joey, at present away in prison, but the interest lies not in the activities of the gang but in the relationship of Rocky to his step-sister, his step-father and his gradual appreciation that perhaps a life of crime is not the exciting and satisfying prospect he had supposed it to be.

For younger children, Leila Berg has attempted to portray the working-class scene, and her series of 'Nipper Books' (Macmillan), which are short and easy to read, was welcomed as a useful antidote to the middle-class suburbia of Janet and John when it first appeared in 1969. An earlier book by Leila Berg, *A box for Benny* (Brockhampton), is a delightful story about a little Jewish boy, living in a Jewish community in Manchester, who one spring decides he is old enough to play the shoe-box game instead of the cupky games played by the younger children. The story is an account of how he manages to acquire a shoe-box by a series of swaps, but into this account is introduced an interesting impression of the whole community. This was published in 1958 but, judging by the things which can be bought for a half-penny and the description of the public library, it was set at a time even earlier than that. The poverty of some children is taken for granted, and there is one stage of the story when the children in Benny's class who have no shoes are supplied with them by the better-off members of the community. All this detail is worked into the story as essential background; Benny thinks that at last he is going to get his shoe-box when Yvette gets her new shoes and is very let-down when he finds that she wants to use it as a bed for her doll.

For stories of really disadvantaged children, it is necessary to turn to books set in other countries.* There is, however, no evidence to suggest that children like reading only about chil-

*see also page 97

dren who live in the same sort of environment as the readers themselves do, though this is often quoted (by adults) as a reason for producing more stories with a working-class background. In fact, since children read fiction for relaxation and escapism, the reverse may well be true. One East End children's librarian put forward Antonia Forest as a favourite author among the children in her library, a popularity stemming largely from her own enthusiasm.

The extremes of poverty and disadvantage can lead to stories reflecting contact with welfare and social services, as seen from the receiving end. In Christine Pullein-Thompson's *Homeless Katie* (H. Hamilton), the situation is fairly desperate. The family has been poor for as long as the four children can remember and their flat, where one tap serves five families, is demolished so that the children and mum have to move into a family hostel while dad lives away from them in a men's hostel. Despite the fairy-tale ending, it is a well-constructed story. The mother is Italian, which is important because it forms a link between her and the old lady who finally provides a satisfactory solution to their problems. Jean, Katie's elder sister, says at one point ' "You can't expect everything to come right. It never does." ' But, of course, in this particular story it does.

The children in Margaret Baker's *Home from the hill* (Methuen) are also made homeless and have to be taken into care, but show enough initiative to find a home for themselves and their parents. It is interesting that the welfare services are shown in an extremely favourable light; at the same time it is clear that they are only a second-best substitute for a proper family life. The story which comes nearest to portraying sympathetically the problems of a child in a home is Catherine Storr's *Rufus* (Faber). Rufus and Rachel, his elder sister, (parents killed in a road accident) live in a children's home; most of the children invent mothers for themselves and tell fantastic tales about them, but Rufus is inhibited from doing this because Rachel remembers too well. Then Rachel, having reached the age of fifteen, leaves the home to live with the family of a school friend and Rufus, left unprotected, is bullied by Mickey, who is undoubtedly a bad lot and leads him astray. Catherine Storr shows very clearly how easily this can happen when one is unhappy, and how Rufus escapes into a fantasy dream life among the Ancient Britons, which helps him through the really bad patch until he can get free of Mickey.

Richard Parker's *Second-hand family* (Brockhampton) is about a rather older boy, Giles, who is in care and boarded out with a succession of families. Although Giles also has his day-dreams, he is past the stage of make-believe. This is a readable story with a happy ending, and girls particularly enjoy the sympathetic exploration of the relationships between Giles and the various members of the family which fosters him. This is not a particularly demanding story to read, but it extends the experience of the child reader a little.

In all these stories, there is a feeling for the importance of the family unit, the necessity to have roots and relations on whom one can depend. Some stories take this feeling one stage further and delve into family history. In Angela Bull's *Way-land's Keep* (Collins) chance brings together three cousins to stay in the house of a mutual ancestor. In unravelling a family mystery they discover that their superficial evaluations of each other were wrong, and they become friends. A similar theme occupies Kate in *Kate and the family tree* by Margaret Storey (Bodley Head). Kate, sent to live with an elderly guardian, traces out her family history from old photographs and other things which she finds in the attic.

In most of the stories so far mentioned, problems of family relationships are minor ones, perhaps looming large for a short period in the minds of the children, but soon solved satisfactorily. Other writers have used the family story as a framework for working out situations not so easily dealt with.

Step-parents are moving away from their traditionally wicked role but their existence can still give rise to problems. In *The battle of Wednesday week* (Longmans Y.B. and Puffin), Barbara Willard brings together two lots of step-children, and a conflict arises between the rival families. In Sheena Porter's *The scape-goat* (O.U.P) Carys, made unhappy by her father's remarriage, acquires the habit of petty thieving, a situation sharpened by her unhappy relationship with her step-mother. She escapes official retribution, but Jimmy in Frederick Grice's *A Severnside story* (O.U.P) is not so lucky. He is similarly led astray, as a result of his rather impoverished home background, and he finds himself in the juvenile court. Frederick Grice is excellent in the way he gets over Jimmy's indifference to school, which contrasts sharply with his enthusiasm for boats.

In Penelope Balogh's *Up with the Joneses* (Gollancz), the Jones family 'as a matter of principle' adopts a coloured baby. This is one of the few stories which looks at adoption from the point of view of the adopting family.

The problem arising from divorce is one which has not yet been tackled successfully in a children's book; Erich Kästner's *Lottie and Lisa* (Cape and Puffin), which is one of the few books which handles it at all, has a rather romantic plot and there is a splendid fairytale reconciliation at the end. In a children's book, a happy ending is a basic requirement, and divorce is a situation in which it is difficult to produce a really satisfactory conclusion from the child's point of view.

The family story also provides a background for stories in which a child suffers from some physical or mental disability. Veronica Robinson's *David in silence* (Deutsch) is at times in danger of becoming too much like a documentary, with the author over-anxious to put across the basic facts about the nature and education of deaf children, but there is enough of a plot to carry this along for most readers. David, born deaf and therefore with speech difficulties, has to readjust to his family and to his hearing companions when his family moves to a new housing estate so that he can leave his special boarding school and live at home. David succeeds in carrying out an exploit—walking through a long, dark canal tunnel—which has defeated all his contemporaries, and he is also proved right about the balance of a raft which they are building to sail on the canal. David is therefore shown to be successful despite his handicap.

In Ivan Southall's *Let the balloon go* (Methuen), there is a description of a spastic boy. Left on his own for the first time in his life, John Sumner resolves to make the most of it, and tries to act out the advice of a stranger who had once said to him ' "Don't let anything stop you from being the boy you want to be. The answer's inside you. A balloon is not a balloon until you cut the string and let it go." ' There is a small amount of action, but the real interest lies in the detailed account of the boy's feelings as he struggles to achieve. Another Australian book, *I own the race-course* by Patricia Wrightson (Hutchinson), includes a sympathetic treatment of a mentally-handicapped boy. Five friends, boys, play a kind of real-life Monopoly with the publicly-owned buildings and open spaces in Sydney. Andy, the mentally-handicapped boy, is one day 'sold' the Beecham Park race course for three dollars by an old tramp, and the men who work there, taking a liking to the boy, play up to the idea. Andy's friends begin to wonder if he really has bought it, but Joe, in particular, is very much afraid that Andy's castle in the air will come crashing down around him and is very much concerned with looking after the boy and protecting him.

In all these stories there is emphasis on coming to terms with disability, instead of the now old-fashioned approach where a cure was required to bring the story to a happy conclusion. These stories, and others like them, are a far cry from *What Katy did* where Susan Coolidge gets all the possible sympathy for Katy's crippled state and then allows her to be cured. The modern attitude is a much healthier approach to life, and the stories have a wider significance in emphasizing the need for adjustment to the situation which presents itself.

Joan G. Robinson's *Charley* (Collins) is a good study of a girl who believes herself to be unwanted, unloved and generally misunderstood. Charley runs away to live by herself in a field for almost a week. Although Charley is quite young and fairly immature, we are here on the edge of the problems caused by adolescence and growing up generally. Some problems only make themselves apparent at the adolescent stage, and a number of stories dealing with these problems in some depth have been written especially for young people.*

Family stories for children should not be too complex. Good characterization is essential to a successful family story, and it should not be crowded with incident to the extent that full development of the characters is hindered. The story which attempts to be a mini-version of the Forsyte saga or the White-oaks chronicles is not really very successful. Elfrida Vipont's

*see also page 182

The pavilion (O.U.P) and Barbara Willard's *The toppling Towers* (Longmans Y.B) both crowd in so much happening to so many people in the family that children are unable to see the development of individual characters, and thus the essential point of family stories is missed. *The toppling Towers* has enough material for six good children's books, and adolescents who can tackle it and get something from it will already have moved on to adult books.

READ ON FROM HERE:

CAMERON, E : The art of Elizabeth Enright. *The Horn Book Magazine*, vol. 45, no. 6, December 1969, continued vol. 46, no. 1, February 1970.

ELLIS, A. W : The family story in the 1960s. Clive Bingley, 1970.

FISHER, M : Writers for children : Barbara Willard. *The School Librarian*, vol. 17, no. 4, December 1969.

FISHER, M : Writers for children : Patricia Wrightson. *The School Librarian*, vol. 17, no. 1, March 1969.

MEIGS, C : Louisa Alcott and the American family story. Bodley Head, 1970. (Bodley Head Monograph.)

TAYLOR, J. K. G : The social background of children's fiction. *The School Librarian*, vol. 11, no. 3, December 1962.

WILNER, I : Laura Ingalls Wilder. *Bookbird*, vol. 5, no. 3, 1968.

See also Reading list, *Chapter 9, for article about William Mayne, and* Read on from here, *Chapter 24, for 'Bodley Head Monographs' about Noel Streatfeild and Ruth Sawyer.*

THE evolution of the school story presents one of the most interesting developments in the last hundred years. The school story for boys emerged in the last twenty or thirty years of the nineteenth century, the great exponent being Talbot Baines Reed whose *The fifth form at St Dominic's* was his best known work and very typical of the genre as a whole. Earlier there had been Thomas Hughes' *Tom Brown's schooldays* (Dent), published in 1856, and Dean Farrar's *Eric; or little by little*, published two years later. *Eric* harked back to the very moral tale typical of the early nineteenth century, while Hughes' book was almost a documentary, shot through with his own admiration for the great Dr Arnold of Rugby. The reader follows both Tom and Eric from the time when they arrive as new boys at their respective schools until they leave. In *Tom Brown's schooldays*, there is much more filling in of the background detail than was usual in later school stories, where events tended to be circumscribed by the school walls. However, even in this book, adults assume a rather minor role and Tom is soon absorbed in a world where the important figures are his contemporaries, led by East, and the older boys, such as Brooke, who can make the sun shine for younger boys by giving a kind word of praise, and where he suffers fagging and learns the schoolboy lore and language.

In the traditional school story, interest lies in the characterization and in the competition and incidents which arise naturally out of school life. A boarding school provides a small, closely-knit world in which there are clearly defined rules and standards. Children can assume an importance which they do not have in the outside world, and small matters loom large in this microcosm.

The boys' school story flourished in the last part of the nineteenth century in the style set by Baines Reed, and stories in the same style were written well into the twentieth century, but they were never really the same after Kipling published *Stalky and Co* (Macmillan) in 1899, in which the heroes drink, smoke and despise games. Young people today can extract as much enjoyment as ever out of Stalky and his friends and the methods by which they contrive to outwit both masters and fellow students, but few think of *Stalky and Co* as a typical school story.

The school story for girls developed rather later, partly because the girls' public schools themselves were a later development. The female equivalent of Baines Reed was Angela Brazil who, between 1906, when she published *The fortunes of Philippa*, and 1947, when she died, was responsible for nearly fifty school stories. Some of them were in print until quite recently and two or three were reprinted as paperbacks in 1969. Angela Brazil made an attempt to move with the times and some of her later books were set against the background of the Second World War, as earlier ones had been set in the First World War, but, on the whole, the schools, the girls and the incidents are much the same whether it is 1914 or 1940.

The reprinting of a few selected titles seems to indicate the reliance which some publishers place, probably quite justifiably, on parental recommendation for selling books to children. Even the modern jackets can hardly compensate for the solid mass of small print inside, and it is hard to imagine what mini- or maxi-skirted misses of the seventies will make of some of Angela Brazil's resounding sentences, the old-fashioned names in which the girls rejoice (would any children's editor nowadays allow an author to give the heroine of a school story the name of 'Lesbia'?) and the way in which the girls talk.

The girls of St Cyprian's (Armada) is one of the titles reprinted and is vintage Brazil. The heroine, Mildred, is an orphan, brought up by a kindly aunt and uncle, and her story is firmly set against the background of St Cyprian's. Mildred is a talented musician, a violinist, but the hard work necessary to making the most of this talent is emphasized, and she is very much concerned in the efforts of the school to excel within the Alliance, formed among the six girls' schools in the town to organize competitions in Drama, Music, Art, Literature and

Games, and with the honour of St Cyprian's in general. When she is made a 'monitress', she 'thoroughly appreciates being a school officer', particularly enjoying the committee meetings! She devotes just as much attention to making juniors behave as she does to winning a scholarship which will give her three years' study at the Paris Conservatoire. It was out of these sorts of priorities that the traditional school story for girls was born. The generations of girls who must have read Angela Brazil in her hey-day are now mothers and grandmothers but will their influence really persuade today's eleven year olds of her charms? Perhaps a very small minority will be attracted to them, as a minority of boys is persuaded by the nostalgic reminiscences of father and grandfather to enjoy the adventures of Billy Bunter, who also features in full-length books, both paperback and hardback, upgraded from the comic where he began and should rightfully have stayed. The world of Billy Bunter is a completely artificial one, and it is difficult to see what appeal the archaic vocabulary and unsophisticated humorous situations can have in book form.

Angela Brazil's footsteps were followed by other prolific writers such as Dorita Fairlie Bruce, Elsie J. Oxenham and Elinor Brent-Dyer, but all these authors tended to lose interest in the school life of their characters and produced long series of books, in which the later heroines are daughters of the earlier ones, who, despite the trials of motherhood and even, in some cases, widowhood, manage to retain the 'jolly hockey-sticks' approach to life which they had at fourteen. Whereas Elsie J. Oxenham and Elinor Brent-Dyer used their school as a sort of background peg for the outside events in which they became more interested as time went on, other writers sought to give added interest to the school story by introducing buried treasure, smugglers, kidnapped princesses, film stars and other unlikely excitements.

These stories linger on in cheap reprints but have little really popular appeal. The market for which they were intended, the twelve to sixteen year old girl, has had her attention directed elsewhere and, although they might be read and enjoyed by the more able girls under twelve, it would be a pity for them to waste time on them.

After the war, there were two new impulses in the school story—the progressive boarding school and the day school. Slightly later, the secondary modern school began to loom large; now it would be the turn of the comprehensive school, but by the 1960s school had begun to take second place to family life and, although children in fiction often attend comprehensive schools, we are unlikely to be treated, in a children's book at least, to a view of the problems arising at a new comprehensive, operating on three separate campuses, each half a mile from the others.

In the stories set in progressive schools, interest centred on the way the children were involved in the running of the school, and some of the stories were daringly co-educational. The several books of this kind written by M. E. Allan in the 1950s are now out of print, and Enid Blyton's books about *The naughtiest girl in the school* (Newnes and Merlin Books), which are less insipid and trite than much of her work, have never achieved the popularity of some of her other series.

In the 1950s A. Stephen Tring, Fielden Hughes and Geoffrey Trease all wrote stories about day schools, followed later by E. W. Hildick with his stories about Jim Starling, but in these one can see the growing importance of life out of school. In *No boats on Bannermere* (Heinemann) and the other four Bannermere titles, Geoffrey Trease introduced girls as well as a number of other, rather glamorous, outside interests.

One schoolboy character who is still going strong is Anthony Buckeridge's Jennings, who first appeared in *Jennings goes to school* (Collins and Puffin), published in 1950. Like Billy Bunter and Greyfriars, Jennings and Linbury Court bear little relation to real life, but are very popular with boys of nine to eleven to whom that type of humour appeals.*

Three contemporary writers have given the traditional school story a completely new look—William Mayne, Mary Harris and Antonia Forest. These writers come nearest to the tradition in those of their stories which are set within the world of school but they are, at the same time, concerned with wider problems and themes.

William Mayne draws on his personal experience of school

*see also page 118

F

life in his stories about the choir school which began with
A swarm in May (O.U.P) in 1955. This tells how the youngest
singing-boy, Owen, is required to carry out the duties of beekeeper at the special annual service—an old tradition maintained, although there are no longer any bees—and how, after
trying to pass the job on to another boy, he gets interested in
real bees and, with the organist's assistance, brings in a swarm
to the service. Not only the boys—Owen, Trevithic, Madington,
Iddingley and Dubnet—but also the masters—Dr Sunderland,
Mr Sutton and Mr Ardent—and Turle, the watchman, come
alive for the reader. Although there is a secret passage for good
measure, it is the small details which build up a complete and
charming picture of life in the school, with schoolboy jokes,
and the odd game of cricket sandwiched between services. But
there are the same old standards; Owen is thought to be 'wet'
because he tries to shirk what is his rightful job.

Both in William Mayne's stories about the choir school and
in Mary Harris's stories about day schools, one can see the
elements of the traditional school story still, but with a difference. The awe-inspiring Miss Wolff in *Penny's way* (Faber) is
a clearly-drawn teacher who puts the fear of God into Penny,
short for Persephone; Penny is involved in problems of friendship, her loyalties divided between the rather unpleasant Mavis
and the much more sympathetic and attractive Nicola, and at
the end of the story Penny, who is in the 'C' stream of the
Grammar School and who is overshadowed by her academi-
cally brilliant elder sister, brings attention to herself by providing an attractive snuff-box for an exhibition and wins a
special essay prize, in the same way that John Owen in *A swarm
in May* triumphs as beekeeper. So in both books the child reader
has a hero or heroine with whom to identify and in whose
success he can take pleasure. At the same time the books are
firmly rooted in the realities of life.

In many of William Mayne's books, school is successfully
integrated into home life and both environments are made
equally important. *Sand* (H. Hamilton) is a good example of this
as the action centres round the friendly rivalry between the
boys' secondary modern school and girls' grammar school in
an East Yorkshire seaside town, which is gradually being buried

by sand blowing in from the dunes. Although the main activity is the digging up of a skeleton of a sperm whale by the boys and its transportation by a once derelict railway, they are anxious to get to know the girls better and their exploits are largely directed to this end, even to the extent of transporting the whale into the grammar school yard. Some of the scenes take place in school, some at home, but in turn, each of these is brought into focus and brought to life. This approach is typical of the modern attitude to school expressed in children's books where school has become, for the most part, just one part of a much larger canvas.

Mary Harris's earliest book, *Gretel of St Bride's*, was a traditional school story, typical of the '30s and '40s. Her later stories illustrate very clearly the evolution of the school story. In *Seraphina* (Faber), the heroine is a boarder at what is primarily a day school; she invents for herself a family, an invention which causes complications, but which finally enables her to come to terms with herself. There is far more depth of feeling here than is seen in earlier school stories. Another of her books, *The bus girls* (Faber), sympathetically explores the relationship between Hetty and her widowed mother who is 'tiny, subdued, permanently worried' while Hetty herself is masterful, clever and bossy and hates to be fussed. Hetty prides herself on her logic in being able to reduce her mother's mountains to molehills but is frequently reduced to an exasperated exclamation of 'Oh mother!' This relationship is shown alongside the development of a friendship between Hetty and Davina, another of the bus girls.

Antonia Forest has been writing about the Marlowe family since 1953 and the majority of the books are family stories, set in holiday times. However, the girls in the family all attend the same boarding school, Kingscote, and two of the books, *Autumn term* (Faber) and *End of term* (Faber) are set, as the titles suggest, in school. *End of term* is set in the Christmas term and the events build up to the climax of the nativity play. There is a lot of discussion, good characterization and a concern with contemporary problems, such as race, religion and divorce.

Elfrida Vipont has also written a complex series of books.

These are concerned with the fortunes of the Kitson and Haverard families* and two of these, at least, are partially school stories. *The lark in the morn* (O.U.P) describes how Kit Haverard finds that she is destined to become a singer and the two or three chapters in which the climax of the story is reached are set against the background of the Quaker boarding school, Heryot. In *The spring of the year* (O.U.P), published a few years later, Elfrida Vipont has moved away from the boarding school world. Admittedly the two eldest girls are also away at Heryot, but Mary is at the local grammar school, and Laura, the youngest, on whom the interest centres, goes to the village school until she fails her eleven-plus and moves to the secondary modern school, where her talent for acting begins to develop.

In these series of stories by Antonia Forest and Elfrida Vipont the reader can see school as an essential part of the whole picture, and this closer relationship between school and family life, which nowadays is the norm in children's fiction, is matched by the acceptance of a school background in many adventure stories.† The decline in the popularity of the school story in its traditional form is perhaps due to a more widespread enjoyment of school by children nowadays; they don't, therefore, need to read books in which children are successful in the school situation in order to compensate for their own insecurity.

The traditional school story frequently used to include at least one chapter or incident which featured an important sporting contest—a vital house match or a match against a rival school, which had not been beaten in living memory. This match was usually won within the last few minutes and the hero or heroine of the story invariably played a vital part, preferably playing in his or her first match for the team or having substituted at the last minute for another player.

These matches have become a less obvious part of the contemporary school story but a new type of story has appeared on the scene—the sports fiction story. It could be thought that these books would be popular with children in view of the constant demand in school and public libraries for books about

sport, but, in fact, when this demand is analysed, it is dis-
covered that the most popular sports to read about are football
and fishing, with cricket a poorish third, and what most boys
want are factual books, well illustrated by photographs, and
containing plenty of information about their real-life heroes.
Sports fiction as such therefore tends to sit on the library shelves
and unless it has some other merit, both literary and as entertainment, it seems hardly worthwhile providing it. Fiction for
girls with a sporting background is also a non-starter, although
Delia Huddy's *Jane plays hockey* (Longman's Y.B) is enjoyed
for its study of personal relationships.

As children, and girls in particular, began to mature at an
earlier age, an interest in a new type of story—career novels—
began to develop. Children were beginning to look beyond the
school walls and to wonder what the future held, once they left
school. Noel Streatfeild's *Ballet shoes*, published in 1936 (Dent
and Puffin), has been called 'the first career novel' and certainly
it was one of the first children's books to show what it was
like to work one's way up in a particular career. A number of
Noel Streatfeild's books are about children who succeed on the
stage and screen, or in glamorous sports such as tennis and
skating. In *The circus is coming* (Dent and Puffin), awarded the
Carnegie Medal for 1939, Peter and Santa run away to find their
uncle who is an artiste in a circus. They have always led very
sheltered lives, but they gradually adapt themselves to their
new life and prove that they are more able children than they
at first appear. It is interesting to compare their path to success
with that of Jimmy Brown in Enid Blyton's *Mr Galliano's circus*
(Merlin Books), which is a warm mish-mash of cosiness and
wish-fulfilment. Although the children in the Streatfeild books
invariably succeed, the necessity for hard work as well as
natural talent is continually emphasized.

Two other books which show young people succeeding in
their chosen careers were awarded the Carnegie Medal at a
time when the 'career novel', as a type, was becoming a
popular success, Richard Armstrong's *Sea change* (Dent and
Knight), in 1948, and Elfrida Vipont's *The lark on the wing*
(O.U.P), in 1950.

The lark on the wing continues the story of Kit Haverard,

which began in *The lark in the morn*. Kit's success as a singer does not come easily, although it must be admitted that she is at an advantage in having impressed the composer, Sir Hugh Cathcart, who chooses her to sing in his new work, but the importance of carrying out one's chosen job, even at great personal inconvenience, comes through quite clearly when Kit, recovering from a cold, travels down to Silverbridge on a foggy November evening to carry out a singing engagement. There is a happy atmosphere of growing up despite family and financial problems, problems of coping with the members of the opposite sex and with life in general. This is a good introduction to the experience of growing up for the twelve or thirteen year old girl.

Sea change is a fine sea story, with plenty of adventurous incident, set during the voyage of a merchant navy ship to the West Indies. Cam Renton, the hero, is a young apprentice, eager to learn the skills of seamanship and to qualify as an officer. As well as the conflict between the men of SS Langdale and the sea, there is conflict between Cam and the mate which reaches a climax during the voyage, and then resolves itself as Cam learns that the mate is just as interested as Cam in furthering the latter's career.

These are first-class stories, well-written, perhaps beginning to seem a little old-fashioned now, although still read and enjoyed. They are very different from the 'career novels' which became a fashion in the early 50s, when Bodley Head and Chatto and Windus both began to publish series of career novels, which served two purposes. They imparted useful information about the qualifications required to follow a particular career and about what it was like to do a particular kind of job, but they also provided stories with a slight romantic interest for the older girl.

There were other similar books published outside these series, notably those by Nancy Martin, such as *Jean behind the counter* (Macmillan), and Collins began a new series of career books as late as 1962. This, like the Bodley Head series, tended to concentrate on the more glamorous careers and it is these titles which deal with fashion, hairdressing, air hostessing and medicine in various forms which have always been the most popular.

A number of these have been reprinted, with the facts up-dated, as Knight paperbacks, and they still make a steady appeal to younger teenage girls.

The Chatto and Windus series included some useful stories about the less glamorous careers, and about half the titles dealt with boys and boys' careers. These seemed to spend most of the time sitting on the shelves, unread except by the occasional girl, and many children's librarians must have discarded them while they were still in good physical condition, despairing of them ever being worn out.

The great popularity of the American series of books about *Sue Barton* (Bodley Head and Knight), who pursues a successful nursing career through several volumes, shows quite clearly the link between the average story of this kind and the light romances which may well be read by the same girls in their late teens and on into middle age unless they are stimulated at this early stage to read more widely and more imaginatively.

However, the career story may be in for a face-lift. Compare Elizabeth Grey's *Pauline becomes a hairdresser* (Bodley Head and Knight) or Marjorie Gayler's *Daphne sets a fashion* (Macdonald and Knight) with the swinging 1969 look to be seen in Josephine Kamm's *First job* (Brockhampton), and one can see how safely old-fashioned the first two have become. *First job* is a down-to-earth account of a girl in her first post, and although Sally succeeds after a fashion, the value of a few appropriate qualifications is briskly pointed out and, at the end of the book, she is about to embark on a part-time secretarial course. Nor does Sally's romantic life follow the traditional pattern of success usually seen in the career novel; it has, one suspects, much more in common with reality!

Realism is taking over from romance at every stage from school to first job, and although it would be a pity to deprive children and young people completely of the opportunity to be vicariously successful through their reading, it is probably better for them to see that success must be achieved through hard work, and that one's plans do not always work out as expected.

READ ON FROM HERE:

BLISHEN, E : Writers for children : William Mayne. *The Use of English*, vol. 20, no. 2, Winter 1968.

THE TIMES LITERARY SUPPLEMENT: Mary K. Harris: the real world of school. 5th December 1968.

MUIR, L : Fifty years of the Hamlet Club. *The Junior Bookshelf*, vol. 30, no. 1, February 1966. *About Elsie J. Oxenham.*

TATHAM, C. S : Yesterday's schoolgirls. *The Junior Bookshelf*, vol. 33, no. 6, December 1969.

See also Read on from here, *Chapter 24, for the 'Bodley Head Monograph' about Noel Streatfeild.*

GOOD stories about children and young people living in other countries can help to make the way of life elsewhere come vividly alive. Jella Lepman, the founder of the International Youth Library, sincerely believes that books can help to bridge the gap between children of different countries. While no one can seriously suppose that stories of the 'mysterious-adventure-in-Armenia' type can be of much help in this direction, those stories which paint a sympathetic picture of life elsewhere, which draw attention to those things which children of different countries have in common, and in which the plot is really dependent on the foreign setting do help to build this bridge.

Many of the best books in this category are produced by non-English writers. English authors who choose to set their stories abroad usually build the plot around English children visiting the country, and the result is either a semi-documentary travel book, with too much undigested information about the country concerned, or a mystery-adventure story, with too little.

Two nineteenth century stories of this kind and one from the early twentieth century have by now become classics. *Hans Brinker; or the silver skates* (Dent), published in 1865, written by the American Mary Mapes Dodge, has a rather romanticized but memorable Dutch setting. Johanna Spyri's *Heidi* (Dent and Puffin) was translated into English in 1884, four years after its original publication in German, and is still extremely popular with girls of nine to eleven. Selma Lagerlöf's *The wonderful adventures of Nils* (Dent) was published in Sweden in 1906-7 and was intended to be a readable guide to Swedish history and geography. Selma Lagerlöf brought to it such creative imaginative skill, however, that it became a very popular story among Swedish children, and was successfully translated into other languages.

These books set a pattern for the current situation in which we find that many of the successful books set in foreign countries are the work of foreign writers. A number of the American writers are first or second generation Americans, and write either from their own experience or from that of their parents or grandparents about their country of origin; other writers, such as the Dutch A. Rutgers Van Der Loeff, even when not writing about their own countries or countries with which they have special ties, seem to be able to capture successfully the feeling of what it is like to be a child in the country concerned.

Some stories, of course, are set in foreign countries where the standards of living and the scenery seem very little different from those at home. From Paul Berna's books children will learn, if they are observant, that French children don't go to school on Thursdays; from Edith Unnerstad's and Astrid Lindgren's they will learn a little about Sweden, but these stories are usually enjoyed as straightforward adventure or family stories, as are those set in the former Dominions. In stories set in Australia, for example, basic ideas and names at least are familiar, and through impressions acquired from books by such writers as Joan Phipson, Patricia Wrightson, H. F. Brinsmead and Eleanor Spence, many English children must feel that Sydney and the Australian outback are as accessible to them as Edinburgh and the Scottish grouse moors.

Younger children enjoy stories in which the children are seen to have much in common with themselves—a secure and happy home even though this is in a mud hut, and pets, although they may be very different from English ones—and in which the story is woven around the incidents of everyday life.

Gwen Westwood uses the kind of incidents and situations that appeal to children in her stories about Africa. *Narni of the desert* (H. Hamilton) is a small boy in the Kalahari desert with an ambition to become a hunter like the adult men of his tribe. In *The red elephant blanket* (H. Hamilton), Bengu, a herd boy in the Transkei, tries to save up the money necessary to replace his grandmother's beautiful new blanket when it is damaged by fire, and his pet goose, Hamba, is instrumental in achieving this goal.

Lots of small girls will sympathize with Yoshiko, the Japanese heroine of Momoko Ishii's *The dolls' day for Yoshiko* (O.U.P), who cannot take part in the annual Festival of the Dolls until her mother is at last able to provide her with a beautiful, hand-made set of paper dolls. In Yoshiko Uchida's *Takao and grandfather's sword* (Chatto, Boyd and Oliver), Takao has to sell his much-prized Samurai sword, inherited from his grandfather, in order to pay for the damage caused by a fire. The same author's *In-between Miya* (Angus and Robertson) is a delightful story, appealing to girls of ten and eleven, who are fascinated by details of life in Japan. The description of the Japanese home and food, the contrasting charms of the 'western style' room and modern electrical gadgets, provide the background to the gently humorous story of Miya's summer the year she is twelve. Even if the moral is a little too obvious, the story does successfully say something about the values and conditions of an ordinary Japanese home, which are shown to be similar to those in any happy home in any part of the world, even if the customs are different.

While young children are satisfied with stories of everyday events, older children demand a stronger element of adventure. The qualities to be looked for can be seen in A. Rutgers Van Der Loeff's *Steffos and his Easter lamb* (Brockhampton). The story is dependent on the Greek setting; the smallest lamb in the flock is to be slaughtered for the Easter festival. Steffos manages to save it by showing a party of Dutch archaeologists a clue to the classical ruined palace for which they are searching, by stowing away on their coach and by persuading them to take the lamb back to Holland. Every part of the story is seen through Steffos' eyes, but there is plenty of comment on the poverty of Greek peasants, the rocky ground and poor soil from which a living has to be scratched, and the honour which is given to Mikali's family because his father has been to the city twice; thus, as well as an enjoyable story, the reader also gets an insight into the way of life in modern rural Greece.

Meindert DeJong, winner of the international Hans Andersen

Award in 1962, spent his childhood in Holland and his sympathy with the Dutch and their country comes through very clearly in *The wheel on the school* (Lutterworth) and *Far out the long canal* (Lutterworth). In the first book, the six children in a little Dutch village school decide to try and bring back the storks to nest in their village. As the story progresses, the landscape around the village is developed as a background to the children's search for a suitable wheel, and the various adult inhabitants of the village come into focus and assume a new importance in the lives of the children. Incidentally, DeJong's books should not be stocked without being read by the librarian. Both *The house of sixty fathers* (Lutterworth and Puffin) and *The journey from Peppermint Street* (Lutterworth) contain passages which many children find unpleasantly disturbing, despite the enthusiastic reception of these books by the critics.

Kate Seredy was also drawing on her own childhood memories when she wrote *The good master* (Harrap and Knight). City Kate is sent from Budapest to stay with relations on their ranch on the Hungarian plains. When she arrives there she is spoilt and bad-tempered, but she gradually settles down and comes to love the life. In any setting, this is a story which would appeal to girls, but its descriptions of the great Hungarian plain, the ranch where the 'good master' runs his farm, the kitchen where his wife makes sausages and stores them in preparation for the long bleak winter give it an added appeal. Then there are the feast days—Easter, Christmas and the excitement of the visiting fair and the round up of the horses beforehand. Above all, Kate is just the sort of heroine who appeals to girls of ten and eleven—tomboyish and holding her own with her cousin Jancsi.

Turi's papa (Gollancz) by another American writer, Elizabeth Borton de Treviño, is also set in Hungary, a rather romanticized Hungary in which vague and ominous references are made to the difficulties of obtaining the all-important papers and the shortage of food, and Turi and his father, who has been asked to go to Cremona to take over the direction of the Institute of Violin Making, have to make their way across two borders in secrecy in order to reach Italy. The time is evidently after the Second World War, but very little attempt is made to set the story precisely in time and place. Children have to rely on the dust jacket to fill in the details, but many of them would have preferred a map and more detail in the story.

There is an increasing number of English authors who can write successfully about life in other countries from the inside. In Roberta Elliott's *The day of the cats* (Macmillan), the Italian food (spaghetti in the first sentence) and architecture (Antonio lives in a marble semi-palace) are an essential part of the background. Antonio would dearly love to have a cat, and strikes up a friendship with an old lady who has fourteen but who lives in an attic (whose poverty contrasts very strongly with Antonio's home) and is threatened with eviction on account of her pets. The story ends happily because the yowling of the cats saves families from drowning, and world-famous paintings in the Uffizi Gallery from damage, when the River Arno floods Florence in the October of 1966.

Sylvia Sherry has written two stories about Malaysia. *The frog in a coconut shell* (Cape) is an adventure story with Yusof, who lives in a small fishing village, getting involved in a raid by the Indonesians. The story begins with Yusof being entrusted with the family heirloom, a sword once used to fight pirates, and ends with him a hero, thanks to the timely use of the sword as a threat.

For older readers, stories in which they can read about young people of their own age facing up to the kind of problems which they themselves have to face are useful. Certain problems of adolescence are common to young adults in any country; other problems may arise because of particular circumstances but the reader can see the process of growing up played out against a different background.

Alan Boucher's *The hornstranders* (Longmans Y.B) shows how a young boy living in a remote district in Iceland is torn between loyalty to his grandfather, who is steeped in the traditions of his Viking ancestors, and the attractions of the modern world to the south. Margaret Balderson's *When jays fly to Barbmo* (O.U.P) shows a heroine disturbed by divided loyalties too—in this case between loyalty to her Norwegian father and loyalty to her Lappish mother. Although both her parents are dead, she feels an overwhelming sympathy for and attraction to her mother's nomad family. Manolo, hero of Maia Rodman's *Shadow of a bull* (H. Hamilton) faces a similar problem. The son of a great bull-fighter, he is expected to become one too, but although he feels he owes it to his dead father, he knows his heart is not in bull-fighting and he is afraid that this is because he is a coward. He learns, however, that 'Real courage, true bravery is doing things in spite of fear, knowing fear.' The author captures the Spanish scene and the Spanish way of life, but the theme of the book has a much wider significance than this.

Books set in the West Indies and India are useful as they give English-born children a view of those countries. This may help them both to understand the cultural background of their immigrant contemporaries and to appreciate the tradition from which it springs; the books are also useful for the children whose roots lie in those countries, to enable them to preserve links with their own traditional heritage.

There are several stories for younger children set in the West Indies. *Lonely Maria* (H. Hamilton) by Elizabeth Coatsworth and two books by S. Gudmundson, *The turtle net* (World's Work) and its sequel, *The hurricane* (World's Work), are all useful for children who are beyond the picture book stage. Ebbie, the hero of *The turtle net* is anxious to be old enough to go fishing with his father, but he learns that he can be just as responsible and useful by staying at home, and he manages to save the village fishing net.

Humphrey's ride (Routledge and Kegan Paul) by R. Abrahams and Virginia Durstine's *Monty of Montego* (Hart-Davis) both have an element of adventure which appeals to ten and eleven year olds. The second book contrasts very clearly life in a Jamaican mountain village with life in the town where there are such conveniences as tap-water and electric light. C. E. Palmer's *The cloud with the silver lining* (Deutsch) uses the ever popular theme of two children restoring the family fortunes, though here the children are West Indians, the time twenty or thirty years ago and the fortunes, even when restored, are quite modest. Timmy tells the story of how he and his brother Milton make enough money to buy a buggy for their crippled grandfather; the climax comes with the Christmas fair when the two boys run a stall, selling goat curry, snow-ball (a drink) and a variety of sweet goodies.

One of the most outstanding writers of stories with a West Indian setting is Andrew Salkey whose first book, *Hurricane* (O.U.P) was published in 1964. This, *Drought* (O.U.P), *Earthquake* (O.U.P) and *Riot* (O.U.P) are all fairly short, focussing on one major incident. His most recent book, *Jonah Simpson* (O.U.P), is rather more complex, the story woven around an eventful summer holiday spent in Port Royal.

India, too, is well covered by children's stories suitable for various age groups. In R. Mehta's *Ramu* (Angus and Robertson), one feels the conflict between old and new India, but Ramu is a boy who will be recognized by children in any country. His ambition is to get a red and gold mouth organ, as his reward for being good, at Diwali, the Festival of the Lights.

In other books, too, Indian children are shown to have much in common with their contemporaries. Lalu, the hero of *The road to Agra* (Brockhampton) by Aimée Sommerfelt, and Rama, the hero of *One rupee and a bundle of rice* (Odhams) both set out on journeys, the one to take his small sister, threatened with blindness, to hospital, the second to make sufficient money to buy a bullock for his family. Although they both accept a lot of responsibility, Lalu only does so because he is goaded into it, while Rama does some stupid things before he achieves his object. In *The road to Agra*, particularly, the poverty of India comes through very clearly. Two books by A. C. Jenkins, *Kingdom of the elephants* (Blackie) and *Storm over the blue hills* (Chatto, Boyd and Oliver) are most likely to appeal to children who enjoy animal stories.

S. L. Arora's *White Shirt* (Blackie) is a useful book for older children, although as there are no illustrations and it is rather slow moving at first, they will need some encouragement to tackle it. This is set in a little fishing village, and through the eyes of Kumanan, one sees the conflict between 'White Shirt', the government official who has come to give advice on new and better fishing methods, and the villagers who do not understand. It is an interesting study of education and experiment ranged against traditional methods and superstition, and shows, quite incidentally, certain aspects of Indian society; Kumanan, for example, although the youngest member of the family, receives from his mother the respect due to a male.

Shanta by M. Thøger (Brockhampton) is a book which appeals to adolescent girls, both those of Indian origin and those living alongside them. Shanta tells her own story of the year when she is twelve and of an age to be married, when a dowry is of more importance than schooling. The arranged marriage, the preparations for it, the importance of having a son, the need to make cakes of dried cow-dung to sell for fuel are all seen as perfectly natural things. Sita Rathnamal's *Beyond the jungle* (Blackwood), although not intended specially for young people, has the same sort of appeal as *Shanta*. Sita tells her own story too; as a child in hospital she meets a young Brahmin doctor, and as she grows up the friendship develops into love on both sides but he cannot bring himself to marry her because she is not of his own caste. This story is very sensitively told, and though girls may be disappointed at the unsatisfactory ending to Sita's romance, it may give them a little more insight into the problems of integration.

Books set in other countries can also be useful for setting squarely before the English child the problems of racial integration. Books of this kind must be chosen with particular care, and ones which may suggest a problem which does not really exist here should be avoided. Dorothy Sterling's *Mary Jane* (Longmans Y.B) has transplanted well. It shows, in the story of Mary Jane who is one of the first negroes to enter a newly integrated High School in one of the Southern states of America, some of the problems which can arise in an area divided by racial prejudice.

Bianca Bradbury's *Lucinda* (Macdonald), set in a small, north American town, is a teen-age novel-with-a-purpose. The arrival of Lucinda, a negro girl, from the South to live with the Lee family as part of a scheme to improve the educational opportunities of the negroes, has unexpected repercussions on the whole community; some people realize that they are not quite so liberal-minded as they had supposed. This provides a good picture of a small American community, and although the author writes with social purpose uppermost in her mind and without having absorbed and recreated her material thoroughly, the story is enjoyed by teenage girls who might be given food for thought as well as enjoyment.

Stories about Jewish children are usually set abroad and are useful for English children when they are set against the background of Nazi-occupied Europe or in the new state of Israel. K. Ambrose's *The story of Peter Cronheim* (Longmans Y.B) describes how Peter, living in Germany in the 1930s, gradually becomes aware of the growing hostility to his race. Margot Benary's *A time to love* (Macmillan) is set in Germany in the period immediately before the Second World War, and shows the heroine's sadness at the growing power of Nazism and her loss, but thankfulness, when her Jewish friend, Esther, departs to England. Aimée Sommerfelt's *Miriam* (Abelard-Schuman) contrasts the lives of two girls, one Jewish, in German-occupied Norway. Leonard De Vries' *The land is bright* (Dobson) paints a more hopeful picture, telling the story of young refugees leaving Europe to make a new home in Israel. All these give children a better understanding of a minority group, but it seems pointless to introduce them to a book such as Emily Neville's *Berries Goodman* (Angus and Robertson), set in America, which shows only too clearly the anti-Semitic feeling which can exist in a country which many English children think of as not very different from their own.

In some of the books with foreign settings, English children will read about children who lead very different lives; such stories may give substance to the Oxfam and Save the Children appeals. Even among the stories of the most impoverished English children there is nothing to compare with the life led by the heroine of Karl Brückner's *Child of the swamps* (Burke), who lives among the rice-workers on the Po delta in conditions which contrast sharply with the affluence of the modern city dwellers. Also set in Italy, M. Oliver's *Five spinning tops of Naples* (Dent) paints a varied picture of life among the Neapolitan urchins who have to scratch together a meagre living. G. Feustel's *José* (Methuen) tells the story of a half-starved Amerindian boy who leaves his home in the Bolivian Andes to seek work and food in the town, while Aimée Sommerfelt's *My name is Pablo* (Abelard-Schuman) is about the efforts of a Mexican shoe-shine boy to overcome the dis-

G

advantages of his poverty-stricken peasant background. Naomi Mitchison in *Friends and enemies* (Collins) contrasts very clearly the rigours of freedom in drought-stricken Bechuanaland with the softer, but police-dominated, life in South Africa. To make satisfactory children's books, a happy ending is necessary and this is usually forthcoming. Well-written stories of this kind appeal to a number of children, whose sense of compassion is aroused, and there is nothing with an English setting of quite this kind.

There is one great lack, however, and this is of books about life as it is really lived at the present time in the USSR and other East European countries. Books set there and published in this country tend to be written by expatriates, so that for the most part they are set in pre-Revolutionary Russia or in the post-Revolutionary period seen with a rather prejudiced eye. E. M. Almedingen in *Little Katia* (O.U.P) and Mara Kay in *Masha* (Macmillan) draw charming pictures of what it was like to be a child in Russia before 1917. In contrast to these, B. Bartos-Höppner provides a vivid account of life in Siberia at the beginning of the century centred around Nikolai, the son of one of the *Hunters of Siberia* (Brockhampton), although the story carries a message of the need for conservation of wild life which has a much wider significance.

In Mara Kay's *The burning candle* (Hart-Davis), set in communist Yugoslavia soon after the end of the Second World War, the plot hinges on the fact that Zora, the heroine, still observes traditional religious festivals and gets involved in helping her cousin, a member of the royalist party, to escape abroad. Although this provides a basis for an exciting story, the author, who was brought up in Yugoslavia but who has lived in America since 1950, seems too much concerned with pointing out the evils of communism, and the book lacks the warmth and sympathy which might have made the characters come alive. Many young readers would be discouraged by the strange names and by the lack of atmosphere and incident.

Marie H. Bloch is also an expatriate, born in the Ukraine and taken to the United States at an early age. Since she has revisited the Ukraine and talked to people who trusted her in the 1960s, the picture shown in *The two worlds of Damian* (Macdonald) may well be true although it is biassed against the communist régime. Damyan is keen on swimming and can see that the passport to success is to throw in his lot with the Party, but he is very much under the influence of his grandmother whose religious beliefs are still strong, and it is her influence which finally wins the day.

One book which does manage to communicate successfully the pleasure which Russian children must surely get from life is Noel Streatfeild's *Lisa goes to Russia* (Collins). Here, admittedly, there is an English child, of Russian descent, going to stay with her Russian cousins in Moscow. At nine, Lisa has a totally uncritical acceptance of the Russian way of life; she soon discovers 'it was impossible to compare things at home with things in Russia because they were so different'. Grisha, the boy cousin nearest to Lisa in age, does enjoy special treats, such as acquiring two pet gold fish and eating chocolate biscuits, because of her arrival, but he is also able to share with her the pleasures that he knows about such as the theatre, the ballet, the circus and the children's festival. Russian ideals and beliefs are accepted; Cousin Sasha would never try to look smart even for a wedding because he preferred to look like 'someone winning a revolution', and the Russians do not celebrate Christmas with Father Christmas, but the New Year with Father Frost. Because of the style in which this book is written, it is enjoyed mainly by the under elevens.

More translations of books written by contemporary East European writers might fill a gap in children's literature, as long as the translator took care to include essential explanations in the text. In Helena Šmahelová's *Youth on the wing* (Brockhampton), set in Czechoslovakia, the communist régime is seen in a favourable light since the reader can easily see the advantages of a society where young people are encouraged to learn to glide without any consideration of the costs involved, and although Masa is pleased to earn money for a bicycle and a new winter coat, there is no suggestion that anyone is deprived in the material sense. Apart from the rather jerky style which makes it a difficult book for many girls to read, there is a rather irritating lack of explanation about what is meant by 'brigade work' or what happens during the 'political' part of the meeting which Masa and her friends attend after the gliding sessions.

Life in other countries seems to come through best in books which rely on a simple adventure story woven around the everyday life of the children who, though they may eat different food or wear different clothes, are not really very unlike English children in their interests, ambitions and outlook on life.

READ ON FROM HERE:

TEACHERS WORLD: J. Adcock. Reading far and wide—Europe. 27th December 1968; Africa, Asia and Australasia. 17th January 1969. *These articles are brief surveys of titles relating to different countries. Books set in the British Isles are covered in an article*, Reading nearer home, *Teacher's World, 12th and 19th December 1968.*

HIGGINS, J. E: Kate Seredy: storyteller. *The Horn Book Magazine*, vol. 44, no. 2, April 1968.

HISTORICAL fiction has been one of the big growth points of children's literature in recent years and nearly every period of history, from prehistoric times up to the Second World War, is now covered. Well written historical novels can be of great value in supplementing the teaching of history by clothing the bare bones of fact in recognizable human forms. In some cases, the most useful information about a specific subject may well be found in a novel rather than an information book. Barbara Leonie Picard's account of the illumination of manuscripts in *One is one* (O.U.P), for example, is far more vivid than any account likely to be found elsewhere in the children's library.

A good historical novel should not be deadened by too many facts. The author needs to be thoroughly at home in his period so that he can use the wealth of detail naturally to capture the right atmosphere without making his story in any way akin to a text-book. The style of dialogue is an especially important factor in the historical novel since it must be credible, thus helping to create the right atmosphere, without being full of either anachronistic phrases on the one hand or incomprehensible, archaic ones on the other.

The readability of a historical novel, as far as most children are concerned, depends on a good, simple style, convincing characters including at least one with whom the child reader can identify and a fast moving, well-developed plot. This need to provide youthful heroes and heroines means that one gets the impression, after looking through a number of historical novels for children, that the whole of world history has been the responsibility of young people under the age of twenty. In two books published recently, set in the Second World War, Jill Paton Walsh's *The Dolphin crossing* (Macmillan) and Hester Burton's *In spite of all terror* (O.U.P), the young hero in one, the young heroine in the other, take part in the evacuation of the army from Dunkirk. This is typical of the approach to writing historical novels for children.

Until Geoffrey Trease, who has, perhaps, been the most influential figure in this particular field of contemporary children's literature, began to write in the 1930s, historical fiction for young people was regarded largely as a means of imparting a romantic cloak and dagger atmosphere to an adventure story, and there was little serious attempt to write convincing stories which captured the real atmosphere of the period. Captain Marryat, in *The children of the New Forest* (Dent), published in 1847, was very much attracted by the Crusoe element in his story of the Royalist family during the English Civil War. In Robert Louis Stevenson's *Kidnapped* (Dent), the emphasis is on romance and adventure, and in most of G. A. Henty's seventy stories, produced between 1871 and 1902, the heroes are essentially Victorian schoolboys with Victorian standards and a Victorian outlook on life, whether they are with Wolfe in Canada, or with Clive in India or even sailing under Drake's flag. The stories by Marryat and Stevenson have survived as classics, and a few of Henty's titles are still in print and are read and enjoyed by a few boys who are probably introduced to him by fathers and grandfathers who remember him with affection. But the attitudes of these writers are very different from those which predominate at the present time.

The type of historical novel against which Geoffrey Trease was reacting is now no longer in print, and the present generation of young librarians may well find it difficult to understand what all the fuss was about and to appreciate the contribution which Trease made to the development of the high quality novel which has reached its peak with the post-war writers of historical fiction for children. *Charmouth Grange: a tale of the seventeenth century* by J. Percy Groves, published by Sampson Low during the 1930s must have been typical of the kind. The hero, Ronald Cathcart, 'of a bright, genial disposition . . .', not 'wanting in the sterner qualities which go to make the man', succeeds to the Charmouth estate on the death of his uncle in 1642, and is (naturally) on the side of the King during the Civil War. The villain of the piece, Captain Philip Ruddach, who hopes to do Ronald out of his inheritance, is a Parliamentarian, and in Ronald's triumph in this personal feud, the fact that he had sided with the losing King can be glossed over to some extent. In any case, his bravery enables him to carry out some deeds which bring about minor victories for the King. Apart from the general attitudes, implicit throughout the book, however, there are some real gems of dialogue of which the following remark by the porter at Charmouth Grange when Ronald arrives to be at the bedside of his dying uncle is a fair sample. ' "I' faith, young sir, thou hast indeed ridden hard! It must have been strange for Bevis to be scored by the rowels and taste the sting of the lash! But what kept that varlet Mark? Surely *he* loitered not on the road?" ' (Bevis is Ronald's horse.) Evidently acceptable by the standards of the 1930s, no reputable publisher would have dared to print such rubbish in the '60s.

Geoffrey Trease realized the importance of having a strong plot, basically adventurous, if the book was to appeal to young people. *Bows against the barons* (Brockhampton), which was first published in 1934 by Lawrence and Wishart, was a milestone in the development of historical fiction for children, for he wrote with some feeling for the social history and ideas of the period in which he set his story. Robin Hood is portrayed as an early socialist, and there is a conscious effort to present the seamier side of life and to play down the more popular, romantic picture by showing what life must have been like without windows, proper sanitation and modern heating and lighting. Trease also set a fashion for dialogue which avoided the use of archaic phrases of the 'zounds' and 'prithee' type.

Trease's finest achievement is, perhaps, *Cue for treason* (Blackwell and Puffin). In this adventure story, the hero has to run away from home because he becomes involved in the attempts of the farmers to prevent the enclosure of their lands. He falls in with a troupe of actor-players and travels with them to London where he uncovers a plot to kill Queen Elizabeth I. This is a most readable story and there are the two central characters of Peter Brownrigg and Kit, the girl whom he meets on the way, with whom the reader can identify. At the same time, Trease never forgets for one moment that he is writing about the late sixteenth century—Peter looks at the sun to tell the time, and later makes use of the timber-frame of a house to climb up and in through a window.

Once Geoffrey Trease had shown the way, the quality of historical fiction for children began to improve, and among the post-war winners of the Carnegie Medal one finds the names of Rosemary Sutcliff, Cynthia Harnett, Ronald Welch and Hester Burton. Leon Garfield was the first winner of the Guardian Award for a novel set in the eighteenth century. Henry Treece was an outstandingly creative writer who was never honoured by either the Guardian or the Library Association, although his posthumous novel, *The dream-time* (Brockhampton) came very near to winning the Carnegie Medal. Apart from these writers, there are others who have produced competent work in this field such as Mary Ray, Barbara Leonie Picard and C. Walter Hodges from England, Elizabeth Speare from the United States, Nan Chauncy and Eleanor Spence from Australia and from elsewhere, in translation, René Guillot, B. Bartos-Höppner and Karl Brückner.

Most historical fiction is written for children of ten and over, since it is necessary to have some sense of history before a historical novel can be properly appreciated. However, there is an increasing number of well-written stories which can be enjoyed by younger children. Hamish Hamilton have included some in their 'Antelope' and 'Reindeer Books' and in 1969 Heinemann began a new series, 'Long Ago Children', with four stories by Leon Garfield, Ruth Manning-Sanders, Elfrida Vipont and Frank Knight.

Although Leon Garfield's *The boy and the monkey* (Heinemann) is a small literary gem, set in London in the mid-eighteenth century, Ruth Manning-Sanders' *The Spaniards are coming*, which is set at the time of the Armada, and Elfrida Vipont's *Children of the Mayflower* are likely to be the most successful with children since they deal with well known historical events and show the involvement of children in them.

Some of the Hamish Hamilton books require quite a lot of maturity in the reader and, for this reason, are often quite useful with the older, reluctant reader. One title which is particularly successful in meeting the needs of its intended public, however, is Jacynth Hope-Simpson's *The great fire*, a 'Reindeer Book' intended for nine to eleven year olds. Jeremy, a boy who lives in the baker's house in which the Fire of London breaks out, is accused of starting the fire and has to run away. His adventures in the burning city provide plenty of scope for references to historical facts and the introduction of contemporary characters such as James, Duke of York, and Christopher Wren.

Rosemary Sutcliff's *The chief's daughter*, set in Prehistoric Britain, although an 'Antelope Book' aimed at seven to nine year olds, would be better appreciated by older children. The two main characters, Nessan and Dara, are ones with whom teenagers of today could easily identify and the story has the sort of pattern which would only be appreciated by older children.

Rosemary Sutcliff is noted particularly for her novels set in the Roman period, and it was for one of these, *The lantern bearers* (O.U.P), that she was awarded the Carnegie Medal for 1959. It is generally agreed, however, that her outstanding achievement is *The Eagle of the Ninth* (O.U.P), and once children have got involved in Marcus' quest for the Eagle of his father's lost legion, they thoroughly enjoy this story. The slight romantic interest in the growing friendship of Marcus and the British Cottia appeals to older girls, but many children have to be helped over the earlier chapters which set the scene.

Rosemary Sutcliff does not, however, restrict herself entirely to the early period, and *Simon* (O.U.P), set during the English Civil War, is a good example of another of the changes in historical writing for children, the movement towards presenting the viewpoint of the underdog rather than of the establishment. Simon, like his father, declares himself to be for Parliament while his life-long friend, Amias, like *his* father, is for the King. The story traces their fortunes during the Civil War seeing the major part of it, however, through Simon's Parliamentarian eyes.

Cynthia Harnett is much concerned with the social life of the times of which she writes, and her own illustrations most usefully supplement her descriptions, but she does not overlook the need for an element of adventure. Although she was awarded the Carnegie Medal for *The woolpack* (Methuen and

Puffin), *The load of unicorn* (Methuen and Puffin) illustrates even more clearly the way in which she uses the social conditions of the time to mould her story. Benedict's father is a retired scrivener who has handed over his business to his two eldest sons, Benedict's step-brothers. Caxton is just setting up his printing press in London and the two scriveners, seeing a threat to their livelihood, are involved in a plot to prevent paper reaching the press. Benedict's father, however, not only encourages him to accept the new invention, and to learn to live with it rather than to fight against it, but even apprentices him to Caxton. The climax of the story comes with Benedict's journey to Warwickshire to get the manuscript of Sir Thomas Malory's *Morte d'Arthur*. *A load of unicorn*, like *Cue for treason* and many other successful historical novels, has a fictional hero whose adventures are integrated into the contemporary historical scene. Real historical personages such as Shakespeare and Queen Elizabeth I, or Caxton and Malory, or Sir Christopher Wren are introduced, but the two elements of fiction and historical fact are skilfully interwoven to make a complete whole.

With the growing interest in environmental studies and the teaching of history being increasingly related to the child's own area, those historical novels which have a strong sense of locality are invaluable. Meriol Trevor's *Lights in a dark town* (Macmillan), set in Birmingham between 1849 and 1851, is a good example. This story contains a fair amount of discussion about Catholic ideas which is likely to appeal most to rather thoughtful girls of about eleven and upwards, but many Birmingham children who do not fall within this category will enjoy tracing out the places described in the book on a modern map and reading the account of Queen Victoria's short visit to the City, of the conditions in the slums and so on; there are many references to places which can still be identified a hundred years later. This is a story full of fact but this is carried along by a plot of basic appeal to children. Emmeline has a happy family background, living with her widowed mother, and is the sort of girl with whom ten and eleven year olds can easily identify, and there is a very satisfactory, happy ending. Phyllis Bentley has written three historical novels for children, set in her own native West Riding. Tom, the fictional hero of *The adventures of Tom Leigh* (Macdonald), is befriended by Daniel Defoe, touring through Yorkshire in the 1720s. Librarians should pick out those stories which have particular relevance for their own area and exploit them to the full.

In the books of K. M. Peyton and Hester Burton one can see the East Anglian countryside during various historical periods. *The Maplin Bird* (O.U.P), *Windfall* (O.U.P) and *Thunder in the sky* (O.U.P) by K. M. Peyton, and Hester Burton's *Castors away!* (O.U.P) and *Time of trial* (O.U.P) are all set, at least partially, in this area but these stories have a more than regional significance and deal with wider issues. In some of them there is concern with the problems of growing up and adjusting to an adult world, particularly from the girl's point of view. Although *Thunder in the sky* is set during the First World War, the questions of pacifism and cowardice which are raised are relevant at any time.

Whereas Hester Burton, Cynthia Harnett and K. M. Peyton are authors very much concerned with people and ideas and appeal mainly to girls, C. Walter Hodges, Ronald Welch and Henry Treece put much more emphasis on action, particularly violent action, and therefore have a special attraction for boys. This does not mean that Treece and Hodges, at any rate, do not have a clear philosophy to communicate to the reader. For his last book, *The dream-time* (Brockhampton), Treece chose for his hero Crookleg, a boy who would rather create things than fight, who expresses a strong belief in humanity and the need for understanding between all men. This is a book which has great relevance for the contemporary adolescent, a relevance which is emphasized by Charles Keeping's illustrations, in some of which today's teenagers might easily recognize themselves. In over twenty historical novels, Treece returned again and again to the Viking period which he made peculiarly his own. These stories too, full of vigorous action, are used to communicate important ideas; in *Viking's dawn* (Bodley Head and Puffin), the first of the books in the trilogy about Harald Sigurdson, the need to respect other people's ideas and different ways of life is clearly pointed out and at the end Harald, the only member of the longship's crew to survive, is saved by John the monk. The evocative northern gloom which dominates the books is relieved by the occasional touch of humour. *Man with a sword* (Bodley Head) provides the most readable story available for children about Hereward the Wake and is a much happier choice than Kingsley's *Hereward the Wake* to which so many children are introduced.

C. Walter Hodges published his first historical novel for children, *Columbus sails* (Bell), in 1939. Then, after a gap of twenty-five years, there appeared *The namesake* (Bell and Puffin) in which he traces the early story of Alfred the Great. This comes vividly alive, told by another Alfred, left with only one leg by a party of plundering Danes, who, as a young man, travels to Wessex from East Anglia and witnesses King Alfred's struggle with the invaders. The King's story is continued in *The marsh king* (Bell).

Ronald Welch was awarded the Carnegie Medal for *Knight Crusader* (O.U.P), published in 1954. Unlike this, most of his stories are woven around various members of the Carey family and cover a wide range of historical periods and geographical locations. The Careys fought at Crécy, during the Civil War, at the Battle of Blenheim, during the Peninsular War and the Crimean War; another Carey was able to render good service to Wolfe before the capture of Quebec. There is plenty of action and excitement in all these stories, and the use of members of the same family (a family tree is included in some of the books) gives the reader a sense of the continuity of history.

Leon Garfield is one of the few historical writers who appeals to both older boys and older girls. His rather strange plots and the Hogarthian eighteenth century atmosphere seem to have a fascination for many children. Children's librarians hesitated over the buying of *Black Jack* (Longmans Y.B) with its horrific opening scenes where young Tolly is left to look after Black Jack's corpse which then comes back to life, and the later scenes involving the mad girl, Belle, and the madhouse, but it proved to be enormously successful with older children, who like this kind of horror, and the book, like all Garfield's, is of the highest literary quality, besides being meticulously accurate in its historical research.

The history of other countries can also be gleaned from the reading of historical novels, and the United States and Australia are particularly well covered by books available to English children. The history of these two countries is closely linked to that of Britain, and English children are therefore aware of the basic situations behind these stories.

Elizabeth Speare's *The witch of Blackbird Pond* (Gollancz and Puffin) is set in the very early days of colonial America, in 1687, when Kit Tyler arrives from a luxurious and exotic home in Barbados to live with her aunt and uncle and two cousins in a Puritan household in a small Connecticut settlement. There is a first-class story for girls with an element of romance but also showing very clearly what it must have been like to live in these hard-working households, struggling for existence, with their puritanical outlook on life and the tendency to look upon anything slightly unusual as witchcraft. This book was awarded the Newbery Medal in 1959.

Ruth M. Underhill's *Antelope singer* (H. Hamilton and Puffin) is set in a later period, the nineteenth century pioneering days, when whole families were moving westwards across America to California. Ted and Mitty Hunt look after a crippled Indian boy, deserted by his companions, and, in return for saving his life, are accepted by his tribe and saved from starvation and almost certain death by being allowed to spend the winter with them before making the final mountain crossing.

Both these stories are full of accurate historical detail, but they both have relevance for the contemporary reader in that they show the need for tolerance and that, given this, people of different beliefs and cultures can live together happily, everyone learning from everyone else.

Although Australia has had a comparatively short span of recorded history, this has been used by a number of writers, amongst them Nan Chauncy and Eleanor Spence. Nan Chauncy has sympathetically dealt with the plight of the aboriginal tribes and the way they were ruthlessly maltreated by the early settlers in Tasmania, briefly in a time-travel story, *Tangara* (O.U.P), and at greater length in the very moving *Mathinna's people* (O.U.P). A work of more popular appeal, *Half a world away* (O.U.P.), contrasts life in England in 1911 with the pioneering life in Tasmania about the same time. In the first half of the story the Lettengar children live in an E. Nesbit world and at a distance from their parents; in the second half the family is very much more of a unit, engaged in making a new home in Tasmania. The hardships of settling new land are also described by Eleanor Spence in *The Switherby pilgrims* (O.U.P), in which a determined Arabella Braithwaite takes ten orphans out to New South Wales in 1825 to make new homes for themselves, and its sequel *Jamberoo Road* (O.U.P). Historical events and historical characters are introduced into these stories and, where necessary, there are notes to explain what is based on fact and what is fiction, but both Nan Chauncy and Eleanor Spence can tell a good story and use historical fact skilfully.

In some historical novels, time-travel is used as a device to provide an element of adventure (as there is always a certain amount of doubt as to whether the twentieth century children will get back to their own time); it can give form to a story which would otherwise lack the qualities which appeal to children, and it is also a useful means of making comment and observation on the past. Ronald Welch used this device in *The gauntlet* (O.U.P) where Peter, wandering on the Welsh hillside in the twentieth century, stumbles across a gauntlet. He is fortunately given a week's grace in which to prepare himself with some basic knowledge of the fourteenth century, so that when he finds himself there in the shape of young Peter de Blois, he is able to hold his own. He is also able to comment and reflect on the squalid and ruthless way of life in medieval Wales, appalled at the table manners which were then considered proper; at times the story is in danger of being too overloaded with fact, but the adventure provided by the time-travel element carries it through. In *The bells of Nendrum* by J. S. Andrews (Bodley Head), Niall is suddenly taken back to the tenth century and witnesses the Viking raid in which the monastery he knows as a twentieth century ruin is burned down. Here the author exploits the humorous possibilities of the situation, and this helps to lighten the tragedy of the situation.

One of the most popular books among children in recent

years has been Clive King's *Stig of the dump* (H. Hamilton and Puffin). Here time-travel happens in reverse, as Kipling uses it in *Puck of Pook's Hill* (Macmillan), for Barney finds Stig, a cave man left over from the Stone Age, living in a twentieth century Sussex chalk pit. Children of seven and over very much enjoy this story, largely because of the humorous accounts of the way in which Stig and Barney use the rubbish which has been thrown into the chalk pit, but on midsummer night Barney and his sister see the ancient Stone Age encampment and the raising of the standing stones on the Sussex Downs.

Apart from historical novels, there are also period novels. Frederick Grice and Geraldine Symons have used the Edwardian period and Gillian Avery has made the Victorian period particularly her own. In Geraldine Symons' novel, *The workhouse child* (Macmillan) and most of Gillian Avery's, where girls are the main characters, a lot of the interest arises from the fact that the girls are very far removed from the sort of young ladies which the fashions of their day demanded. In 1875 Maria, the heroine of Gillian Avery's *The warden's niece* (Collins), runs away from her boarding school in a Midland spa town and seeks refuge with her uncle, Warden of an Oxford college. Her taste for research, very appropriate for a don's niece, leads her into trouble, aided and abetted by Professor Smith's three boys. Maria's sacrifices in the cause of research include at one point crawling out of the Bodleian on hands and knees. Mr Copplestone, the tutor, is a great comic character who subsequently figures in some of Gillian Avery's later books. These novels are not historical in the strict sense of the word, but they do convey perfectly the charm and atmosphere of a by-gone period.

Historical novels are more plentiful than any other category, and it is impossible to do more than scratch the surface by mentioning a few names. In those written for younger children, up to the age of about eleven or twelve, the emphasis must be on adventure; most of the books which appeal to the over twelves are really most likely to be enjoyed by girls, and this fits in well with the pattern of popular reading. Adult historical novels are read mainly by women, and many girls in fact cross the bridge into adult reading by means of the novels of

Georgette Heyer, Margaret Campbell Barnes, Jean Plaidy and Margaret Irwin.

READ ON FROM HERE:

ALDERSON, B. W : Properly alive. *Children's Book News*, vol. 4, no. 2, March/April 1969. *About Nan Chauncy*.

BLISHEN, E : Leon Garfield—a remarkable children's writer. *Where*, 39, September 1968.

BURTON, H : How I came to write Time of trial. *The Junior Bookshelf*, vol. 28, no. 3, July 1964.

BURTON, H : The writing of historical novels. *The Horn Book Magazine*, vol. 45, no. 3, June 1969.

BUTTS, D : Writers for children : Gillian Avery. *The School Librarian*, vol. 16, no. 2, July 1968.

CHARLTON, K : Recent historical fiction for secondary school children. *Historical Association*, 1969.

CROUCH, M : Half a world away. *The Junior Bookshelf*, vol. 29, no. 3, June 1965. *About Nan Chauncy*.

GARFIELD, L : And so it grows. *The Horn Book Magazine*, vol. 44, no. 6, December 1968.

HODGES, C. W : On writing about King Alfred. *The Junior Bookshelf*, vol. 31, no. 3. June 1967.

MARDER, J. V : The historical novels of Rosemary Sutcliff. *The use of English*, vol. 20, no. 1, Autumn 1968.

MEEK, M : Rosemary Sutcliff. Bodley Head, 1962. (Bodley Head Monograph.)

MEEK, M : Writers for children : Geoffrey Trease. *The School Librarian*, vol. 13, no. 2, July 1965.

STEWART, C. D : 'More songs tomorrow'. *The Junior Bookshelf*, vol. 28, no. 5, November 1964. *About Rosemary Sutcliff*.

TREASE, G : Why write for children? *The School Librarian*, vol. 10, no. 2, July 1960.

See also Reading list, *Chapter 22, for article about K. M. Peyton and Read on from here, Chapter 24, for the 'Bodley Head Monographs' about R. L. Stevenson, Geoffrey Trease and Henry Treece.*

APART from adventure, humour is perhaps the most essential ingredient in popular and successful children's fiction, since children generally expect to be amused in their recreational reading. Humour is a very personal taste and a book which will cause some children to laugh out loud will not raise the faintest titter from others. The books considered in this chapter depend, to quite a large extent, on their own particular brand of humour and unless this happens to appeal to a particular reader, that reader is unlikely to get much pleasure from reading the book.

Some of these books serve the same purpose as children's comics in that they enable children to live out their fantasies in a perfectly harmless manner by reading about, and thus sharing vicariously, the experience of animals or humans doing the kind of things which they themselves would like to do but are usually prevented from doing by authority.

A good example of this can be seen in Michael Bond's *A bear called Paddington* (Collins and Puffin) and its sequels. If, instead of a small brown bear from darkest Peru, the Brown family had found a small boy of seven on Paddington station, none of the subsequent comic situations would have arisen. Paddington, although he can talk in the language of humans, is a bear and can behave with the innocence of a child, but at the same time can enjoy the sort of independence which is usually only granted to adults. Paddington is a contemporary phenomenon. Since he made his first appearance in 1958, he has achieved the kind of status enjoyed by Pooh and he is just as well known as Pooh to many children. It is strange that another bear, Mary Plain, featured in a series of books by Gwynedd Rae in a similar sort of way, never achieved the fame of Paddington.

H

Perhaps Mary Plain made her first appearance, in the 1930s, at a time less appropriate, and the original format of the books probably did nothing to promote her popularity. Paddington and Mary Plain, who features in *All Mary* (Routledge and Knight) and twelve sequels, both indulge in the sort of well-intentioned mischief that children themselves would enjoy perpetrating but cannot with impunity. As Jonathan says to Paddington fairly soon after the latter's arrival in the Brown family, ' "Fancy you making all this mess. Even I've never made as much mess as this!" '

The same effect can be achieved through a human character. *Pippi Longstocking*, the heroine of Astrid Lindgren's books (O.U.P) is a Swedish nine year old who lives all by herself and behaves exactly as she likes. She is an extremely competent cook (since food is important to children) and, moreover, cooks on a grand scale, rolling out her ginger-snaps on the floor because a pastry board is no use to someone who is proposing to make at least five hundred. On the other hand, she's not too fussy about housework and her pets (a monkey and a horse) live in the house with her. Pippi is very strong, has an endless supply of money to supply her needs, and does and says as she wishes. The effect of this, attractive to children in itself, is enhanced by the presence of Tommy and Annika, the two admiring children who live next door.

One of the appeals of comics is that so many of the comic strip characters are children or apparently weak and defenceless beings who manage to outwit or outshine their elders and betters. Vicke, also of Swedish origin, in Runer Jonsson's *Vicke the Viking* (Brockhampton) has much in common with comic strip characters in that, although he is expected to be brave and bold and to enjoy fighting, he prefers to rely on his cunning and this cunning enables his strong-armed but dim-witted father and friends to outwit their opponents in a series of comic situations; the humour of this book is perfectly matched by the illustrations.

In some stories, the humour arises from just one impossible happening which is described and documented in such a way that it seems quite credible and is certainly accepted as perfectly normal by the characters in the book. In John Yeoman's

The boy who sprouted antlers (Faber), Billy Dexter is told by his exasperated handwork teacher, Miss Beddows, that he can do anything if only he will try hard enough. Convinced of the truth of this statement, Billy, challenged by one of his friends, grows antlers, a curious and unnatural event which is accepted by his parents, friends and teachers. Miss Beddows cleverly makes use of Billy and his antlers in the Abbots Bromley horn dance at the end of term concert and, then, in the natural course of events, Billy's antlers fall off. The reader is left at the point when one of Billy's classmates is challenged to grow an elephant's trunk.

Another example of a comedy of situation is Richard and Florence Atwater's *Mr Popper's penguins* (Bodley Head). Mr Popper has never been outside the small American town of Stilwater where he is a house painter, although he dreams of far-away places, and particularly of the North and South Poles. Then, one day, he acquires a penguin sent to him by an Antarctic expedition, and from then on fantasy takes over. The penguin, named Mr Cook by the Popper family, proves to be a sensational pet, but when he starts to pine from loneliness another penguin, Greta, arrives to keep him company. Mr Popper obligingly floods the basement and lets it freeze over while the family sit around in their overcoats. One problem which the author has with this kind of comic fantasy is to extract himself from it at the end and to bring the story to a satisfactory conclusion, without an anti-climax. In this case, after a season as performing penguins (for Captain Cook and Greta produce eight lively babies), Mr Popper sets off with them to the North Pole to found a new breed of Arctic penguins.

Clive King's *The town that went south* (H. Hamilton) also hangs on a single impossible circumstance; a south coast town, Ramsly, breaks away from the English mainland and cruises south as if it were a ship. Gargoyle, the Rectory cat, suddenly realizes that something is amiss one wild night in March and finds that Ramsly has cast itself off. Gradually Ramsly moves south, making a temporary stay off the French coast and then slowly moving into warmer waters, where it becomes a tourist feature. The Ramsly housewives, led by Mrs Guffle, make an entertaining picture, bargaining in the markets of Tarboosh.

The novelty of the situation, however, begins to wear off, the inhabitants stay behind at the various stopping-places and only Gargoyle remains to the bitter end and reaches the South Pole.

These events—the growing of antlers by Billy, the arrival of the penguins in the Popper household, the floating town of Ramsly—are treated as normal and quite understandable happenings, and the humour arises from this matter-of-fact acceptance, which appeals greatly to children. It is also a type of humour which appeals to many adults, and these three books are all good for reading aloud to children, because of this adult appeal.

Some humorous books for children centre on the existence of one comic character. Norman Hunter's Professor Branestawm, for instance, is the epitome of the inventive but absentminded professor. A story which is particularly likely to appeal to children in the library is *The professor borrows a book*, one of the stories included in *The incredible adventures of Professor Branestawm* (Bodley Head), in which strange things happen in the libraries around Great Pagwell. This is a good story for telling or reading to children at the end of a group visit to the library.

Christianna Brand's *Nurse Matilda* (Brockhampton) is a kind of comic Mary Poppins, who herself is a fairly humorous character; Nurse Matilda descends upon the extremely large Brown family and tames the very naughty children by unorthodox methods. When the children gobble down their breakfast, Nurse Matilda causes their plates to be filled up time and time again until at last they manage to write 'Stop' in treacle on their porridge—although she doesn't stop until they add 'please'. When they pretend to be ill and won't get up, she makes them really ill so that they have to stay in hot and scratchy beds all day. The children, in being naughty, do the kind of things which many children like to imagine themselves doing, and the child reader also appreciates the rough justice meted out to the offenders.

Tove Jansson's *Finn family Moomintroll* (Benn and Puffin) is very closely related to the characters found in comic strips. The moomintrolls mingle with all kinds of fantasy creatures and have very amusing adventures. Moominmamma always carries a handbag and refuses to be parted from it, sleeping with it under her pillow, for instance, when they are stranded over-night on an island. Moomintroll and his friends, The Snork, Snork Maiden, the Hemulen, Sniff and Snuffkin indulge in child-like tricks and humorous back-chat, but are essentially good-hearted. Thingumy and Bob, two mysterious small creatures, turn up speaking in a language made up of spoonerisms and carrying an enormous and mysterious suitcase. Their dialogue is just the sort of thing that many children enjoy, and most children will soon catch on to the trick of it. In the book, only the Hemulen seems to be able to understand it, and he conse-quently becomes very proud of his rôle as interpreter.

Barbara Euphan Todd's *Worzel Gummidge* (Evans and Puffin) is a scarecrow who can scarcely avoid being comic, dressed as he is in a shabby black coat discarded by the Vicar, the Squire's trousers, carrying a green silk umbrella and with his face carved out of a turnip. Through their friendship with Gummidge, John and Susan are involved in a series of unfortunate incidents for which they receive the entire blame, but the enjoyment which they get from keeping Gummidge's human qualities a secret from adults is shown to be well worth the trouble. This kind of humour demands a more objective appreciation from the reader, and as children grow older and mature they are more able to regard it in this light.

William Mayne's *No more school* (H. Hamilton and Puffin) is a 'Reindeer Book', intended for seven to nine year olds, but because it demands more of this objective approach from readers, some girls, at any rate, will enjoy it well beyond the age of nine. The opening situation is basically promising. Miss Oldroyd, the sole teacher in the little village school, is taken ill and the children decide to run the school themselves. The first day Shirley and Ruth, two bossy little girls, who undertake the teaching turn and turn about, nearly have a strike on their hands when there is no school dinner. The second day they remedy this deficiency by cooking it themselves with ingredi-ents which they buy out of the children's dinner money. By the second week, the novelty has worn off for Shirley who says ' "I'd rather teach a crocodile than boil a potato." ' This story can be read by quite young children, though older girls will be better able fully to appreciate the humour of the situation. Mayne's *The Gobbling Billy* (Brockhampton and Knight) is hardly a children's book at all, although John and Norah, through whose eyes most of the events are seen, are children. Mr Diarty, their rather eccentric father, is strongly opposed to all forms of cars so that when a lodger, whose great passion in life they are, moves in and proceeds to renovate an ancient Gobelin-Billet racing car, plenty of fun can be expected.

The books which come nearest to reproducing the sort of humorous dialogue in which children themselves indulge, or would like to indulge, are probably those by Anthony Buckeridge. His Jennings is a prime example of a character who provides all the more popular elements of schoolboy humour. Elementary word play and slapstick comedy result from the doings of this well-intentioned schoolboy in the same way that they do from the activities of William, Lemon Kelly and Jim Starling. In the books about Jennings, much of the humour arises from the fact that the inevitable outcome of events can be seen well in advance by the least sophisticated of readers. In *Just like Jennings* (Collins), for example, it is obvious, from the moment when Miss Wilkins arrives at the school to deliver her Siamese cat into the safekeeping of her brother, that the said cat will somehow become involved in the doings of Jennings and his friends with disastrous, but comic, consequences. This point is quite clearly made by the author and the reader has only got to sit back in comfortable expectation to await the inevitable. Linbury Court may be an unrealistic picture of a prep school, but the right attitudes are preserved towards Mr Wilkins who, although essentially a comic character, is nevertheless always in control of the situation.

Peter Paul Hilbert's *Zoo on the first floor* (Brockhampton) depends, for its humour, very much on the style in which it is told. This is reminiscent of the many adult first-person true sagas of adventures with animals, and as children begin to move towards adulthood, they are likely to be better able to appreciate a more sophisticated humorous style. In Hilbert's book, Chico's family, consisting of mother and sister, in addition to Chico himself, live at the mouth of the Amazon; they are broke, so what better way of repairing the family fortunes than collecting animals for zoos? Chico's account of their subsequent adventures is very entertaining.

It is the more mature children who are most likely to enjoy Rosemary Harris's *The moon in the cloud* (Faber), winner of the 1968 Carnegie Medal, with its slightly irreverent humour, full appreciation of which is dependent on a knowledge of the Biblical account of the Flood— '... the Lord God stirred and grumbled, "They're all bad down there, except the Noahs, I'll have a flood" '. The relationship between Noah and his wife and their conversation is reminiscent of the dialogues between them which provided an element of humour in the medieval mystery plays. Older children will also be able fully to appreciate the High Priest's rhyme which enables him to remember the gods of Ancient Egypt.

One splendid nonsense story, which has been sadly neglected, is Norman Lindsay's Australian classic, *The magic pudding* (Angus and Robertson), first published in 1918. The hero, Bunyip Bluegum, decides to leave home because of his Uncle Wattleberry's whiskers which get in the soup. He meets two other characters, Bill Barnacle, a sailor, and Sam Sawnoff, a penguin, who own a magic pudding. Bunyip becomes a fellow puddin' owner to help them outwit the puddin' thieves, which they manage to do on several occasions before finally retiring to a tree-house with a little puddin' paddock for the puddin' to exercise in. The story is interspersed with comic nonsense rhymes which make the story ideal for reading aloud and in the new 1963 edition the illustrations are generous pagefuls in a large format, which makes it possible to show them to a group of children during a reading of the story.

Recreational reading for children is an entertainment, not a chore, and even where there is sadness in a story, this needs to be compensated for, so that even the saddest children's book tends to be lightened by the occasional humorous incident or remark. The books described in this chapter, however, are those in which the humour is paramount and appeals to a wide range of children. They can safely be introduced to a whole group in the knowledge that so many children will show their amusement spontaneously that the other children, at first more doubtful about the appeal, will soon be joining in the laughter.

READ ON FROM HERE:

BAMBERGER, R : Astrid Lindgren and a new kind of book for children. *Bookbird*, vol. 5, no 3, 1967.

BATEMAN, R : Children and humorous literature. *The School Librarian*, vol. 15, no. 2, July 1967.

CROUCH, M : Moomin-sagas. *The Junior Bookshelf*, vol. 30, no. 6, December 1966.

HARRIS, R : The moon in the cloud. *The Junior Bookshelf*, vol. 33, no. 4, August 1969.

ROE, M : A magic pudding from Australia. *Bookbird*, vol. 6, no. 3, September 1968.

THERE are plenty of short stories for the under eights, and children of about twelve upwards enjoy collections made up of suitable adult material, but there seems to be a lack of good short stories for the children who are between these two stages. There is a great demand for short story collections from parents, play group leaders, teachers and librarians in search of bed-time, classroom and story hour reading material, and children themselves like this kind of collection which can provide a satisfying read for short periods of relaxation.

Folk tales appeal to a wide range of children and most of these have the characteristics of a successful short story— simplicity of plot, sometimes with an unusual twist to add interest, characterization and style.* Some of the most successful literary short stories have been written in the style of the folk tale—Kipling's *Just so stories* (Macmillan), Walter de la Mare's *Collected stories for children* (Faber), Eleanor Farjeon's *The little bookroom* (O.U.P) and James Reeves' *Pigeons and princesses* (H. Hamilton) all contain many stories whose inspiration has been the traditional tale.

It is also fairly easy to find short stories about everyday life which will satisfy younger children, though some of the collections are series of stories written about the same characters, which saves time in establishing the basic facts for each story. There are, for example, Leila Berg's *Little Peter stories* (Puffin) and Dorothy Edwards' stories about *My naughty little sister* (Methuen and Puffin). The collections by Eileen Colwell, *Tell me a story* (Puffin) and *Tell me another story* (Puffin), are two of the best buys for parents of young children and playgroup leaders, and should always be included in library exhibitions intended to recommend books for personal buying. Ruth Ains-

*see also chapter 2

worth is a writer who can make everyday life seem exciting for small children, and some of the best items in her collection, *Do, look and listen* (Heinemann), are those stories which she has written herself. Other particularly successful writers for young children are Anita Hewett and Charlotte Hough who in *The bull beneath the walnut tree* (Bodley Head) and *Red Biddy* (Faber) respectively mingle everyday stories with tales in traditional style.

Writing short stories is a difficult art. Every word must add something to the story. Character must be established quickly and economically, and neither time nor words can be wasted in developing a plot. The way-out twists or inconclusive ends which often give point to an adult story are usually inappropriate in a story for children.

Even those writers producing short stories which are enjoyed by children of nine to thirteen who do move away from the pattern of the traditional tale, tend to stick closely to fantasy— Janet McNeill in her stories about Specs McCann in *Various Specs* (Faber) and Joan Aiken in *A small pinch of weather* (Cape). These authors are enjoyed by children of up to the age of about thirteen since their humour is on a fairly sophisticated level, but Bill Naughton's *The goalkeeper's revenge and other stories* (Puffin) seems to stand on its own as a book of stories for older children with roots firmly in everyday life. Real-life pursuits such as football and fishing provide the background interest of these stories.

Collections aimed at older children usually include a high proportion of adult short stories, and reference has already been made to the most successful collections of science fiction stories which do just this.* Stories of the supernatural are extremely popular with children of nine or ten upwards, and there are a number of useful collections of ghost stories, which help to meet this demand. The short story lends itself particularly well to the maintenance of a bloodcurdling suspense, and adult and traditional stories provide a rich source of material. Kathleen Lines' collection, *The house of the nightmare and other eerie tales* (Bodley Head) is a good example. It has an attractive title for children who want this kind of

*see also page 65

story; it draws almost entirely on stories written for adults and is, incidentally, a good way of introducing young people to such writers as Elizabeth Bowen, W. W. Jacobs, M. R. James and Margaret Irwin. The title story, by Edward Lucas White, is a splendidly creepy narrative, told in the first person, with an unexpected denouement in the last sentence.

In *Terror by night* (H. Hamilton), Elfrida Vipont has woven a succession of strange stories into the framework of a holiday at a music course at a north country adult education centre. The atmosphere of the old house, Thwaite Howe, provides a good and evidently inspiring background but although a few girls enjoy this touch most children will be deterred by the way in which the framework holds up the action of the stories which are the real meat of the book.

Every children's library should include Dickens' *A Christmas carol* which is available in a number of well-produced and illus- trated editions, one (Heinemann) by Arthur Rackham. With surprising and, one suspects, totally unjustified regularity, Dickens appears at the head of children's lists of favourite authors; *A Christmas carol* seems to be the best introduction to him and in fact the only one of his works, apart from *The magic fishbone*, which has a real place in the children's library.

Leon Garfield's title story in *Mr Corbett's ghost and other stories* (Longmans Y.B) has something of the Dickensian spirit in it, and the title gives it an immediate attraction for many children. The events take place one New Year's Eve when Ben Partridge, an apothecary's apprentice, pays for a spell to kill his unkind master, Mr Corbett. He then finds the corpse on Hampstead Heath, takes pity on it and wishes his evil deed undone. Leon Garfield's style is just right for this kind of story.

How can short stories be presented to children? Volumes of stories written by different authors tend, for economic reasons, to draw on traditional and non-copyright material which has appeared elsewhere. There are few outlets for new, well-written short stories for children at the present time, and the situation is very different from that in the nineteenth century when there were a number of good quality magazines for children and many notable children's books appeared first as serials in the children's periodicals of the period—Robert Louis Stevenson's *Treasure Island*, which appeared in *Young folks*, is an outstanding example of this. The periodicals also provided a convenient vehicle for the publication of short stories. The separate issues of the periodicals were often cumulated in time for Christmas, producing a generous volume of entertainment for a wide range of children.

During the 1930s Basil Blackwell produced an annual called *Joy Street* which drew on the work of distinguished writers of the period, including Eleanor Farjeon and Walter de la Mare, but, on the whole, in the twentieth century the standards of the Christmas Annual deteriorated steadily until by the 1950s the term 'annuals' had become, in the minds of librarians at any rate, synonymous with trashy publication at its worst, and were linked with the weekly comics. Both comics and annuals are subjects which frequently crop up in discussions following on talks given by librarians to adults and although most public libraries do not include either in their stock, librarians should know that there are exceptions to the general picture. The annual *Blue Peter* (B.B.C. Publications), linked to the successful television programme, is, for example, both extremely popular with children of about seven upwards and of a much higher standard than most of the other annuals.

At the moment, there is only one quality periodical, *The Elizabethan*, but during the last few years Macmillan have published an annual *Winter's tales for children* and O.U.P have produced *Miscellany*, both of which have contained contributions from significant contemporary writers for children, and, in time for Christmas 1968, there appeared the first volume of *Allsorts* (Macmillan), edited by Ann Thwaite and intended for the eight and nine year olds, a deliberate attempt to provide a quality alternative to the cheap (both in contents and price) annuals which flood the bookshops just before Christmas. These are attractive (in terms of quality) productions with poems, stories, various miscellaneous items and—in the case of *Allsorts*—puzzles. Their main drawback is the high price it is necessary to charge in order to produce material of this quality, and they still lack the brash visual appeal of the cheaper annual, which also gets wide publicity from its weekly comic. *Winter's tales for children*, *Miscellany* and *Allsorts* are competing in a difficult market and will never replace the popular 'annual' in the lives of the majority of children. In fact *Winter's tales* did not appear in 1969, and according to John Rowe Townsend, writing in *The Guardian* in December, 1969, the 1969 volume of *Miscellany* (the sixth) is to be the last. These books fall between two stools—they are too expensive for the private market, and they don't seem quite right for the library shelves (though, of course, some libraries do buy them) for the price is high and usually most of the stories, although the work of distinguished contemporary writers, do not represent the authors' best work.

Two interesting collections have appeared in recent years which seem to emphasize the difficulty of writing short stories for children—*The Friday miracle and other stories*, edited by Kaye Webb (Puffin), published in aid of The Save the Children Fund, and *The Eleanor Farjeon Book*, edited by Naomi Lewis, published as a festschrift to Eleanor Farjeon. To both these, outstanding contemporary writers have contributed.

Short stories which have appeared in these collections have subsequently appeared as 'full-length' books for younger children. Rosemary Sutcliff's *The chief's daughter*, which appears in the Hamish Hamilton 'Antelope Book' series,* was first published in *The Eleanor Farjeon Book*. Eleanor Farjeon's own *Mr Garden*, one of her last stories, was first published in a volume of *Winter's tales for children* and later came out as a picture story book, illustrated by Jane Paton (H. Hamilton). This corresponds to the use of stories, which appeared in the *Joy Street* annuals of the 1930s, by Kaye and Ward for their 'Early Bird' series. These short, 'full-length' stories are a much more successful proposition in both the publishing and the library world.

Finally, the librarian in search of material for reading aloud to older children should not overlook the usefulness of collections such as Margery Fisher's *Open the door* (Brockhampton) which includes tempting excerpts from longer books. This provides useful guidance for the inexperienced librarian who wants to introduce a full-length novel to children during a library club programme.

see also pages 105, 169, 170

READ ON FROM HERE:

FLETCHER, D: Strolling down Joy Street. *The Junior Bookshelf*, vol. 32, no. 4, August 1968.

See also Reading list, *Chapter 2, for article about James Reeves, and* Read on from here, *Chapter 24, for the 'Bodley Head Monographs' about Eleanor Farjeon and Walter de la Mare.*

Classics of fiction

OVER the years certain books have come to be regarded as children's classics. Some publishers have interpreted this term in a very liberal way and have included in their series of classics not only books such as *Robinson Crusoe*, *The Pilgrim's progress* and *Gulliver's travels* which, although written for adults, have become generally accepted as stories for children, but also books such as *Moby Dick*, *Jane Eyre*, *The tale of two cities* and similar literary works, which are in a different category.

Publishers are also given to bestowing the title of 'classic' on books, both new and old, but the term, if it is to mean anything, is one which must be earned. What makes a classic? The book must establish itself sufficiently well at the time of its first publication to ensure that it remains in print more or less continuously. A certain element of chance is involved here, as a book's immediate success depends on the moment at which it is published, the format in which it is produced, the publisher and his means of publicity, and the illustrations. Once a book is established as a classic, these details become relatively unimportant as far as the status of the classic is concerned. However poorly produced, however badly illustrated the newer editions, a book such as *Alice in Wonderland* is going to remain a classic.

Although certain conditions at the time of original publication could cause a book which had classic qualities to sink without trace, these conditions, operating favourably, could not give a poor book classic qualities. The most important factor is the quality of the book, and here the normal criteria used to judge any novel must come into play and consideration be given to characterization, plot and style. As a classic is a book which is going to stand the test of time and is therefore meaningful to more than one generation, it must also have something of lasting value and interest to say.

Asked for titles of nineteenth century children's classics, the first that most people suggest are *Alice in Wonderland*, *Treasure Island* and *Little women*. Each of these illustrates the fact that good plot, characterization and style are important elements, although in varying degrees. In *Treasure Island*, the plot is probably the element which catches at the child's imagination, though the style in which it is unfolded and characters such as Long John Silver and Benn Gunn are memorable too. In *Little women*, Louisa M. Alcott drew her characters in such a way that girls ever since have been able to recognize themselves, their failings and their aspirations. She wrote the story in a style which makes everyday life interesting and at times almost exciting.

The case of *Alice in Wonderland* is particularly interesting. Why did this become a classic while Jean Ingelow's *Mopsa the fairy*, published only four years later, did not? Alice is a household word while Mopsa is known to comparatively few people. It was not that Carroll benefited from his social and intellectual position; Jean Ingelow enjoyed the friendship of Ruskin, Browning and Christina Rossetti and was even suggested as Poetess Laureate in succession to Tennyson. The plot of the two stories is similar—here Carroll may have gained from the fact that he was first in the field. Tenniel's illustrations may also have helped to establish *Alice*, and *Alice* may owe her immortality to the fact that there is a heroine (which appeals to girls who are the great readers of fiction and perhaps have more influence on the books which their children later read), whereas the real hero of *Mopsa* is a boy, Jack. Setting aside these points, however, one can see that the characters in *Alice* are more memorable than those in *Mopsa*, and that Carroll's style has worn well. The opening paragraphs could have been written yesterday and Alice, sitting by her sister on the bank, bored, is in a situation which any child in any age can recognize. A good style is one of the essentials of great literature.

Certain books establish themselves quite quickly as classics. *Peter Pan*, *The wind in the willows* and *Winnie the Pooh* are books from the early part of the twentieth century which have clearly done so, while Mary Norton's *The Borrowers* was very quickly hailed as a classic and will almost certainly be on the shelves in children's libraries (if there still are such things) in the twenty-first century. There is little doubt that fantasy stories wear the best of all. Qualities which tie a book to its own time become an extension of the fantasy with the passing of the years, and where the author has something of universal significance to say, his message can be reinterpreted by successive generations in their own contemporary terms.

Children may well be put off reading for life by having too many classics thrust upon them by well-meaning adults who think they remember, probably quite erroneously, reading and enjoying the books themselves at the same age. On the other hand, classics can be successfully introduced as stories read at bedtime, or in class, or in the library story hour. Since they are books with qualities which appeal to adults, parents, teachers and librarians can communicate some of their own enjoyment in the reading of those classics which they particularly like.

Certain children's classics, such as the titles already mentioned, are basic requirements for any collection of children's books, but no collection should be overweighted with them. As the size of the collection grows, the number of classics which ought to be included can be increased. Certain titles must be stocked to saturation point, for in an ideal library a copy of *Treasure Island*, for example, should always be on the shelves, available for borrowing at exactly the right moment.

In selecting an edition of a classic, what should one look for? In the children's library, classics should be provided in attractive and, at the same time, authoritative editions. The child will not be automatically attracted to a book which the adult knows to be worthwhile, and the external appearance and attractiveness therefore require the same kind of attention as any new novel. Within the book, the type-face should be well-spaced and of a size appropriate to the age of the children to whom the book is likely to appeal, the paper of good quality and the illustrations in keeping with the book, done by an artist of distinction. Since royalties no longer have to be paid to the authors of nineteenth century classic titles, and since these titles are well known among adults who know them to be

I

'good books', cheap classic reprints are a good commercial proposition from the publisher's point of view. The children's library is a source from which children should be able to borrow good editions of the stories which are available in plenty elsewhere in cheap editions, ruthlessly abridged or rewritten, and garishly illustrated.

Some cheap reprints of classics are furnished with sugary illustrations in the hope that this will make them more palatable to children. One must, of course, be careful to distinguish between what is artistically poor taste, and what is rejected because of intellectual snobbery. Most librarians shuddered at the rewritten editions of the Pooh stories, illustrated in Disney style, which appeared hot on the heels of the commercial success of the Disney film of *Winnie the Pooh*. It seems pointless to rewrite what is already simple and to replace the exactly right E. H. Shepard illustrations. At the same time, it is sobering to reflect that many of those who shuddered would accept a Disney-illustrated *Snow White* because their first introduction to the story was through the Disney film, and that the younger of them, those in their twenties, are likely to accept Disney illustrations for *Peter Pan*; perhaps, at this rate, children's librarians in the 1990s will quite happily stock Disney-illustrated *Winnie the Pooh* and think nothing of it. Adults are very much influenced by what they themselves enjoyed in childhood, and classics are particularly subject to these influences because they have such a long existence.

If a classic has sufficient appeal and a sufficiently high reputation, it can overcome an unattractive format. How else can one explain the continuous demand for L. M. Montgomery's *Anne of Green Gables* (Harrap) which looks, in its hardback edition, most unappealing? Yet girls not only read and enjoy it, but are stimulated to ask for the other books in the series, a sure sign of success.

There is a great temptation to urge children to read books which require of the reader far more maturity than he can give. The librarian is frequently under pressure to provide children's editions of adult classics which have been filmed or televised; thus one gets, in the children's library, requests for *Jane Eyre* for a girl of eight or *Moby Dick* for a boy of seven. These pressures should be strongly resisted by the children's librarian; not only would it be a pity for children to be introduced to these books at too early an age, but the reading of them would prevent the reading of some of the fine literature that is much more appropriate to their stage of development. In the case of the adult asking on the child's behalf, a tactful explanation of the policy should be made; in the case of the child, it is a good idea to show him the full edition if this is available in the library and then make some helpful suggestions about books he might enjoy at once.

Although it is fashionable to turn up one's nose at abridgements, *Gulliver's travels*, for example, would be quite unacceptable for children in anything but an abridged edition, and books such as *Robinson Crusoe* would, for the most part, remain unread unless they were abridged. But while some abridgement is justified in certain cases as long as the extent of the abridgement is indicated (as it usually is in reputable editions), rewriting is certainly not. Children with normal reading ability should wait until they can appreciate the original style. Other children, less able, can enjoy excerpts from the right classics, read aloud.

The most extensive series of classics is Dent's 'Children's Illustrated Classics', a series which includes well over seventy titles and is still being added to. This series contains most of the well-known classics, as well as many minor ones, and provides editions for young adults of a number of adult titles. Oxford University Press have a series of 'Oxford Illustrated Classics'. This includes some volumes of traditional stories, but there are half-a-dozen classics and the series has a *Treasure Island*, illustrated by Rowland Hilder, and *The Swiss family Robinson*, illustrated by C. Walter Hodges.

Blackie's 'Chosen Books' are unabridged classics, well designed and illustrated, and there are pleasant editions of *Little women*, *What Katy did* and *Treasure Island*. Some of the titles in the series are clearly adult, and although they provide good editions for young people, they really have no place in the children's library. 'Chosen Books from Abroad', good translations of foreign classics, are also useful for the teenage library.

The 'Nonesuch Cygnets' from the Nonesuch Press, part of

the Bodley Head, are superb examples of book production and, in an ideal world, would be best suited as gifts for children to own themselves, especially as their external appearance has little immediate appeal and they do not compete well standing on the shelves alongside editions with colourful jackets. They are really the contemporary equivalent of the 'gift book' from the early part of this century. Many children will not, however, have the opportunity to handle them unless they do so in the library. Reference has been made elsewhere to one outstanding volume from the series,* *Fifty favourite fairy tales*, a selection of tales from the Andrew Lang collections, made by Kathleen Lines. Kathleen Lines is editorial adviser for the series, which also includes *Treasure Island*, *Robinson Crusoe* and E. Nesbit's *The Bastables*, and the books are designed by Sir Francis Meynell. The price of the volumes is appropriately high. If there seems justification for buying editions of this quality, there is also a fine Folio Society edition of *Treasure Island*.

Some titles are still issued by their original publishers or by publishers who have had long associations with certain authors. The most readable-looking edition of *Alice in Wonderland* is, for example, that published by Macmillan. *Peter Pan* is available in nearly a dozen different editions, all but one (a Puffin) emanating from Brockhampton, who inherited the title from Hodder and Stoughton. *Peter Pan* has had a chequered publishing career since Barrie authorized retellings of the story of the play before he produced one himself, and, by now, it has almost the status of folk-lore. Barrie's own version of the story, written seven years after the play was first performed on the stage, has a lot of adult humour and comment in it. The text of *Peter Pan: the story of the play*, presented by Eleanor Graham and Edward Ardizzone, is the most likely to appeal to children, but *Peter Pan and Wendy*, retold by May Byron and illustrated by Mabel Lucie Attwell, is both readable and much nearer to the spirit of Barrie's own text.

If librarians want to encourage children to read the best children's classics, there is a lot to be said for providing them in good quality paperback editions as well as hardback editions.

*see also page 12

Some librarians have found that the most popular hardback editions of children's classics are those from good American publishers, particularly Macmillan of New York; the Macmillan editions are attractive, with well-spaced type, and although they are expensive, the extra cost has been more than justified in terms of issues.

During the last few years publishers have started series of new editions of books which can conveniently be considered under the heading of classics. Brockhampton, in fact, call their series 'Twentieth Century Classics'. These are most likely to appeal to young adults, although boys and girls from about ten upwards enjoy Baroness Orczy's *The Scarlet Pimpernel*. Max Brand's *Destry rides again* is a good introduction to the first-class western story and O. Douglas' *Penny plain* and Jean Webster's *Daddy-long-legs* are both romances much enjoyed by adolescent girls.

The 'Gollancz Revivals', a series edited by Gillian Avery, are books which are of most interest to the student of children's literature. Their uniform dust-jackets (different colours but uninspired design) do not stimulate interest among children. These are books which evidently did not have those essential qualities which keep the classic alive although some of them can still be appreciated by a minority of children today. Mrs Ewing's *A great emergency* appeals to E. Nesbit fans, and Mrs Molesworth's *My new home* has got a lot in common with some of today's soul-searching, teen-age novels for girls.

Hart-Davis' 'The Keepsake Library' is a short series. F. L. Shaw's *Castle Blair* is a family story set in Ireland, but its length seems formidable to the majority of children today and, although entertaining to read for the adult reader, it seems pointless to encourage children of today to read it when there is so much of contemporary interest. 'The Keepsake Library' also includes two of Louisa M. Alcott's books, *Eight cousins* and *Rose in bloom* which, when compared with *Little women*, show only too clearly their lack of classic qualities.

There have been other isolated instances of revivals of minor books by well-known authors. Heinemann, for instance, have produced a charming reprint of Frances Hodgson Burnett's *Editha's burglar*, but this has not the qualities nor the imaginative power which have enabled *The secret garden* or *Little Lord Fauntleroy* to survive.

These revivals and reprints help to illuminate the reasons why certain books have attained the status of classics and are still read with as much appreciation and enjoyment as when they were first published. Each children's librarian will have her own particular favourites among the classics, but it is essential to distinguish between those which still have something to offer to children of the '70s, and those which are stocked merely because they are old and must therefore be good. It does not follow at all!

READ ON FROM HERE :

BLISHEN, E : The classics. *Books for your children*, vol. 4, no. 3, Spring 1969.

THERE are two kinds of fiction series. In a publisher's series the books may be by different authors but they are linked by a common purpose, all being the same type of book or all being aimed at a specific age group. The second kind of series consists of stories about the same character or group of characters. Fiction series have advantages for both the publisher and the consumer. Publication in a standard format means economies in production so that a series book represents good value for money and, once a series is established, the publisher knows that the titles added to the series will have a ready-made market. The buyer or borrower, on the other hand, knows that a book is likely to meet his specific need or taste.

Reference has already been made to publishers' series which are related to specific types of fiction. There are, for example, a number of series which consist of traditional tales and legends,* and others which provide good editions of classics.†

A very helpful type of series is that which caters for children of a particular level of reading ability. During recent years publishers have produced a number of series, suitable for library stock, which cater for children in the process of learning to read. Even now most of the books published for this group to read themselves are intended as class readers or supplementary readers, but there are a few really imaginative books. It is difficult to produce great literature when working within the limits of a controlled vocabulary but the American Dr Seuss showed what could be done, and some of his titles are available here in the 'Beginner Books' (Collins). Also American in origin are the 'I Can Read' books (World's Work). Benn's 'Beginning to Read' series, however, is English; there are titles by some of our more distinguished writers for older children,

*see also page 14   †see also pages 131, 132

such as Helen Cresswell, and this series is beautifully illustrated by some of our most outstanding illustrators. An even simpler series published by Benn is 'First Steps in Reading'. The most recent arrival of this kind is the 'Nipper Books' series from Macmillan, edited by Leila Berg, which was designed and published to provide stories with a working-class background. Library editions of all these books are available and they are clearly distinguishable from the books which belong to reading schemes.

The biggest range of publishers' fiction series is produced for the seven to nine year olds, children who have got beyond the picture book or easy reader stage but who are not yet fluent enough to read a full-length children's novel.

'Read Aloud Books' (Methuen) are intended both for reading aloud by teacher, parent or librarian and for 'beginning readers' to return to and to read themselves. Quite a number of the books consist of short stories featuring a central character, which fits them well for their declared purpose. Most of them have a humorous touch which adds to their appeal.

Hamish Hamilton was one of the first publishers to do notable work in this field. There are now 'Gazelle Books' for five to eight year olds, 'Antelope Books' for seven to nine year olds, 'Reindeer Books' for nine to eleven year olds, and 'Big Reindeer Books' for ten to twelve year olds. Some of the titles have been reprinted in a cheaper series, 'Red Bison Books', but the production standards of these are correspondingly poor and they are not really suitable for library stock. These series are of increasing difficulty and length but they all have a strong, simple plot, a few, clearly distinguished characters and large, clear print, and they are all much shorter than the average children's story book. There is, however, some attempt to widen children's horizons, and many of the titles are written by distinguished children's authors whose names, it is hoped, the children will recognize when they move on to novels for older children.

There are a number of other series along the same lines— the 'Acorn Library' (Bodley Head), 'Pied Piper Books' (Methuen), 'Early Birds' (Kaye and Ward), 'Flying Foal Books' (Harrap), 'Brock Books' (Brockhampton), 'Wren Books' (Burke) and 'Salamander Books' (Nelson). The 'Salamander Books' are graded into three age groups. Each of the series has a distinctive device which is clearly displayed on the spine of the book, facilitating identification by the library assistants and finding by the children or their parents. Many libraries shelve the books in these series together in one place under some such heading as 'For younger readers', and librarians have found that shelving titles in the same series together is a good way of encouraging children to go on reading at a time when practice is particularly important.

As the books in these series are short and aim at simplicity of subject matter and approach, few of them reach great literary heights, but many of them do represent competent writing. The titles cover the whole range of children's fiction—fantasy, adventure and historical—but the most successful seem to be those which have their roots firmly in everyday life, however improbable the happenings which are described. Many of the stories in these series demonstrate quite clearly that it is possible to write for this age group in a way which appeals to them but which is not watered down for their benefit.

Elizabeth Beresford's *Knights of the cardboard castle* (Methuen), a 'Pied Piper Book', which is enormously successful with children, is a good example of this type of story. The four children build a castle, complete with drawbridge and throne, and then find that they are in danger of losing it because they have built it on the spot scheduled for the town's rubbish tip. It is a simple plot but the children are all quite clearly drawn characters, the adults are reasonably credible and the dialogue and situation are realistic. Denise Hill's *The clever car* (Methuen) in the same series uses the appealing theme of children playing with an old car, restoring it to pristine condition and then nearly losing it.

Pamela Sykes' *Billy's monster* (Bodley Head), in the 'Acorn Library', appeals to the current interest in prehistoric monsters and archaeology. Billy's school is organizing a natural history museum. Billy, his elder brother and friend go out to look for skulls and Billy, on his own, finds an enormous one which he takes along in triumph for the museum. Finding it, digging it up and bringing it home involve adventure and excitement; this is a well constructed story, full of quiet humour.

Barbara Sleigh's *The snowball* (Brockhampton) and Helen Cresswell's *A gift from Winklesea* (Brockhampton) are two recent 'Brock Books', both fantasies, showing an interesting reflection of contemporary culture. In *The snowball* a plastic daffodil which came with the washing powder is used to decorate a snow woman; in *A gift from Winklesea*, decimal currency is used. Both stories show a matter-of-fact approach to fantastic happenings. A snowball hatches out into a snowbaby whom Tom and Tilda keep in the 'fridge. The gift is a stone brought back from a day trip to the seaside which hatches out into something suspiciously like a potential Loch Ness monster. Both Flump, the snowbaby, and the Gift grow at an alarming rate, giving rise to tremendous problems which have to be solved. There is delightful detail such as Tilda rolling out frozen pastry for Flump's bed-clothes with Tom saying helpfully ' "You will be able to squish it out a bit more each evening as he grows bigger ... We can always have it for dinner later on." '

The length of these books also provides a good means of re-introducing short stories. The 'Acorn Library' includes Kenneth Grahame's *The reluctant dragon* (Bodley Head) and Charles Dickens' *The magic fishbone* (Bodley Head). The Kaye and Ward 'Early Birds' include several stories which were first published in the Basil Blackwell *Joy Street* annuals in the 1920s.* One of these is Compton Mackenzie's *The stairs that kept going down*, an amusing adventure told in a style well suited to this age group.

For older children, series provide a useful way of reprinting books at reasonable prices, partly because of the economies of standardized production and partly because of the 'self-advertising' effect of the series image.

Dent have two series, 'Pennant Books' which are cheap editions of their better-known, quality titles, and 'Signal Books' which cover titles of rather lower quality. The 'Oxford Children's Library' is an inexpensive reprint series of stories by distinguished writers, and for their 'Evergreen Library' Collins have chosen some of their best back-list titles which are attractively produced. Cape have a 'New Adventure Library', which

*see also page 125

includes titles by authors such as Ian Serraillier, Mary Tread-gold and Frederick Grice. Brockhampton issue the 'Super Hampton Library' which includes both new titles and some reprints of popular stories such as Pamela Brown's *The brides-maids*. These series appear to be one way of making available at an economic cost in hard-back editions the sort of good, com-petently-written children's stories which should form the hard core of the stock of the children's library.

Even with these economies, however, there are titles which the librarian would like to represent but which the publisher cannot economically produce as a business proposition because of the limited market. In December, 1969, Cedric Chivers pub-lished the first batch of 'Portway Junior Reprints' and it is planned to publish six titles every two months. These reprints are produced by means of photolithography and have been given new, attractively designed jackets. Whereas the original publisher would have to reprint at least two thousand copies to make a reprint a viable proposition, Chivers, because they reprint to satisfy a known demand and sell direct to libraries, can afford to produce short runs of only five hundred copies. Titles so far selected for the 'Portway Junior Reprints' include early titles by still popular writers such as Monica Edwards, Noel Streatfeild and Christine Pullein-Thompson. There is an early historical novel by Richard Parker, *The sword of Ganelon*, and one of the less well-known of E. Nesbit's books, *Five of us —and Madeline* (the rather modern jacket design of this may well give it appeal for those children who would be deterred by the rather old-fashioned publisher's jacket). Suggestions for titles needing reprinting have been made by children's librarians and on the basis of books recommended by Margery Fisher in *Intent upon reading*.

Series which are limited to a special category of fiction for older children, and which are composed of stories by different authors, do not seem to be outstandingly successful with the notable exception of the 'Career Books' series from Bodley Head, Chatto and Windus (for girls) and Collins. These are a prime example of letting the customer know what she is going to get, and here the fact that each volume in a series follows much the same pattern is not a handicap.

Attempts to attract to fiction reading those children who are more interested in doing and in active pursuits have been made by Longmans Young Books with their 'Out and About Books', edited by Robert Bateman, and 'Sports Fiction Series' and by Brockhampton with their 'Real Life Adventure' series, consisting of novels with a semi-documentary background of modern life. These work quite well as individual books, but children do not seem to demand them as a type, and the reading of one title in the series does not normally lead to a request for others.

The least successful series of this kind seem to be those which are restricted to historical novels. Titles in three different series, 'Time, Place and Action Series' (Deutsch), 'Pageant of History Series' (Phoenix House) and 'Adventures in History Series' (Macdonald) are in print, but it seems a pity to handicap the author of a historical novel by requiring him to write to a specific length and to meet a pre-determined formula.

The other kind of fiction series is that in which the books are all written around a particular character or group of characters. This is a good way of establishing a book's popularity among children, for once they have really enjoyed a book about a character, they will always want to read the other titles in the same series.

An author can adopt one of two approaches. He can keep his central character or characters always at the same age and in the same surroundings, sometimes (if the series goes on for many years) making concessions to the changes in external social and economic conditions. This is the approach which seems to appeal to younger children. The long series of books about the 'Lone Piners' by Malcolm Saville (Collins, Merlin and Armada), Kathleen Fidler's books about the Brydons and the Deans (Lutterworth) and Enid Blyton's stories about the 'Famous Five' (Brockhampton and Knight), the 'Secret Seven' (Brockhampton and Knight) and the 'Find-outers' (Methuen and Dragon) must have encouraged many eight to ten year olds to 'carry on reading' at a critical point in their reading lives.

This approach also appeals to boys and so we have William (Newnes, Armada and Merlin) and Jennings (Collins, Armada and Puffin), permanently around the age of eleven, though in the William books one can see changes in the environment and in the Jennings books a reflection of the changes in slang fashions. Similarly Biggles adapted his doings to the contemporary political conditions, although one observes no real change or development in the main character himself.

Alternatively—and this is the approach which seems to appeal most to girls—the characters are seen to be growing older, marrying, having families and in turn their children grow up. In some of the series the girls change only physically —their emotional age remains round about the age of fifteen or sixteen, and even though they reach the age of forty and have three sets of twins (as in the 'Abbey Books' by Elsie J. Oxenham or the 'Chalet School' stories by Elinor M. Brent-Dyer) they tend to act and react much as they did in their teens. Both Elsie Oxenham and Elinor Brent-Dyer are now dead, and the last long series of this kind is probably that of the books by Lorna Hill which began with *A dream of Sadlers Wells* (Evans) and which flourished during the 1950s and early '60s, combining those two chief interests of many ten to thirteen year old girls—ballet and ponies.

In recent years, however, as it has become permissable to introduce adolescent problems and more adult attitudes into children's books, one can see a real attempt, on the part of some authors, to show their characters developing emotionally as well as physically. In the 'Bannermere Books' by Geoffrey Trease (Heinemann), published between 1949 and 1956, one could see the beginning of this, but it has been done to an even greater extent by Monica Edwards in her books about the Romney Marsh and Punchbowl Farm families (Collins) and by Antonia Forest in her books about the Marlowes (Faber).

Where a librarian decides to stock a particular series at all, it is sensible to stock sufficient copies of each title in the series to meet demand, particularly in the case of the progressive series where there are likely to be references in the later books to incidents which have been described and characters who have appeared in earlier ones. The 'Junior Portway Reprints', it seems to me, may well perform their most useful function by making available library editions of early out-of-print titles in still flourishing series such as the books by Monica Edwards, so that children can follow through the adventures of these characters.

Although there are dangers inherent in allowing children to read on and on in the same pattern, series do encourage children in the reading habit and this tends to outweigh the disadvantages. The careful librarian will select only those series which maintain a reasonably high standard throughout and will encourage children to move on to something else at the right psychological moment.

READ ON FROM HERE:

DOYLE, B: Blyton and Biggles. *Books and Bookmen*, May 1969.

FORD, B, ed: Young writers, young readers: an anthology of children's reading and writing. Hutchinson, rev. ed, 1963. *This contains two particularly useful chapters,* The work of Enid Blyton, *by Janice Dohm, and* Captain Johns and the adult world, *by T. R. Barnes.*

LINES, A BULLETIN FROM THE ESSEX BRANCH OF THE SCHOOL LIBRARY ASSOCIATION: vol. 2, no. 7, Autumn 1969. *This issue has as its theme* Blyton revisited *and includes a number of excellent articles on Enid Blyton by a college lecturer, two teachers, a student and a psychologist.*

PEARSALL, R: That boy William. *Books and Bookmen*, May 1969.

THE USE OF ENGLISH: Problems. vol. 18, no. 1, Autumn 1966. *Suggests ways, successfully adopted by teachers in different schools, of weaning children from Enid Blyton.*

THE firm of Penguin Books published the first Puffin Story Book,
Barbara Euphan Todd's *Worzel Gummidge*, for children in 1941,
not many years after they had first launched Penguins on the
market. Puffin Picture Books, consisting of thirty-two pages of
pictures combined with a simple descriptive text, usually with
half the pictures in colour, were produced under the direction
of Noel Carrington and were an important landmark in the
reproduction of original colour illustrations, but these, of
course, were non-fiction books. Early attempts to publish story
books for very young children were evidently not a success for
Baby Puffins were published only between 1943 and 1948, and
only four Porpoise books appeared, in 1948. One of these was
Ardizzone's *Paul, the hero of the fire*, later published as a hardback and later still, in 1969, as a Picture Puffin.

Thanks to the standards set by Eleanor Graham and maintained by the present editor, Kaye Webb, the quality of Puffin
Story Books has always been high in terms of literary merit.
Penguins had the children's paperback market virtually to themselves for many years and this meant that any children's book,
which the original hardback publishers were prepared to release,
could be selected by the Puffin editor.

The next paperback series of any size to come on to the
market was the Armada series, which catered for a rather
different reading public, with the emphasis on the popular children's authors. Armada Books were started by Gordon Landsborough in 1961 and sold out to Collins in 1966, by which time
they were very well established. Armadas are distributed much
more widely than Puffins and nearly every small newsagent and
supermarket seems to include a quota, which means that
Armadas get into the hands of many children who would never

go into the kind of bookshop where Puffins are mostly sold. Dominated by Enid Blyton and pony stories, Armadas have also included school stories by Elinor Brent-Dyer and Angela Brazil.

In the mid-1960s the market for children's paperbacks expanded considerably. With the increasing costs of hardback publishing, publishers had to face the fact that the hardback market for children's books was becoming more and more an institutional one, the bulk of sales being to schools and public libraries, and that if books were going to get into the hands of children directly, it was going to be in a paperback format. Moreover it was obvious that the pre-teen children had control of more pocket-money than ever before and that with good advertising and marketing, some of this might be steered in the direction of paperbacks.

A few publishers were able to produce paperback editions of their own children's books. Faber, for example, published Mary Harris, Walter de la Mare, Henry Treece and Lucy Boston in paperback and then, in 1967, launched one of the most exciting developments of the '60s, the Faber picture books, reduced in size but otherwise faithful to the original. This move made it possible for a great number of small children to have their own copies of books such as Virginia Lee Burton's *Mike Mulligan and his steam shovel* for the first time. This development was soon followed by other publishers such as Penguin Books and Sphere Books and, at last, good quality picture books came on to the market at a price that most people were prepared to afford, filling what had hitherto been a real gap.

Methuen published the A. A. Milne books and Kenneth Grahame's *Wind in the willows* in paperback editions, Dent published Mary Norton's four books about the Borrowers as Aldine Paperbacks and Macmillan published Kipling as Papermacs.

Some publishers launched new series. The attractively produced Zebras came from Evans, Collie Books from Transworld and Jackanory Books from the B.B.C. Collie Books, by publishing paperback editions of Antelope books, catered for the younger age-group of seven to nine year olds and Kaye and Ward have now started publishing some of their Early Bird titles in this form, so that children of all ages can now buy paperbacks suited to their tastes and reading skills. Macmillan started a series called 'Topliners' which was aimed specifically at the teenage market.

Gordon Landsborough, having sold Armadas to Collins, started Dragons in part ownership with Associated Book Publishers Ltd. in the autumn of 1966. These, like Armadas, are designed to appeal mainly to the popular market. They do, in fact, cover a wide range of titles and are graded as Blue Dragons (for six to eight year olds), Red Dragons (for eight to twelve year olds) and Green Dragons (for twelve to fifteen year olds). The first eight titles included *My friend Flicka* by Mary O'Hara, in two parts, and advertised a competition. As well as a selection of Blyton titles, Dragons have included some reprints of above-average children's fiction such as M. E. Atkinson's *Castaway Camp*, Noel Streatfeild's *The house in Cornwall* and David Severn's *Drumbeats*. They also include P. C. Wren and Henty titles and the emphasis is very much on adventure stories.

Merlins, from Paul Hamlyn, draw on popular authors such as Blyton, Saville and Crompton and include Billy Bunter titles, but in addition there are some original Merlin titles, most of which are aimed at girls and seem fairly closely related to the old paperback schoolgirl novels.

Brockhampton, in 1967, launched Knight Books, which are classified in four different categories—Green Knights, frankly 'pop', Black Knights, good quality stories for older children over ten, Red Knights, good quality stories for the under tens, and White Knights, which are non-fiction. The covers of Knight Books are outstandingly attractive and the colour distinction means that children's librarians, when talking to parents or teachers, can give a general recommendation to Black and Red Knights. This is an admirable idea but, unfortunately, it is possible to find many Green Knights in retail outlets where no Red or Black Knight ever ventures.

Not aimed specifically at children but certainly including children's titles are the more expensive Dover Books, issued in this country by Constable. The cost of these books is high but some of the less well-known classic children's books such as the original Andrew Lang colour fairy book collections and the Palmer Cox Brownie books as well as novels by such writers as

K

Edgar Rice Burroughs have now become available in this format.

It is some indication of the market for paperbacks that Blackie, a firm which has always specialized in cheap hardback editions of the classics, has also launched a series of Star Classics in paperback.

Meanwhile, the various Penguin series for children and young people have also expanded. As well as the Picture Puffins and the standard Puffin Story Books, there are Young Puffins, for children up to eight or nine, Puffins in ita and Peacock Books, aimed at teenagers. In March, 1967, Penguin Books started the Puffin Club with a quarterly magazine, *Puffin Post*, a badge and a wide range of activities and competitions. In 1968, the first Puffin films were made; these are short, ten to fifteen minute films, in colour, about Puffin authors, designed to answer the sort of questions children ask about favourite authors and also, of course, to stimulate them into reading the books. There are now four films featuring Leon Garfield, Michael Bond, Alan Garner and Joan Aiken and a fifth, about William Mayne, is in production. The films are available for hire or purchase and are ideal for use in library-based activities.

How can paperbacks be used in school and children's libraries? The paperback format does appeal to many children and may encourage them to tackle books which they would not be prepared to look at in a hardback edition. It is not now possible to buy most paperbacks in pre-bound editions but even when it was, it scarcely seemed justifiable since the poor quality of the paper meant that the reinforced cover tended to outlast the inside which deteriorated fairly rapidly. Some children's librarians and school librarians will feel that it is not economically possible to maintain an attractive collection of paperbacks: others will feel that the expenditure can be justified if it encourages children and young people to read worthwhile books. In this case the collection should be exploited as such by bringing all the paperbacks together and displaying them attractively in a stand or rack similar to those used in shops. Processing should be kept to a minimum and the books discarded as soon as they become worn and shabby.

Paperbacks can also meet another need in libraries. So many

titles are now available in this form that when a book receives publicity through being made into a film (*Doctor Dolittle* or *Mary Poppins*) or through being serialized on television (*The silver sword* or *The railway children*) or, on a local scale, through being introduced to a group of children by teacher or librarian, additional copies can be bought to meet the requests of those children who want to read the book. This is an economical way of supplementing the normal library stock and coping with a comparatively short-lived burst of popularity.

However, the main advantage of the paperback is that children can be encouraged to build up their own collections. Teachers can do this directly by selling paperbacks in schools. A relatively easy and straightforward way of doing this is through Scholastic Publications who run a series of paperback book clubs for various age groups—the See-Saw Club for the under fives, the Lucky Club for the infants, the Chip Club for the juniors and the Scoop Club for secondary school children. Each month there is a choice of titles to be selected and a Club newsheet is issued for each individual member of the Club, as well as a memorandum for the teacher, which gives more detailed information about the books on offer.

Some teachers dislike this limitation of choice and prefer to run a school bookshop where they can exercise a preliminary control of choice themselves and then give children complete freedom within this range of titles. This takes more organization but Penguin Books have produced a useful leaflet called *The school paperback bookshop* which offers helpful hints, as does the pamphlet on school book agencies distributed by W. H. Smith.

It is more difficult for the librarian to encourage buying directly in this way but it is often possible when organizing a big children's book exhibition to get the co-operation of the local bookseller who will set up and run a bookstall, stocked largely with paperbacks, within the exhibition. Children's librarians also have an opportunity to encourage the buying of paperbacks by drawing attention to the wide range of worthwhile titles in talks to groups of adults or children and by including examples in lists or exhibitions of books intended to stimulate book-buying as well as book-borrowing.

In some Scandinavian libraries, for example at Helsingborg in Sweden, small bookshops have been set up, in cooperation with local booksellers, within the library. This has not yet been done by any public library in the British Isles but such a development may well come in the not too far distant future.

READ ON FROM HERE:

RUDGE, K: Not a hard sell. *Teachers World*, 5th September 1969.
About selling books, mainly paperbacks, in school.

SOME books have become so much a part of English children's literature that we forget they are translations. Not only do our favourite fairy tales come from the French Perrault, the German Grimm and the Danish Hans Andersen, but books such as Johanna Spyri's *Heidi* (Blackie and Puffin) and Johann Wyss's *Swiss family Robinson* (O.U.P) have long since had the status of children's classics in this country.

However, the main developments in this field have taken place since the end of the Second World War. Since 1945 the part which children's books can play in improving international understanding has been increasingly appreciated in many different countries. Jella Lepman was very much aware of this when she set up the International Youth Library in Munich just after the war and one of the main functions of the International Board on Books for Young People (I.B.B.Y), which was also due to her inspiration, has been to encourage the translation of worthwhile children's books. *Bookbird*, the English language periodical, published at the International Institute in Vienna, regularly includes reviews of books recommended for translation.

Some authors, such as A. Rutgers Van Der Loeff, Paul Berna, René Guillot and Astrid Lindgren have, in translation, acquired international reputations, and their stories are of universal interest. Some translated books are useful because of the insight they give into the life and customs of other countries. Sometimes authors write stories set in their own countries but some, such as Karl Brückner and Aimée Sommerfelt, write about many different countries. It may be that European writers have a more cosmopolitan background than English writers and can convey more successfully the feeling of what it is like to be a child in another country. Other translations are a useful contribution to a particular type of fiction; Leif Hamre's fine adventure stories translated from the Norwegian are an example, and it is interesting to see how many humorous books* are translations since humour is the most difficult quality to convey in translation.

Most British publishers now include some translated books in their lists, but one of the most significant lists has been that of the University of London Press which, in the 1950s, began to publish a series of 'Foreign Award Winners', books which had won prizes in their original language. The first titles in the series were A. Rutgers Van Der Loeff's *Avalanche* and P–J. Bonzon's *Orphans of Simitra*. In 1968, in a reorganization of publishing functions, this list was taken over by the Brockhampton Press.

There is little point in recommending books for translation unless publishers are going to act on suggestions. Publishers are, after all, in business and are not going to publish translations unless there is a market for them. From an economic point of view translations at picture book level are a distinct advantage and many publishers are now selling picture books to foreign publishers before publication so that the cost of the reproduction of the colour art work can be shared and in addition the colour printed for several countries at once, thus reducing the cost of those two expensive items in picture book production; the text, in English, Swedish, French or German can be added afterwards as appropriate. This enables any problems in the story to be ironed out before publication and the pictures rendered acceptable to different nations. This may not be altogether desirable if it results in the texts becoming devoid of all spirit and character but it is one answer to the problem of producing picture books at a reasonable price.

Countries with small populations but with highly developed library services do depend to quite a large extent on translations and in such countries as Sweden and Denmark, a high proportion of the books on the shelves in the children's library tends to be in translation—from English, German, French and Dutch.

The quality of books translated into English seems to be higher than the general level of English books translated into

see also chapter 12

other languages. We are not inflicted with other nations' pot-boilers and this seems to reflect fairly accurately the claim of British publishers that they aim to publish translations only of the 'best' foreign writers.

Problems do arise, of course, in the translation of children's books into English. There seems to be little doubt that children and young people in other countries are prepared to accept much more discussion of ideas and beliefs in their stories than are their English counterparts. There is also the fact that certain subjects have relevance for children in one country and not in another. In 1967, *That summer with Ora* by R. Lampel (Harrap) was translated from German into English, providing a sensitive story about relationships between young people and between a girl and her mother. The sequel to it, *Eleanor*, was not published here in translation because its interest was felt to be too dependent on Jewish problems and Jewish inter-relationships which would be meaningless to the majority of young people in this country. The story also includes a non-Jewish German girl who wishes to make amends for her Nazi grandfather by trying to serve the Jewish people, and is a slightly sentimentalized portrait. This again would be of very limited significance to young people here.

There is, therefore, a need to select stories which have relevance to English children. The book must be a translation and not a 'rewrite', yet the translator must have an awareness of what English children will read. He needs to be able to conjure up a series of pictures from the original text and translate these pictures into words in such a way that they mean the same to English children as they do to their foreign con-temporaries. Although it is desirable that the translation should stick as closely as possible to the original, the first essential is to produce a book that is readable to the English child. As well as a knowledge of the original language, the translator must have an awareness of the children's book field because, as well as being true to the spirit of the original, he has got to be able to judge how much of the original style will be acceptable to an English child. In the case of books translated from the French, for example, where the translator has stuck too closely to the original, many children will soon be deterred by the phraseology which reads rather oddly in English. Paul-Jacques Bonzon's *The friends of Croix-Rousse* (Brockhampton), translated by Godfrey Burston, is a good gang story about the boys of the Croix-Rousse district of Lyons tracking down a missing dog and falling across some jewel thieves in the process. But what English child is going to sympathise with Tidou, who tells the story, when he says ' "I began to tremble like an almond tree branch in the mistral. I looked at my mother, entreating her with my eyes to speak for me" '? Yet it is phrases like this which give atmosphere to the whole story.

The translator has got to be able to write well in his own language as well as to understand the original language. Skilled translators whose names, although they appear on the title page, are often uncelebrated, can make a real contribution to children's literature in English. A translated book is going to be judged on its own merits by the child reader, who is not going to make any of the allowances which an adult might make in similar circumstances. Some English children seem to have a built-in resistance to books set in foreign countries and if, in addition, they have to cope with a lot of foreign-sounding or difficult-to-pronounce names, they are soon going to be discouraged from reading the book.

Necessary explanations of strange, untranslatable words and phrases must be worked into the text. Both footnotes and forewords giving explanations appear to deter many children because they delay or interrupt the essential business of reading a good story. The only really acceptable addition is a glossary at the end of the book for the more curious child, but an understanding of the story should not be dependent on reference to this.

What do children gain from reading books translated from other languages? Apart from an insight into life elsewhere, children in English-speaking countries undoubtedly benefit from a more compassionate attitude towards human problems. There is no English writer who writes in quite the way that Karl Brückner does in *Child of the swamps* (Burke) or as M. Gripe does in *Pappa Pellerin's daughter* (Chatto and Puffin). One has only to compare A. Holm's *I am David* (Methuen and Puffin), translated from the Danish, and Ian Serraillier's *The silver sword* (Cape and Puffin) to see the difference between the continental approach and the English one.

Continental writers are also, on the whole, more successful at showing attitudes towards war and a positive attitude towards the importance of international peace. This may be because it is these books which are selected for translation, but also, one suspects, because continental writers, not living in countries protected by Channel or Ocean, are much more conscious of the fragility of national boundaries. There is more political consciousness, in Margot Benary's books, for instance, and, more recently, in Alki Zei's *Wildcat under glass* (Gollancz). In stories translated from the French, Spanish or Italian languages, with their Roman Catholic background, there is likely to be much more religious consciousness than one finds in the average English book.

At the present time, standards of translation are high in that translators try to stay very close to the original, both in style and spirit, but this may well mean that these books will appeal to a smaller minority of children than would otherwise be the case. The children's librarian therefore needs to select carefully and to be prepared to promote thoroughly those books originating in other countries which she believes to be of help and interest to English children.

READ ON FROM HERE:

PERSSON, L-C, ed: Translations of children's books. Sweden, Lund, Bibliotekstjänst, 1962.
WEAR, W. H: A study of a selection of translations of foreign children's fiction, published 1950–1959, with special reference to the social attitudes expressed in them. *Education Libraries Bulletin*, no. 27, Autumn 1966 continued no. 28, Spring 1967.

THE first prize to be given for children's books was the Newbery Medal, established in 1921. It was endowed by Frederick G. Melcher, to be awarded each year to the author of the most distinguished contribution to American literature for children, and it was named after John Newbery, the first English publisher to print books especially for children. The responsibility for selecting the author to receive the award lies with a committee appointed by the Children's Services Division of the American Library Association.

Since 1921, many awards have been established, the majority of them since the end of the Second World War, and almost every country with even a small annual output of children's books now has at least one award in this field. This reflects the growing importance of children's literature throughout the world.

There are three international prizes. The major one is the Hans Christian Andersen Medal, which has been presented biennially since 1956 to an author whose works have made an outstanding contribution to children's literature. This award is sponsored by the International Board on Books for Young People and has been awarded to Eleanor Farjeon, René Guillot, Meindert DeJong, Erich Kästner, Astrid Lindgren, James Krüss and José Maria Sanchez-Silva. Krüss and Sanchez-Silva received the prize jointly in 1968 and in the same year an award to an artist, Jiri Trnka of Czechoslovakia, was made for the first time.

The Caorle European Prize for children's literature was instituted in 1962 and is awarded by an international jury, presided over by the Director of the Institute of Education, Padua, Italy. The Biennale of Illustrations, Bratislava, is held every two years and awards are made by an international jury for distinguished work in the illustration of children's books.

In 1936, the Library Association established the Carnegie Medal to mark the centenary of the birth of Andrew Carnegie and, as in the case of the Newbery Medal, the aim was to improve the standards of children's books and to encourage authors and publishers to devote their best efforts to creating children's literature. The Library Association Kate Greenaway Medal, given for distinguished work in the illustration of children's books, was established in 1955.

In Great Britain, there are now two other awards in the field. The Eleanor Farjeon Award was instituted in 1965, in memory of Eleanor Farjeon, by the Children's Book Circle, an informal group of people working as editors in the children's book departments of publishing firms. This award is slightly different in that it is given for distinguished services to children's literature; the first award was given to Margery Fisher, author of *Intent upon reading* (Brockhampton). The Guardian Award has been given annually since 1967, when the first prize went to Leon Garfield for *Devil-in-the-fog* (Longmans Y.B. and Puffin). In the following year Alan Garner received both the Guardian Award and the Carnegie Medal for *The owl service* (Collins and Puffin).

Many of the books which have been awarded prizes in English-speaking countries are available to English children. The majority of the American Newbery Medal winners are available in English editions and the Australian children's writers who have been recognized with the Australian Book Council Children's Book of the Year prize include Joan Phipson, Patricia Wrightson and Nan Chauncy, who are as well known in England as they are in their own country.

Books which have won prizes in many European countries are available here in translation. René Guillot's *Sama* (O.U.P) was awarded the French Prix Jeunesse, Runer Jonsson's *Vicke the Viking* (Brockhampton) the German Youth Book Award, Karl Bruckner's *Child of the swamps* (Burke) the Austrian City of Vienna Prize, Miep Diekmann's *Just a street* (Brockhampton) the Dutch Best Children's Book of the Year Award, and Aimée Sommerfelt's *The road to Agra* (Brockhampton) the Norwegian State Prize, and these are only a few examples.

What criteria are used to select a prize-winning children's book? Most committees look for literary merit and since, as a result, prizes most often go to works of fiction, characterization, plot and style are all taken into account. The first awards were established to improve the quality of children's literature and book production. This they have undoubtedly helped to do, encouraging both authors and publishers, and particularly publishers, to produce good children's literature. A look at E. P Kelly's *The Trumpeter of Krakow* (Chatto), winner of the Newbery Medal in 1929, only recently published for the first time in this country, shows very clearly how standards have improved over the years; the rather turgid style and didacticism of this book would result in little serious critical attention being given to it nowadays.

The emphasis placed on the various criteria by which the awards are made has changed over the years. In 1936, when the Carnegie Medal was instituted, great attention was paid to the format of the book but by the middle of the 1960s, book production standards had improved so much that it seemed unlikely that any poorly produced book would be in the running for the Medal on other grounds so, although this consideration is not omitted from the conditions completely, it is not given so much importance as it once was.

Little attention seems to be paid to whether or not a book is popular with the children themselves, and this fact is a criticism frequently levelled against children's book awards. The selection is done by librarians, teachers or other suitably qualified adults with an almost total disregard of children's likes and dislikes. It would, of course, be difficult, in the case of awards made shortly after the end of the year in which the books were published, to decide whether or not a book was really popular with children, since a new book takes a little while to become established in this respect. The Carnegie Medal selection committee does now always include some children's librarians who are in day-to-day contact with children, so that some attention to this aspect of the matter can be given.

Most awards are made soon after the conclusion of the year of publication, and it is difficult for any person to survey a whole year's output within six months of the end of the year and to select from it the 'most outstanding' book, the 'best book' or the 'most promising' book. However, it does seem something of an anti-climax if an award is announced a long time after the book itself has been published. The Hans Andersen Award is now made for the whole body of an author's work so far published, and this seems the only acceptable solution in the case of an international prize which is awarded only once in two years.

In fact, in the awarding of the Carnegie Medal, it has often been the case that the award has been made, not for the author's best or most noteworthy book, but for one which has happened to be published in a year when there was no other serious contender. Rosemary Sutcliff's *The lantern bearers* (O.U.P) is certainly not her finest achievement, nor the one most likely to be read by children. The Carnegie Medal was awarded to C. S. Lewis for *The last battle* (Bodley Head and Puffin), the last in the series of Narnia books, but the whole series must obviously have been in the minds of the committee when it made the decision.

The Carnegie Medal selection committee chooses 'an outstanding book', not 'the most oustanding book' nor 'the best book', and over the years selection has tended to favour those authors who have already made a notable contribution to children's literature. An exception to this was in 1968, when Rosemary Harris received the Medal for *The moon in the cloud* (Faber), her first book for children. The Guardian Award selection committee looks for a book by an author of promise but, in fact, the lists of winners and runners-up produced by the Guardian and Library Association committees, drawing on the same potential, tend to overlap considerably.

In 1932 the American Library Association approved a resolution that the book of a previous recipient of the Newbery Medal should receive the award 'only upon the unanimous vote of the Newbery Committee' and this was done because, it was pointed out, 'the Newbery Medal is intended to encourage an increasing number of authors'. In Great Britain, a tradition grew up that the same person should not receive the Carnegie or Greenaway Medals for a second time, although this had never officially been laid down. When the conditions were revised slightly in 1968, it was specifically stated that a person could receive the Medals a second time. Although no one has yet received the Carnegie Medal twice, Elizabeth Speare received the Newbery Medal for *The witch of Blackbird Pond* (Gollancz and Puffin) in 1959 and for *The bronze bow* (Gollancz and Peacock) in 1962.

Some prizes are restricted to authors living in the country concerned and they are not usually given to translations. This reflects the aim of encouraging and promoting a country's own authors and publishers. The German Youth Book Award is a notable exception to this practice and can be awarded in any of its three categories—picture book, children's book and youth book—to a German translation, published in West Germany, Austria or Switzerland, of a book from another country. In 1965, for example, the children's books selected for the short list included six American, three English, one Dutch, two Swedish and three German and the award went to the Swedish Runer Jonsson for *Vicke the Viking*, translated into German as *Vicke und die Starken Männer*, one third of the prize money being given to the translators. Extra, bonus awards were given in 1965 for 'artistic design', for 'a brilliant translation' and for 'the representation of a contemporary topic in a youth book'. It is clear that there is scope for prizes for qualities apart from the more conventional literary ones. In 1966, the American Library Association established the Mildred L. Batchelder Award in honour of the former Executive Secretary of the Children's Services Division. This is given to the American publisher of the most outstanding children's book originally published abroad in a language other than English and subsequently published in the United States. The first award was made to the firm of Knopf for Erich Kästner's *The little man* (published in England by Cape).

In 1968 it was possible for the Carnegie Committee to consider for the first time, the possibility of awarding the Medal to someone other than a British citizen domiciled in the United Kingdom and, as a result of these new conditions, Margaret Balderson, an Australian, was among the list of runners-up for *When jays fly to Barbmo* (O.U.P). The terms of the Carnegie Medal, however, still require that books eligible for the Medal should have had their first publication in the United Kingdom.

It would be interesting to have a complete record of the deliberations of a prize-awarding committee. The Arbeitkreis für Jugendschriftum in Munich each year publishes an annotated list of the books selected for final consideration for the German Youth Book Award. These are not only of contemporary interest but should also prove to be of immense value to the scholar looking back in later years.

What is the value of a prize? Financially, it varies, but even the Carnegie Medal, which carries no monetary award, has some built-in financial value. Although the winning of the Medal will not guarantee permanent financial security to the author, it does mean that his Medal-winning book and probably other titles by him are likely to remain in print and that there will be a steady annual sale. Of the Newbery Medal winners, going back to 1922, all are still in print in their American editions while of the Carnegie Medal winners since 1936, only Kitty Barne's *Visitors from London*, the winner in 1940, has gone out of print, and that quite recently. This particular book has dated because of its war-time setting on which it is entirely dependent, unlike Mary Treadgold's *We couldn't leave Dinah* (Cape and Puffin), the winner for 1941, which has a strong element of adventure in it. *The family from One End Street* (Muller), published in 1937, has also, to people in their late 30s who first read it as children, dated, but to contemporary children it appears to have something of the timeless charm of *Little women*. This charm is due to the characters and the way in which the story is told rather than to its social significance which may well have drawn it to the attention of the selection committee at the time. But it might not have stayed in print had it not been for the winning of the Medal—and what, incidentally, were the members of the committee doing that year to overlook Tolkien's *The hobbit* (Allen and Unwin)?

The prizes are also valuable publicity, not only for the authors and the books which win them, but for children's literature as a whole. During the 1960s there have been increasing efforts made to obtain maximum publicity for the Carnegie and Greenaway Medals and in 1969 the Youth Libraries Group of the Library Association for the first time produced book marks and gold medals to help librarians, booksellers and publishers who wanted to draw attention to Medal-winning books.

In 1969, children's writers both in the United States and in Great Britain were for the first time recognized by national awards given not specifically for children's books. Leon Garfield, for *Smith* (Longmans Y.B), and Kevin Crossley-Holland, for *The green children* (Macmillan), were included amongst the recipients of awards given by the Arts Council, while Meindert DeJong's *Journey from Peppermint Street* (Lutterworth) was given the National Book Award of America. This is an indication of the generally growing appreciation of children's literature, and no doubt the awarding of honours to children's books as such has been instrumental in bringing this about.

READ ON FROM HERE :

HUTTON, M : A clutch of Carnegies. *The School Librarian*, vol. 11, no. 5, July 1963.
INTERNATIONAL YOUTH LIBRARY, MUNICH : Children's book prizes. Munich, Verlag Dokumentation, 1969.
LIBRARY ASSOCIATION : Chosen for children : an account of the books which have been awarded the Library Association Carnegie Medal, 1936–1965. rev. ed, Library Association, 1967.

Illustration in fiction

MOST fiction published for children is illustrated and the illustrations play a major part in attracting a child to a particular book in the first place. Often, the dust-jacket will provide the only colour illustration and should, as the first thing a child sees, give some indication of what the book is about. Children, having been attracted by the dust-jacket, will then look at the illustrations to see if they confirm a favourable first impression. Most children prefer books in which the characters appear a little older than themselves, although girls are less exacting about this than boys. Children are usually stretching forward for experience in their reading and, for this reason, once they are past the picture book stage, seem to prefer their story books to be demonstrably different, that is, in a crown octavo or similar format.

The function of the illustrations changes as the age of the potential reader increases. For younger children, the illustrations can enlarge upon the text or increase their understanding of it. Once children can read fluently, it seems likely that some of them do not really look at the illustrations at all, although they might complain or reject a book if it had none. Here the illustrations should aim to capture the mood rather than to supplement the understanding of the text although, even at this stage, they can help by providing accurate visual details of buildings, dress and landscape in the case of stories set in unfamiliar foreign countries or in historical periods. Jenny Dalenoord's illustrations for A. Rutgers Van Der Loeff's *Steffos and his Easter lamb* (Brockhampton)* and Cynthia Harnett's for her own historical novels show how useful this kind of help can be.

As well as illustrations of incidents and characters from the

*see also page 91

story, maps, plans and family trees are an extremely useful addition to many stories, helping to elucidate the plot or fill in the background. These important aids should not be relegated to end-papers since if the book is bought in a pre-bound edition or subsequently rebound, this vital material may well be lost.

From a fairly early period, artists of considerable ability have turned their attention to the illustration of children's books. In the early nineteenth century, for example, Thomas Bewick and George Cruikshank were two well-known professional book illustrators who worked on children's books and helped to improve the standards in this field.

There are some children's books where the work of one particular illustrator has become almost inseparable from the author's text. An early example of this close sympathy between illustrator and author is to be found in Lewis Carroll's *Alice in Wonderland* (Macmillan), for which, in 1865, Sir John Tenniel created Alice and all the strange creatures of Wonderland. In the same way, E. H. Shepard later created Pooh and his friends for A. A. Milne and, more recently, Peggy Fortnum the incomparable Paddington in Michael Bond's stories.

Some children's classics can be successfully illustrated afresh for every generation. Arthur Rackham turned his attention to many well-known children's books when looking round for inspiration. As well as *Peter Pan* and *Gulliver's travels*, which have not become closely associated with any special set of illustrations, he also managed to produce acceptable illustrations for *Alice in Wonderland* and for *The wind in the willows*, for which he was Grahame's original choice of illustrator, and editions of these, with the Rackham illustrations, should be included in the stock of the children's library alongside the more usual editions with illustrations by Tenniel and Shepard respectively.

The Dent's 'Children's Illustrated Classics' series includes the work of such contemporary illustrators as Victor Ambrus for Ballantyne's *The dog Crusoe*, Margery Gill for *What Katy did*, Charles Keeping for *The tale of Ancient Israel* and Joan Kiddell-Monroe for *Song of Hiawatha*. Shirley Hughes has produced attractive illustrations for the 'Chosen Books' edition of *Little women* (Blackie), while Rex Whistler's illustrations for Hans

Andersen's *Fairy tales and legends* (Bodley Head), published in 1935, nearly a hundred years after the Andersen stories made their first appearance here, are widely admired and seem delightfully appropriate.

At present, there is little recognition of the part played by book illustrators, and even the most outstanding of them have had to produce a picture book or to work in colour before being awarded the Library Association Kate Greenaway Medal, which is the only award given for illustration work in children's books in this country. Good picture books tend, of course, to be more eye-catching than well illustrated story books, but it seems a pity that Charles Keeping should not have received due honour for his fine work in historical novels, Pauline Baynes for her part in the chronicles of Narnia, and Antony Maitland for his contribution to Leon Garfield's books, all of which represent work just as interesting as that for which they were awarded the Medal. Brian Wildsmith had done some excellent work in book illustration, notably in a fine edition of *Tales from the Arabian nights* (O.U.P), before he became widely recognized as a picture book artist. Joan Kiddell-Monroe, who produced one outstanding picture book, *In his little black waistcoat*, just before the war, has never been honoured for her outstanding work in the volumes of folk tales in the 'Oxford Myths and Legends' series. The work of Robin Jacques, an English illustrator, who uses mainly black and white, notably in the series of folk tale collections published by Methuen, was, in 1969, recognized by the award of a Plaque at the Biennale of Illustrations, Bratislava, for his contribution to Ruth Manning-Sanders' *A book of ghosts and goblins* (Methuen).

To produce a well illustrated book, the illustrator must be in sympathy with the text, and some publishers prefer and encourage close co-operation between an author and his illustrator. The choice of incidents for illustration is usually left to the artist, although it is stipulated that, if the book is to be illustrated throughout, the incidents should be evenly distributed.

The best illustrators have a distinctive style. This is good as long as the illustrator is well chosen in the first place and his style is appropriate to the author and the text he is illustrating.

Papas' style seems quite suitable in Frederick Grice's *A Severn-side story* (O.U.P), but is too cartoon-like and exaggerated in H. F. Brinsmead's *The beat of the city* (O.U.P). Edward Ardizzone is a prolific illustrator and usually successful but he is not really the ideal person to illustrate Buchan's *The thirty-nine steps* (Dent), where he makes Richard Hannay look rather too much like Little Tim. Even in C. Day Lewis' *The Otterbury incident* (Bodley Head), his illustrations may deter the twelve year old boy who might otherwise enjoy the story. On the other hand, his illustrations capture the mood perfectly in a book like Christianna Brand's *Nurse Matilda* (Brockhampton).

A good way of ensuring that illustration and text are complementary is for the author to illustrate his own text, as Arthur Ransome, Hugh Lofting, Cynthia Harnett and Eve Garnett did. Arthur Ransome did his own illustrations to achieve accuracy, especially important where technical details and semaphore messages are involved; they are childlike in appearance and are attributed to Captain Nancy Blackett herself. *Columbus sails* (Bell), written and illustrated by C. Walter Hodges, is a good example of what can be achieved by the expert author-illustrator.

Charles Keeping and William Stobbs have both established reputations for their outstanding work in illustrating historical novels; some of Stobbs' best work can be seen in Ronald Welch's novels, while Keeping has done some interesting work in the books of Henry Treece and Rosemary Sutcliff. Keeping is also successful in capturing the atmosphere of contemporary stories, as he does in Garner's *Elidor* (Collins and Puffin), for example, or in Eric Allen's *The latchkey children* (O.U.P). Victor Ambrus, who came to this country from Hungary in 1956, produced his first set of illustrations here for Alan Jenkins' *White horses and black bulls* (Blackie), a story set in the Camargue district of France, and since then has gone on to do a wide range of work for a number of different publishers.

Book illustration is, of course, affected by the techniques available to the printer and by the cost of employing them. Line-blocks can be printed on the same paper as the text and at the same time, and this is the process used in most of the fiction published for children of nine to twelve at the present time. Many of the cheaper children's books published in the 1930s were accompanied by half-tone illustrations, printed on art paper, sewn or, more usually, stuck into the book, and with a reference given to the page on which the incident illustrated was described. Today the standard of children's book illustration is high, with line used flexibly so that text and pictures become a homogeneous whole. Chapter headpieces and tailpieces, and drawings set into and around the text, often form part of a carefully designed book.

This approach to the illustration of children's books became much more common in the 1950s, and since then there has been a growing number of artists doing work of a high quality in this field.

READ ON FROM HERE:

CROUCH, M: Arthur Rackham, 1867–1939. *The Junior Bookshelf*, vol. 31, no. 5 October 1967.

HODGKIN, M. R: Introducing illustrators: Victor G. Ambrus. *The Junior Bookshelf*, vol. 28, no. 2, March 1964.

HOGARTH, G: Illustration? *Children's Book News*, vol. 5, no. 1, January/February 1970.

KEEPING, C: Illustration: another approach. *Children's Book News*, vol. 5, no. 2, March/April 1970.

RYDER, J: Artists of a certain line: a selection of illustrators for children's books. Bodley Head, 1960.

TAYLOR, J: Introducing illustrators: Margery Gill. *The Junior Bookshelf*, vol. 30, no. 5, October 1966.

THERE are some children who are perfectly able to read, albeit slowly through lack of practice, but who do not really enjoy it and therefore require considerable encouragement. These children should be thought of as 'reluctant' rather than 'backward' readers. Backward readers are those who for various reasons have been late in learning to read and who are at least two years behind most of their contemporaries as far as reading skills are concerned.

Whether or not the children's librarian sees many children from either of these two groups depends very much on the siting of the library. If it is situated in the middle of a housing estate, with easy access for the children, and is a welcoming and attractive building, with sympathetic staff, children who are not really interested in books and reading may well come in to enjoy the friendly atmosphere and for lack of other places to go outside their homes. Otherwise, contact with these children, as far as the librarian is concerned, is likely to be through other adults such as parents, teachers and, to a lesser extent, youth leaders.

If contact is established, either directly or indirectly, it is important that the children's librarian should have suitable books to meet the requirements of these children, who will need to be persuaded of the value of reading for enjoyment and pleasure. They are more likely to borrow information books which their interest in a particular subject may well stimulate them to read. Their fiction reading will depend to a very large extent on the enthusiasm with which a particular book is introduced to them.

The teacher in the primary school or the interested parent is in the best position to prevent all but a small handful of children from becoming backward readers, by reading aloud, by introducing well-chosen books and by encouraging children to use the local public library where staff may be able to supplement their efforts by introducing children to a wider range of suitable books. As the less able children get older and their chronological age begins to get further and further ahead of their reading age, the problem becomes more acute. An eight year old may be prepared to have a go at a book intended for a six year old learning to read, but a ten year old will be less than enthusiastic and a twelve year old will almost certainly reject it, put off by what seem to him childish illustrations and interests.

Backward readers require a short story, written in simple words and a style which is not too complex, with a few clearly drawn characters and, above all, a plot which is relevant to their interests and chronological age. The type-face should be reasonably large, clear and well-spaced but outwardly the books should not look too different from those which their more able contemporaries are reading.

Unfortunately few of the series which are designed specially for backward readers are really suitable for library stock. Many of them are appalling examples of book production and give the impression that anything is considered good enough for children who are not very good at reading; they look both different and inferior. The series which are mentioned here are ones which are available either in library editions or pre-bound editions and which maintain reasonable levels of production. They are also series which have proved successful with the children at whom they are aimed.

The simplest books which are designed to appeal to older backward readers are the 'Inner Ring Books' (Benn). These have been criticized for their urban, working-class background with its implication that the problem lies only with the children from this particular environment. These books were planned and written by Alan Pullen with long experience of teaching in the 'inner ring' area of Birmingham, and they are an attempt to provide stories with a setting which is recognizable to the children concerned. There is considerable difficulty in finding suitable material to stimulate the imagination of these children, and it is even less easy to do this when you are limited to short simple words. In *Devil's dump* some young people are renovating a cottage to use as a club-room. There is a misunderstanding between Lin and her boy-friend, Sam, with reconciliation brought about through a small lost sister. The story is well-constructed, short, with teenage characters and is told in a very simple vocabulary. There is a second series, slightly more difficult, but with similar appeal. In *Shilling a mile* by M. Hardcastle, Tony wants to go to a football match, while Jan wants to go on a charity walk. These books are fairly lavishly illustrated with black and white line drawings. The covers are not very exciting, but the difference of appearance at least makes it easy to pick them out from other books on the library shelves.

The 'Tempo Books' (Longmans) are slightly longer and more attractive in appearance, but unfortunately have a 'word list' at the back which gives them the appearance of class readers. *The big drop* consists of seven stories woven around two young people, Linda and Jim. The stories are short and simple, with plenty of action.

The 'Joan Tate Books' (Heinemann) need rather more reading skill, but they too are short, set in working-class areas and have secondary modern children, motor mechanics and shop assistants for their main characters. The vocabulary is simple but the style flows much more easily than in the two series already mentioned.

'Bandit Books' (Benn) are written for twelve to fifteen year olds who have the reading ability of seven to eight year olds. There is no indication in the books themselves that the stories are simple or specially written; the main characters are young people or young adults, and the illustrations reflect this. The stories have a bias towards mystery and adventure. The text is well broken up, with plenty of dialogue. They serve their purpose well but, put on the open library shelves, they might get into the hands of younger children for whom they are not intended. The 'One Star Bandit Books', which have a very limited vocabulary indeed, and the main series of 'Bandit Books' are full of slang, and written in a style and about themes which younger children of normal ability would find puzzling.

One of the most attractive and successful series of books for older backward readers is the 'Jets' series, edited by Margaret Kamm (Cape). They are designed to look like adult paperbacks, though there are a few illustrations scattered through the text, and the type-face is large. 'Red Jets' are simple, 'Blue Jets' slightly more advanced, but apart from a distinctive coloured spine and the device on the cover, there is nothing to mark them out from other books. The majority of the titles are likely to appeal to boys, and they deal with the kind of topics in which boys with reading problems are likely to be interested. For example, Robert Bateman's *Skid pan* is about Joe, aged sixteen and crazy about motor-bikes, who gets involved in a plan to break into a warehouse. There is a lot of quite detailed information about motor-bikes woven into the story, which is well-told.

The 'Bright Arrow Series' (Heinemann), edited by Ian Serraillier, consists of retold versions of adventure stories by R. M. Ballantyne. The retellings are of a high standard and inside the covers the books look attractive, but the dust-jackets are poor and do not attract the eye. Oxford University Press publish a series of 'English Picture Readers', some of which are simplified versions of adult classics such as *Jane Eyre*, *Great expectations* and *David Copperfield*. These are attractively produced and, used as educational tools under skilled guidance, can be helpful for backward readers of thirteen and fourteen who are never going to be able to tackle the original.

The most useful contribution which a children's librarian can make is to look out for books, especially from the series aimed at the six to ten year olds,* which, because of their subject matter and characters, seem particularly suited for older backward readers.

Between the ages of eight and ten, backward readers who can be tempted into the library, can be offered some of the 'I Can Read Books' (World's Work) and 'Beginner Books' (Collins) without much embarrassment and some of these, such as Bennet Cerf's *The book of riddles* (Collins) can even be used with the over elevens. The four Hamish Hamilton series† each contain titles which are useful. Rosemary Sutcliff's *The chief's*

*see also pages 135–137 †see also page 136

*daughter** (H. Hamilton) is an 'Antelope Book' which has characters with whom teenagers can identify and a rather sophisticated twist to the plot. Among the 'Reindeer Books' are Honor Arundel's *The high house* and Christine Pullein-Thompson's *Homeless Katie*, which are both well-constructed stories with plots of interest to older girls. Those 'Salamander Books' (Nelson) which are intended for nine to eleven year olds are short, attractively produced and written by authors such as Eric Allen, Richard Armstrong and Mary Treadgold. Eric Allen's *Smitty and the plural of cactus*, for example, is not at all childish; Smitty looks and behaves like a secondary school boy and the story has a humorous appeal. Some of the 'Brock Books' (Brockhampton) aimed at the eight to eleven year olds can also be used with rather older children; examples are Clive Dalton's *Malay Cruise* and its sequels, Paul Buddee's *The unwilling adventurers†*, Henry Treece's *War dog* and, for girls, Geraldine Kaye's *The pony raffle*.

There are three grades of 'Crown Books' (Macmillan), the most difficult grade ('Three Crown') being intended for the nine to eleven reading age group. In fact, the 'Two Crown Books', intended for children with a reading age of eight to nine and a half, can also be used for older children. Some of the books contain one full-length story; others contain three shorter ones. R. E. Masters' *North for adventure* consists of three fairly short stories, each with plenty of action and dialogue. The third story *The Geordie foresters* is the best, partly because the boy in the illustrations is shown to be wearing long trousers. (This is a point which publishers might be encouraged to bear in mind—children don't mind reading stories about children who appear to be slightly older than themselves, but the reverse is not true.) Ruth Park's *Airlift for Grandee* is a full-length story set in New South Wales, woven around a valuable sheep, missing in the bush, and the search for him. 'Crown Books' are nicely produced, written by well-known people such as Nancy Martin and Malcolm Saville and illustrated (in two cases) by William Stobbs; but the dust-jackets are disappointing and have an air of the class reader about them.

The 'Briggs Books' (H. Hamilton) are intended for seven to

*see also page 105 †see also page 53

nine year olds, and are accounts, well-illustrated in both full-colour and black and white, of modern exploits by such people as Lindbergh, Shackleton, Hillary, Nuvolari and Richthofen. They are written in the form of stories, and those titles which deal with aircraft and racing cars have a particular appeal for older boys.

Armstrong Sperry's *The boy who was afraid* (Bodley Head and Knight) is a non-series book which can also be used with these children. Mafatu, the son of a Chief, overcomes his fear of the sea by leaving his own island in the South Seas and proving his manhood by leading a Robinson Crusoe existence on another island. This is a fairly short book, well produced and meaningful, about the overcoming of fear and the importance of establishing one's self-respect.

One of the big problems which faces the children's librarian is how to get these books into the hands of the children who need them. If the children come in a group with their class teacher, then suitable books can be displayed for the occasion; but where individual children are concerned it is important to build up a close personal relationship, for it is obviously undesirable to label a special section of books; no one has yet thought of an appropriate but tactful heading for such a collection. If the books are shelved with the main fiction sequence, they are difficult to find and may fall into the hands of children for whom they are not appropriate. The style and format of the 'Jets', for example, make them extremely popular with boys of eight and nine and while there is no reason why the eight and nine year olds should not read them, a seven year old tackling an 'Inner Ring Book' might well cause raised eyebrows. The most satisfactory solution seems to be a compromise one—putting 'Jets', 'Briggs Books' and suitable series books on the open shelves, and providing the children who need them with well-produced reading lists and guides, and keeping 'Inner Ring Books', the 'English Picture Readers' and other 'class reader' type books in a special corner, available only on request. This is not an ideal solution by any means but a better alternative has yet to be found.

READ ON FROM HERE:

TEACHERS WORLD: Reluctant readers. 6 articles by Michael Pollard, Vera Michaelson, Angus Stewart, J. A. Gordon and Aidan Chambers. 13th, 20th and 27th February, 6th, 20th and 27th March, 1970. *The authors of some of these articles use the term 'reluctant reader' to denote children who can read, but who need encouragement, others to denote children who have reading difficulties.*

TUCKER, M: Literature for backward readers. *The Use of English*, vol. 18, no. 1, Autumn 1966.

CHILDREN'S librarians working in areas where there are immigrant children can help by finding stories which are meaningful to these children. The same books will help the native-born English children to understand more readily the countries and cultures from which some of their contemporaries come. This is one approach which is recommended by the Plowden Report, although so far little research has been done into the reading needs and tastes of immigrant children and the problem, in so far as one arises, tends to be concentrated in the areas served by a comparatively few urban libraries.

Folk tales provide a good starting point. There are good collections from most of the countries of the world and as integration is, after all, a two-way process, the telling of stories to a child audience of mixed cultures would help to bring the children together in a mood of relaxation and enjoyment. It must be remembered that immigrant children come from many countries; there are not only the coloured children from Commonwealth countries, of whom we tend to be most conscious, but also, in certain parts of the country, quite substantial numbers of children of Italian, Cypriot, Greek and other European origins as well. Some children's librarians will need to use John Hampden's *The house of cats* (Deutsch), a selection of Italian stories, or Ruth Manning-Sanders' *Damian and the dragon* (O.U.P), a collection of modern Greek fairy tales, just as others will tell the West Indian stories about Ananse* or the Indian legends about Rama and Sita.†

Stories set in the countries from which the children come are also useful and, through translation, more of these are becoming available each year. Publishers seem particularly conscious of the needs of children from the West Indies and India and there is a growing number of books set in these countries.‡

see also page 20   †*see also page* 20   ‡*see also pages* 94–96

Since one of the problems met by teachers in secondary schools is the difficulty which adolescent Indian girls have in adjusting between the strict, enclosed life of their home and the relatively permissive atmosphere in which most English girls of their age live, a book such as M. Thøger's *Shanta** (Brockhampton), is particularly useful. One of the most suprising suggestions, however, came from a teacher who found that Kipling's *Kim* (Macmillan) was a great success with a secondary school class of Indian children. Kipling is not the first author one would have thought of in this context, but the descriptions of the Indian crowds and the outlook on life apparently brought a whiff of home to some boys.

A growing number of children are not immigrants themselves but children who have been born in this country of immigrant parents. During the last ten years, stories with English settings have begun to include coloured children, usually West Indians. The West Indian child is normally portrayed in a favourable light but is not, as a rule, a leader. The situation which arises in Nicholas Fisk's *Space hostages* (H. Hamilton),† where Brylo, the coloured boy, assumes the leadership in a time of crisis, is fairly uncommon in children's books, and this book is useful, therefore, for introducing to children of about ten or eleven.

Outstanding for small children are Ezra Keats' picture books about Peter, a little negro boy, beginning with *The snowy day* (Bodley Head and Puffin). In 1967, Longmans Young Books published two small picture books by J. R. Joseph. *Judy and Jasmin* hangs on the fact that the two little girls, one Indian, the other English, change dresses at school and apparently fool their mothers into mistaking them for each other. The other, *Tim and Terry*, is rather more successful; here the two boys, one English, the other West Indian, look for each other around the school because they are friends.

For many years *Little Black Sambo*, by Helen Bannerman, (Chatto) has been extremely popular with small children. In the early '60s, English children's librarians, doubtful about its reception amongst coloured children, found it was equally successful with them. It is possible to be too sensitive. In *Tales of Joe and Timothy* (Methuen), Dorothy Edwards writes about

**see also page 96 †see also page 62*

two small boys who live in the same block of flats, one at the very top, the other in the basement. Half-way up is Jessie, a 'little brown girl', who sometimes joins their expeditions to the park and elsewhere. This phrase, 'a little brown girl', which could be taken amiss, is typical of Dorothy Edwards' style, but it is rather a pity that Jessie's father is referred to by his Christian name whereas the fathers of the two boys are not.

Late in 1969, there appeared Mary Cockett's *Another home, another country* (Chatto), the first story to be written for younger children which admitted there was a problem. Luke is shown at home in the West Indies, living with his elder brother and mother who doesn't seem to want him very much; the joy of his life is a pet mongoose and it is the thought of parting with Mixy, the mongoose, that nearly prevents him from taking the opportunity of going to England when it comes. He does go, however, and finds it cold and wet and disappointing at first. Then he gets a chance to show the other children in his class that he knows about something of which they have no experience—life in Jamaica. The final seal is set on his happiness and that of his adopted parents when he is chosen to act Balthazar in the school nativity play. It is a simple story but well-done, with the problems seen clearly through Luke's eyes.

Children's librarians hold diametrically opposed views about some of the books available for older children. To one the plot and style of Prudence Andrew's *Ginger and no 10* (Lutterworth) is quite unacceptable, while another feels that the attitudes shown in it can only help. One children's librarian welcomes and appreciates Joan Tate's *Out of the sun* (Heinemann), which describes how Jenny, from the West Indies, works first in a supermarket and then as a nurse before settling down to married life, while another feels that it merely accentuates the differences.

For older girls, too, there is Josephine Kamm's *Out of step* (Brockhampton), in which a young English girl falls in love with a West Indian boy and experiences the resentment and hostility which result from this relationship.

Apart from books which deal directly with the situation in this country, there are other books which illustrate the problems of racial integration in other countries.* Other books show young people adjusting to a strange and sometimes hostile environment. A. Huston and J. Yolen's *Trust a city kid* (Dent) reflects the problems of settling down in a strange community. Reg, a coloured boy (though this fact is never stated, it is clear from the illustrations) from the town, goes to spend the summer with a Quaker family on a farm in Pennsylvania. It is also a good story about a boy keen on horses. Betty Cavanna's *Jenny Kimura* (Brockhampton) shows Jenny, with an American father and a Japanese mother, spending a holiday with her American grandmother and coping with the problems which arise. A. Holden's *Rata* (Whitcomb and Toombs) demonstrates even more clearly the situation of a girl with mixed parentage, in this case, Maori and European, who is desperately trying to find a culture into which she can fit. H. F. Brinsmead's *Pastures of the blue crane* (O.U.P) deals with the same sort of situation in an Australian setting.

A useful book in this field is K. Haugaard's *Myeko's gift* (Abelard-Schuman), in which Myeko, a small Japanese girl, an immigrant in the United States, learns that she can offer something of her traditional culture to her school friends. Jade Snow Wong's *Fifth Chinese daughter* (Peacock) is an interesting biographical account of Jade Snow, brought up in a Chinese culture in San Francisco's Chinatown. These books are well-written and interesting for any child but may be specially helpful for any children or young people faced with the problem of settling into a strange environment and these may include some English children as well as Italian, Greek and Cypriot ones.

Finally, children's librarians working in communities where there is a high proportion of immigrant children might be well advised to have another look at some old favourites. Is *The story of Dr Dolittle* (Cape and Puffin), for example, really a suitable book to include in library stock, with its chapters about Prince Bumpo and his desire to be white and Polynesia's remarks about knowing 'these darkies'?

*see also pages 96, 97

LIBRARIANS and teachers have never yet really come to terms with the question of whether or not there is a need for fiction specially written for adolescents. In the nineteenth and early twentieth centuries, there was no very clear cut division between the books read by older children and those read by adults; books such as Haggard's *King Solomon's mines* (Dent and Puffin) and A. Conan Doyle's *The adventures of Sherlock Holmes* (Murray) were intended to be read by anyone who would enjoy them between the ages of eight and eighty; the same was true to some extent of the books more likely to be read by girls and although adult women would not be very likely to read *Little women* (Blackie and Puffin) and its sequels, they might well have enjoyed the books of Charlotte Yonge. Some books which are now thought of as children's classics would almost certainly be labelled teenage novels were they to be newly published today and books such as John Buchan's *The thirty-nine steps* and Jean Webster's *Daddy-long-legs* are included in the series of Dent's Children's Illustrated Classics.

Teenage fiction is an artificial category which has really been imposed on publishers and authors by the administrative organization of public libraries which divides their stock into adult and children's sections. This, in turn, has led to a problem in getting children to move from the children's section to the adult section at the right psychological moment and hence to the realization that there is a place for one section of the library which could bring together books from both these sections so that the change does not have to be a sudden and complete one and so that children, or young people, are gradually introduced to books that they might enjoy.

This problem of progression from children's books to adult

M

books also arises in the school library, and is increased by the fact that so many modern, adult novels, which are reading of desirable quality for sixth formers, are considered unsuitable for young people under the age of fifteen and sixteen by parents, teachers and librarians.

What constitutes a book that will appeal to a majority of teenagers? There must be a good plot, which needs to be unfolded skilfully and in the most interesting way possible, at not too great a length and in a vigorous and fairly simple style. The story should be about things which are both relevant and interesting. It is clear that there are a number of adult writers who meet these requirements admirably and authors such as Nevil Shute, John Wyndham, Mary Stewart and Agatha Christie are extremely popular with a wide range of teenagers, both those who are even more likely to read magazines and with the academic ones who are at the same time enjoying Jane Austen, D. H. Lawrence and Margaret Drabble.

The in-between stage spans the ages of twelve to eighteen and most young people go through a stage somewhere between these ages of reading both children's and adult books before moving on completely to adult fiction. The age of making the change will vary according to the ability and interests of individual children and will also reflect to some extent the sort of help and guidance they have received in school, at home or in the public library.

The first teenage fiction in this country was seen in the early '50s in the shape of career novels, which not only put over information about possible careers but also included a little romantic interest and showed, in the pleasantest possible way, the problems of growing up. These books could be shelved in the children's library without any fear of complaint from indignant parents. The first book to appear on the children's list of a publisher which gave many children's librarians food for thought was Josephine Kamm's *Young mother* (Brockhampton), published in 1965; this story of an unmarried, sixteen year old schoolgirl who becomes pregnant aroused immediate controversy; here was a book which dealt, although in fairly innocent terms, with a subject which might be considered unsuitable for many ten, eleven and even twelve year old girls. It was a book which, if placed on the shelves of the children's library, might give rise to complaints from indignant parents; on the other hand, if it was merely stocked in the adult section of the library, it would be lost to the majority of those who might gain from reading it. A sound knowledge of the children's book-stock is helpful in dealing with complaints from adults and since *Young mother* does not put unmarried motherhood in a favourable light nor tell any child anything which she should not know, it is possible to answer these complaints in a tactful manner. It is, however, useful to try and ensure that books are found by those who will both enjoy them and benefit from them and, even at that time, children's librarians could look round the shelves of the children's library and find a number of other books which might conveniently join *Young mother* on the shelves of a special teenage or bridge section of the library. Nowadays there are considerably more books which are only going to be fully used in the public library if attention is drawn to them in this way. In the time which elapsed between the first edition of the County Libraries Group booklist, *Attitudes and adventure*, in 1965 and the second, published in 1968, many more books intended for older children or young adults were published and the second edition included a much higher pro-portion of this type of book.

The first notable series of books to be published specially for the teenager was the Penguin Books Peacock series, which began to appear in 1962. This series sticks to fairly safe titles, drawing on established works from both the adult and children's side of the fence and there are no special efforts to attract the reluctant reader. Two other series, Topliners, published by Macmillan, and Pyramid Books, from Heinemann, however, are geared to the needs of the teenager who needs persuasion to read; both are associated with Aidan Chambers, an experienced secondary modern school teacher, who has been one of the most articu-late advocates of the need for teenage fiction. He has given much thought to the problem of encouraging young people to read, but titles in both series show the difficulties of selecting or writing the right kind of book. Pyramids include titles as widely varied as John Steinbeck's *The red pony*, an adult long short story, marked both by good writing and appeal for this particular group of young people, Julia Cunningham's *Dorp dead*, excellently written but with a young hero of about twelve and probably rather too subtle for the average reader of this age, and Honor Arundel's *The two sisters* which, although well written and with excellent characterization, is really *Good wives* brought up to date, with long white boots as the modern equivalent of the length of dress silk which was Meg's undoing in the 1860s.

The Topliners have an attractive paperback format and include a wide variety of titles. Some, such as the ones about Birdy Jones, the successful pop whistler, by E. W. Hildick are reasonably appropriate for the younger end of the age group, but some of the early titles in the series, such as the two about *Louie's lot*, also by E. W. Hildick, are really intended for and are certainly enjoyed by much younger children. Joan Tate's *Sam and me* is short but requires a fair amount of intellectual co-operation on the part of the reader since it is told in a series of flashbacks. Ray Pope's *The drum* is a science fiction story, set in the ruins of a Sussex laid waste by some future war; this has considerable quality but the beginning moves slowly and nearly five pages have to be read before there is any dialogue; most reluctant readers demand action more quickly than this and lose interest if they do not get it.

It looks, however, as if both series are finding their feet and containing titles which are likely to attract readers. Irma Chilton's *String of time* is a most successful Topliner, a time-travel story, told in the first person by Gill Bradwell who, as the result of a motor-bicycle accident, finds herself for a short, terrifying time back in the middle ages, hunted as a witch. On her return to the present, she is used by a sinister woman doctor, Dr Edith Palmer, in time-travel experiments. The story is short, told racily in a way which is likely to appeal to those who find reading a chore. The plot is clear, but has originality and, despite its female heroine and female author, this is a book which might well appeal to boys just as much as girls. The boys are more difficult to attract and since they are, on the whole, more reluctant readers of fiction than girls, this is a field in which there is scope for development. Robert Lipsyte's *The contender*, imported as a Topliner from the United States, has an almost wholly male appeal, with its story of Alfred Brooks, a young negro, and his career in boxing. The fact that he retires after only four fights because he doesn't have the 'killer instinct' does to some extent compensate for the brutality of the boxing ring, which comes through very clearly and tends to overshadow the more thoughtful and reflective aspects of the book.

Apart from these two series, most publishers include on their lists some fiction which is likely to appeal to young people who are ready to move on to adult books. Some authors of notable series have allowed their characters to grow up and develop emotionally as well as physically. Geoffrey Trease concluded his series of Bannermere books with the *Gates of Bannerdale* (Heinemann), in which two of the characters fall in love and decide to marry and both Monica Edwards, in her stories about Punchbowl Farm and Romney Marsh, and Antonia Forest, in hers about the Marlowes, allow the characters to discover that some of them are more than just good friends and explore this maturing feeling with some sympathy.

Girls have been much better catered for than boys, and most of the novels written for young people, even where they have male authors and male characters, appeal to them rather than to the boys. That some of the teenage romances are more likely to lead to a reading of women's magazine stories and light romances than to an enjoyment of Iris Murdoch and Margaret Drabble seems only too probable. One of the most successful Peacock titles has been Beverly Cleary's *Fifteen* which describes, in a cheerful but sympathetic way, the trials of young love. This and Mary Stolz's *Goodbye my shadow* (Peacock) are both American in origin and there is little doubt that the American teenage girl is better equipped with this type of reading than her English counterpart. At the same time, the English book market is not yet flooded with teenage romances of little worth. M. E. Allan's output of teenage mystery romances is now considerable, and although the heroines of these tend to be quite indistinguishable one from another, the author has a strong sense of place or background, which helps to compensate for this. *A play to the festival* (Heinemann), set against the background of the Edinburgh Festival, is a good example; the theatrical interest offsets the sentimental reflections of the rather romantic heroine. Most of these stories are one step away from Mary Stewart.

Girls who enjoy the books of Ruth Arthur are likely to be reading, almost at the same period, books by Victoria Holt, Daphne du Maurier and probably Charlotte Brontë's *Jane Eyre*, since they all have much in common. *Portrait of Margarita* (Gollancz) and *A candle in her room* (Gollancz) have a romantic theme, shot through with a sinister element. *Portrait of Margarita*, for good measure, includes an autistic child and Margarita herself is much troubled by her mixed blood, though comfortably cushioned against the worst effects by a kind and rich guardian. One of Winifred Finlay's most recent books, *The cry of the peacock* (Harrap), also combines mystery and romance and has a well-described setting and good characterization, both of which help to give it rather more depth than some of her earlier novels.

Malcolm Saville has made a useful contribution in his series of Marston Baines thrillers, beginning with *Three towers in Tuscany* (Heinemann). He deals with topics such as drugs, in *The purple valley* (Heinemann), and black magic, in *Dark danger*, and these stories are about as near as it is possible to get to Ian Fleming's James Bond stories without the sex and the sadism. It seems, however, that these books are usually read and enjoyed by sophisticated and able eleven year olds rather than by older children who, if they like this type of suspense thriller, much prefer James Bond, the sex and the sadism.

Books dealing with social problems and problems associated with growing up are now written in a way that was not possible or not acceptable a few years ago. The breakthrough came with *Young mother*, although its author had already dealt with another problem in an equally sensitive way; the story of a young white girl falling in love with a West Indian negro formed the basis of *Out of step* (Brockhampton). The developing permissiveness in this field is clearly indicated by a comparison of *Young mother* with Honor Arundel's *The longest weekend* (H. Hamilton), published four years later. Eileen not only discovers that she is pregnant, although unmarried, but is so, not because of unpremeditated passion after too much drink at a party, but as a result of a steady, continuous relationship of some months with Joel, who had previously taken contraceptive precautions himself, but on this occasion had been under the impression that Eileen was now on the pill. Eileen also discusses the possibility of having an abortion, decides, with the support of her parents, to keep the baby and, three years later, with the baby grown into a small, capricious girl and Joel qualified as a doctor, they decide to marry after all. This is a story which will be enjoyed by many girls, not only for the story but also for the picture of the relationships which is painted, between Eileen and her mother, and between Eileen and her daughter.

A trio of books deal with the problems of the adopted girl. Ruth Arthur, in *Requiem for a princess* (Gollancz), does this in a rather romantic way, enabling the girl to reconcile herself to the fact of adoption through identification with a girl living in the same house nearly three hundred years earlier, at the time of the Spanish Armada. Illegitimacy is the reason for the adoption in both Dorothy Clewes' *A girl like Cathy* (Collins) and Josephine Kamm's *No strangers here* (Longmans Y.B.) and the adoption gives rise to adolescent uncertainty. In both these books the problem of drug-taking among young people is raised but this is a theme which has not yet been successfully tackled, perhaps because of a lack of personal experience on the part of possible authors! Cathy's relatives merely imagine that she is taking drugs, and the chapters in which the matter is discussed seem rather artificial in relation to the rest of the book. Josephine Kamm is more successful in showing how easy it might be for someone who is unhappy and insecure to drift into drug-taking.

There is a danger that drugs will merely become a substitute for stolen jewels and smuggled goods in the thriller type of story and that insufficient attention will be paid to the sociological side. For example, both Malcolm Saville in *The purple valley* (Heinemann) and Madelaine Duke in *The sugar cube trap* (Brockhampton), while emphasizing the dangers and evils of drug-taking, have produced thriller-type stories in which the message is easily ignored.

Other themes are treated in a way that would not have been

acceptable a few years ago. In Jean MacGibbon's *Liz* (H. Hamilton), one of the main characters is drowned in a flood with quite shattering effects upon Liz herself. Young people are shown coping with sudden blindness in Dorothy Clewes' *Guide dog* (H. Hamilton) or with being orphaned in Barbara Willard's *Charity at home* (Longmans Y.B). The treatment of the Jews in pre-war Nazi Germany is discussed in Margot Benary's *A time to love* (Macmillan) and the rights and wrongs of a strange religious sect are dealt with by Nan Chauncy in *High and haunted island* (O.U.P). Not only are these subjects being used as the basis of well-written and readable stories, but they are treated much more thoughtfully and in a more mature and sophisticated way which shows recognition of the fact that children are maturing at an earlier age and can therefore cope with and require greater depth of thought in their reading.

Another change can be seen in the kind of language which nowadays is freely used in these books. Dependent upon a use of rather unconventional language are several books written in the style of Salinger's *The catcher in the rye* which is, itself, popular with many young people. Barbara Wershba's *The dream watcher* (Longmans Y.B) tells of the friendship between young Albert Scully and a strange old woman, Mrs Woodfin, and shows how the experience which he gains from this relationship helps him to grow up. Emily Neville's Newbery Medal winner, *It's like this, cat* (Angus & Robertson) and Paul Zindel's *The pigman* (Bodley Head) are also written in a style which is likely to attract young readers. Like *The catcher in the rye*, they are all told in the first person, by young people, and in a racy style which invites the sympathy of the reader.

Lastly, there are those books of very high quality which could be read and enjoyed by many discriminating adults, if they only knew of their existence—books which seem to have been published as books for young people and as the responsibility of children's editors only by chance. In this category come some of the books by Rosemary Sutcliff, Hester Burton, K. M. Peyton, H. F. Brinsmead, Ivan Southall, Alan Garner, John Rowe Townsend, Jill Paton Walsh and two books recently imported from the United States, one by Richard E. Drdek, the other by Esther Hautzig.

It seems purely arbitrary that Rosemary Sutcliff's *The lantern bearers* (O.U.P) and *The mark of the horse lord* (O.U.P) should be published as historical novels for young people when *Sword at sunset* and *The rider of the white horse* were originally published as adult novels, though they subsequently appeared as Peacocks. Hester Burton's *Time of trial* (O.U.P), it is true, has young central characters and an element of adventure in the smuggling activities which is likely to appeal to the young, but the story is a long one and the reader needs some maturity in order to read and appreciate it.

There must be many adults who enjoy stories about the Forsytes and the Whiteoaks who would derive equal pleasure from K. M. Peyton's trilogy of novels about Christina of Flambards, which show Christina growing up through adolescence, marriage and finally in *Flambards in summer* (O.U.P) experiencing early widowhood.

H. F. Brinsmead, an Australian, writes very sympathetically from the viewpoint of the teenage girl, and in a number of her books the teenage girl in question is not of any great academic ability. It is a pity that most of the many girls who read teenage love comics are unlikely to meet Binny Flambeau, the sixteen year old heroine of *A sapphire for September* who, when the activities of her friends become too intellectual for her, retires to her tent to read a *Real Romances* comic by torchlight. At the same time Binny is attracted by architectural student Adam and by his hobby of gem-collecting and, in going on a gem-hunting expedition, she comes to appreciate the values which are really important in life.

Ivan Southall, another Australian, in *To the wild sky* (Angus and Robertson) wrote a novel which comes near to Golding's *Lord of the flies*. In *Finn's folly* (Angus and Robertson) he has gone even beyond this and has produced a horrifying story about a situation which makes tremendous demands upon the young reader. This is undoubtedly a powerful book but it should never have been published as a book for young people since few of them will be able to cope with the effect of helplessness and horror which descends on this group of children who are suddenly isolated in the Australian countryside on a foggy winter night.

And what of *The owl service* (Collins), that splendidly strange award-winning book of 1968 by Alan Garner, in which the relationships between three young people, two boys and a girl, are worked out in the terms of a story from the Welsh Mabinogion? The sinister power, bottled up in a patterned dinner service and a wall-painting by a previous generation, has to be released through the actions of the three adolescents. It would be a pity if children who have enjoyed Garner's earlier books come to *The owl service* before they are really ready for it; it has a lot to say about the experiences of adolescence in a way that is gripping for the reader of the right maturity but would be puzzling for one who was not.

Another novel which makes new demands on the child reader is John Rowe Townsend's *The intruder* (O.U.P), a story about a boy searching for his real identity. Arnold Haithwaite, too, is adopted, living with his grandfather in a dying seaside town in South Cumberland; he is not very bright, although he understands the ways of the tide which can roll unexpectedly up the river mouth, and he is quite unable to deal with the situation which arises when a strange, psychopathic character turns up, claiming to be his uncle, another Arnold Haithwaite. It is horrifying for the reader to witness Arnold's helplessness in the face of the intruder's cunning attempts to ingratiate himself into the old man's favour.

Jill Paton Walsh's *Fireweed* (Macmillan) is set during the Second World War at the height of the air raids on London. Two young people, Bill, who tells the story, and Julie, are on the run, one from an unsatisfactory evacuation home, the other as a result of an abortive evacuation to Canada. They are about fifteen but on Bill's side, at any rate, there is a feeling of more than a straightforward friendship, and the moment at which this delicate feeling is shattered by Julie's rejection of him is most poignant. Before this break comes in their relationship, they set up a home together in the basement of a bombed house, combining a practical working relationship with their growing feeling for each other.

Drdek's novel, *The game* (Bodley Head), was one of two titles, the other being *The pigman*, which were published by Bodley Head in 1969 and given adult-looking dust jackets in a deliberate attempt to woo the more mature reader. There are no illustrations but the books are well-produced with spaciously set text. Sonny, a boy of twelve, has grown up in the care of Frank, an odd job man, watched over by Raymond Jindra, his godfather, the parish priest. The neighbourhood is busily concerned about Sonny's unorthodox upbringing but, gradually, very carefully, it is shown to be a valid one.

Perhaps one of the most moving stories to be published in the late '60s was Esther Hautzig's *The endless steppe* (H. Hamilton), created out of her own childhood experiences in Siberia, after she and some of her family were taken there from Poland in the early days of the Second World War. The fascinating account of events, the contrast between the prosperous Jewish home in Vilna and the hardships of mere existence in Siberia, make compelling reading. What comes through is the resilience of young people in time of stress and many girls will identify with Esther as she grows into young adulthood during the course of the book. From this is a step not forward, but sideways, to *Anne Frank's diary*, which has proved enormously popular with young people.

There is a very real danger that these books, especially the ones in the last group, may be overlooked if they are not exploited by the librarian. They are not filling a gap but they may well fall through one; there is a real need for this type of material and the reading of books such as these is a valuable experience which can extend the horizons of young people.

READ ON FROM HERE:

BRINSMEAD, H. F : How and why I write for young people. *Bookbird*, vol. 7, no. 4, December 1969. A slightly shorter version of this article appeared in *Y.L.G. News*, vol. 13, no. 2, June 1969.

CHAMBERS, A : The reluctant reader. Pergamon Press, 1969.

CROUCH, M : Streets ahead in experience. *The Junior Bookshelf*, vol. 33, no. 3, June 1969. *About K. M. Peyton*.

HOLBROOK, D : Teenage fiction—a closer look. *Books for your children*, vol. 5, no. 2, Winter 1969/1970.

KAMM, A : Teen-pagers. *Teachers World*, 3rd October 1969.

LIBRARY ASSOCIATION, COUNTY LIBRARIES GROUP : Attitudes and adventure. 2nd ed, 1968.

THE official organization of the publishing industry is the Publishers Association, incorporating also the Book Development Council, whose main function is to promote British books overseas. Within the Publishers Association are Groups covering specialist interests, and publishers who produce books for children form the Children's Book Group, many of whose members also belong to the Educational Publishers Council, a division of the Publishers Association concerned with books in schools. There is an informal association of publishers of children's books, the Children's Book Circle, which also sponsors the annual Eleanor Farjeon Award for services to children's literature.

During the 1950s children's books were mainly published through a department of a company under the children's editor. Today, though many firms still retain the post of children's editor, the status and importance of the children's book market has been recognized to the extent that large firms have established separate divisions and in some cases separate companies to publish children's books. The editors of children's books are responsible for working closely with the authors on the one hand and for keeping in touch with the potential market on the other; they are also involved in the commissioning of illustrations and for negotiating arrangements for joint editions, which are becoming increasingly common in the case of picture books, with other countries.

Few authors come fully-fledged into the world of children's books with their first book. Too many people appear to think that writing a book for children is child's play, and many of the unsolicited manuscripts which reach the desk of the children's editor give the impression that the author has no idea at all of what is acceptable as a book for children in the contemporary world. Other new authors, potentially promising, may need quite a lot of guidance in order to realize this potential. In the words of Jock Curle of Macdonald, 'My contribution to children's fiction is simply to be a third eye to as many authors as possible who are open to life, have things they really want to say, and possess the literary and other qualities necessary to show them true.'

The publishing of children's fiction in hardback is not an easy business. The best fiction cannot be written to order or commissioned in quite the same way that non-fiction can; yet it must meet the standards demanded by the institutional market of public libraries and schools, since the number of hardback children's books sold to private individuals is relatively small.

In the early 1920s Jonathan Cape himself waged a campaign to get children's books taken seriously in the literary world, demanding adequate space and proper critical treatment from the press and from reviewers. He wanted the book trade to establish special children's book shops and called on publishers to produce volumes whose 'price must be moderate, the format attractive and the book itself first rate'. He wanted an end to the philosophy of playing safe with the popular annual and the hackneyed, undemanding story. Although Cape now publish less than a dozen new children's titles each year, Jonathan Cape's philosophy is reflected in the fact that Hugh Lofting, Erich Kästner and Arthur Ransome, authors published by Cape before the Second World War, are still going strong.

Today Jonathan Cape would find plenty of support for his views among the leading publishers of fiction for children, who, for the most part, maintain good standards, both in the physical production of the book and in the content. Children's editors are agreed that a good plot line, convincing characterization and literary merit are desirable qualities, and that fiction should be universal in its themes and understanding. They are very conscious of their moral obligation to communicate to children, not overtly but implicitly, certain standards of morality and behaviour. Children's fiction as a whole has humane and liberal attitudes, and there is a traditional avoidance of inessential violence, sadism and sex. The best of children's fiction embodies a real attempt to provide books which widen children's horizons, stimulate their imagination, deepen their emotional awareness, sharpen their moral sense and increase their mastery of language. Not all children's fiction achieves these high standards, but the children's editors are not necessarily to blame for this. As Antony Kamm, speaking at a Conference in Birmingham in 1967, said, 'What is happening is not so much that books are getting worse, but that the better books are not being demanded hard enough. Or, to put it in another way, those who are not buying the worthwhile books are subsidizing the second-rate. And as long as second-rate books are bought, they will continue to be published.'

Going round the shelves of a well-stocked children's library, the observer soon realizes that, while some children's books come from each of a wide range of publishers, less than a dozen imprints tend to dominate the fiction shelves. Each of the thirty or so publishers represented in this book seems to include at least one outstanding author; the acquisition of a successful and significant author is largely the luck of the draw, and some authors have a long association with certain publishers. Children's writers tend to be faithful to the publisher who gave them their start and where an author writes for more than one publisher, it is usually because he writes several different kinds of books, or for different age groups. For example, Bell, who publish very little children's fiction, published C. Walter Hodges' first historical novel, *Columbus sails*, in 1939 and have subsequently, in the last few years, published *The namesake* and *The marsh king*, although Hodges has done illustration work for a number of publishers, and has written non-fiction books, published by the O.U.P.

During the last twenty years the Oxford University Press has built up, among librarians, an enviable reputation; the high quality of book production appeals to the adult connoisseur (though some children seem to find it daunting) and has set new standards in this field. It has also built up a list of books by outstanding authors. In 1950, an O.U.P. book, Elfrida Vipont's *The lark on the wing*, received a Carnegie Medal for the first time; in 1969 another O.U.P. book, K. M. Peyton's *The edge of the cloud*, was the recipient, and during this twenty year period, out of the nineteen Carnegie Medals awarded, ten have been given to O.U.P. books, a fair reflection of this publisher's contribution to children's fiction in the 1950s and 1960s.

The principal publishers of children's fiction, producing as they are for the same market, tend to have a wide area of activities in common. Most of them publish at least some books for each age level, although they may pay special attention to particular age groups. The mainstay of the publisher is, of course, a steady-selling back list such as that of Faber, which includes such authors as Walter de la Mare, Lucy Boston and Alison Uttley. This enables a firm to risk a little experiment and publish an unusual work even though it may not seem likely to be a runaway success. This no doubt led to Faber's publication of Rosemary Harris' *The moon in the cloud* which was such a complete outsider in the Carnegie Medal stakes in 1968 that many children's librarians had not, in fact, bought it and had to hasten to do so when the announcement was made.

The recent trend in publishing towards the amalgamation and grouping of companies means not only that some firms have been able to extend their back lists by absorption, but also that some well-known authors pass into the hands of firms with whom they have not previously been associated. An example of the first of these situations is Chatto, Boyd and Oliver, the firm which resulted from the amalgamation, in 1968, of Chatto and Windus and the children's list of Oliver and Boyd. This has produced an extensive combined backlist which seems to include a high proportion of books about children in other countries. Brockhampton Press, which is one of the five associated publishers in the Hodder Group, specializes in publishing children's books. Reorganization within the Group in the late 1960s meant that Brockhampton, itself only established just before the Second World War, took over such distinguished authors as J. M. Barrie from Hodder and Stoughton and Elizabeth Goudge from the University of London Press. Methuen, now part of Associated Book Publishers, has taken over the children's books, *The little grey men* and *Down the bright stream*, written by B. B. (Denys Watkins-Pitchford), originally published by Eyre and Spottiswoode. This has given them two distinguished 'modern classics' to add to those written by A. A. Milne and Kenneth Grahame, who are also on their list.

There has been a long tradition of buying the rights of children's books from America and the number of American authors published in this country in English editions has increased steadily since the Second World War. A high proportion of the books from The World's Work are of American origin, but a number of English publishers includes some American authors; for example, The Bodley Head publishes the books of Eleanor Estes, Heinemann those of Elizabeth Enright and Macmillan those of Edward Eager.

Angus and Robertson, with its close Australian ties (the children's editor, Barbara Ker Wilson, herself lives there), publishes books by Australian writers, notably the books written for older children by Ivan Southall but other publishers too, such as O.U.P. and Longmans Y.B., draw increasingly on Australian-domiciled authors.

Children's editors feel that the interchange of books through translation is important, and most now include some authors in translation from other languages on their lists. A particular contribution in this field was made by the University of London Press, with its series, 'Foreign Award Winners' (now taken over by the Brockhampton Press), but Methuen introduced Anne Holm from Denmark to English readers and The Bodley Head introduced Paul Berna from France in the same way.

Of the publishers who predominate, The Bodley Head, Brockhampton Press, Hamish Hamilton and Methuen have all made a notable contribution in the field of good quality, readable fiction series for younger children; their books have met a real need and are widely known among the children as well as among librarians.

Collins seems to cater particularly fully for girls in the ten to twelve age range (some of the most enthusiastic users of children's libraries), and has on the back list a number of competent writers of family stories, such as Gillian Avery, Monica Edwards, Joan Robinson, Margaret McPherson and Noel Streatfeild. During the 1960s Collins also managed to hit two bulls-eyes with two of their new authors, Michael (Paddington) Bond and Alan Garner.

Gollancz, who entered the children's book publishing field rather later than some of the other firms mentioned, seems to put a special emphasis on science fiction. The publication of novels of this type by André Norton, Robert Heinlein, Peter Dickinson and Richard Parker reflects the Gollancz interest in the publication of science fiction for adults.

There is a general appreciation among the children's editors of the need to cater for the fact that children's reading tastes begin to mature earlier than they did ten years ago, and many of the books which are now published 'for children' can be thoroughly enjoyed by adults as well. Certain publishers however have paid special attention to the need, expressed by teachers and librarians. The break-through may be dated from the publication of Josephine Kamm's *Young mother* by the Brockhampton Press in 1965. In 1969 The Bodley Head published two books specially aimed at the over twelves, and in 1970 announced that a new imprint would be introduced— Books for New Adults—to distinguish books of this kind. Heinemann has produced the special series, 'Pyramid Books', while the Oxford University Press, looking for a more mature and adult attitude in its novelists, has made a notable contribution in this field by publishing the books of K. M. Peyton, Hester Burton and H. F. Brinsmead. Longmans Young Books has also provided for this age group by publishing such books as V. Breck's *Maggie* and Vian Smith's *The Lord Mayor's show*.

Some publishers of children's books have extended their range to include books about the literature and its authors. Predominant among these have been the Brockhampton Press with the notable survey *Intent upon reading* by Margery Fisher, published in 1961, and the translation of Jella Lepman's *A bridge of children's books*, and The Bodley Head with its series of Monographs about children's writers. Catering for the growing interest in early children's books, the Oxford University Press has produced four volumes in the 'Oxford Juvenile Library' series; these are facsimile editions of key books in the history and development of children's literature and include John Newbery's *A pretty little pocket book*.

N

In 1967, Macmillan produced a useful pamphlet, *Off the shelf: a library guide at home and at school, 1967-68*. This is an imaginative way of drawing attention to books from both the children's and adult lists which are suitable for young people. The only other pamphlet of this kind which seems to have emerged from a publisher in recent years has been the even more useful *Timely reading*, produced by Hodder and Stoughton (4th edition, 1970), listing recreational reading for teenagers.

The most immediate and up-to-date source of information about children's books is the publisher's catalogue. These catalogues are useful as a source of advance information, for checking titles in a given series and for surveying the output of an individual publisher as a whole. The publisher's catalogue can take various forms. There is the stock list or complete catalogue which may contain both adult and children's books. Some publishers produce lists of books suitable for school libraries, and the larger publishers may produce one version for primary schools and another for secondary schools; these lists, especially if aimed at the secondary school market, may also include adult books. Some publishers produce subject lists so that, in an educational institution, the lists may be distributed to the appropriate subject departments. Those publishers who produce many children's books usually issue a separate stock list of these each year, and this is often supplemented by twice-yearly catalogues introducing the books due for publication; these usually cover a six month period, from January to June and from July to December. There are sometimes special and separate lists for important or extensive series, and publicity leaflets for individual books. Publishers' catalogues are, of course, primarily instruments of sales promotion, and their usefulness as a guide to selection is therefore a limited one since they are not critical. The children's librarian should, however, maintain a complete and up to date file of the catalogues for reference.

In 1968 the Children's Book Group of the Publishers' Association, under the chairmanship of Antony Kamm of the Brockhampton Press, worked out, with the assistance of children's librarians and specialist booksellers, a scheme by which the

reading ability and interest age required to appreciate a particular book could be coded. This is called the *Key System for
indicating reading ability and interest age* and the books are
graded as follows:

Reading ability		Interest age	
Under 6	1	Under 6	A
6 – 8	2	6 – 8	B
8 – 10	3	8 – 10	C
10+	4	10 – 12	D
		12+	E

A book is coded for only one reading ability group, but may
be suitable for two or three interest age groups. The system was
produced for *Children's books in print* and a number of publishers now code all the books listed in their catalogues according to it. It is an improvement on the old method whereby a
book was labelled, for example, 'for 8 to 14' but it would be a
pity if it prevented or discouraged a potential buyer from
examining a book and assessing it for himself.

Certain publishers—Methuen, Collins, The Bodley Head and
the Oxford University Press, for example—produce attractive
posters, drawing attention to their books and authors, which
are available free of charge to libraries and schools. Brockhampton Press has produced a wall chart, *How a book is made*,
and Longmans Y.B. a wall chart, *How a picture book is made*.
Although these have to be bought, they make attractive and
useful decorations for the wall of the school or children's
library.

Many publishers are willing to lend, for exhibition, original
art work from books, or to provide material which demonstrates
the making of a book. This kind of exhibit can add interest to
a book display and it is well worth approaching publishers for
help. Publishers are also extremely helpful in putting librarians
into touch with those of their authors who are prepared to
speak to groups of children or adults. Children's editors themselves often make excellent speakers for Book Weeks and other
special events. It is usual to offer a fee and expenses for this
kind of help. Another kind of help is suggested by The Bodley
Head who draw attention in their catalogue to the film strips

and records which tie up with the books which they publish. This firm also offers to lend Bodley Head books in other languages for exhibition purposes; the sight of familiar illustrations or authors' names accompanied by a strange and incomprehensible text makes an exhibition feature which appeals to many children.

READ ON FROM HERE:

LIBRARY ASSOCIATION, YOUTH LIBRARIES GROUP: Children's libraries and the book market, 1967. *A selection of papers delivered at conferences at Holborn in June 1966 and at Birmingham in February 1967. Papers by Antony Kamm and Julia MacRae.*
KAMM, A: The age group thing. *The Bookseller*, 16th October 1967.
TAYLOR, J. and GERAGHTY, A: The Children's Book Group of The Publishers Association and The Children's Book Circle. *Y.L.G. News*, vol. 13, no. 3, October 1969.

DURING the 1960s there was a steadily growing interest in children's literature, not only in the United Kingdom but throughout the world, and this is reflected in the development of associations, societies and special collections in this field, in the increasing number of bibliographies, books and periodicals concerned with children's literature and in the fact that a greater number of critical lists of children's books is now being produced.

In Great Britain, the associations which are concerned with children's books as an important part of their activities are the Library Association through its Youth Libraries Group, the School Library Association, the National Book League, the Publishers Association through its Children's Book Group, the Children's Book Circle, and the Federation of Children's Book Groups. These associations represent librarians, teachers, publishers and parents; they issue publications, disseminate information and organize meetings. There has always been close co-operation, on an informal basis, between these groups of people, and this informal co-operation was, in 1969, recognized by the formation of the Joint Consultative Committee on Children's Books, which consists of representatives of each of the associations mentioned, together with representatives of the Booksellers Association, the Society of Authors, the B.B.C., London Weekend Television, the Colleges, Institutes and Schools of Education Group of the Library Association, the British Branch of the Friends of the Osborne Collection and the National Association of Teachers of English. This Committee, however, acts mainly as a stimulus and as a means of exchanging information about the activities of the groups represented on it; it lacks the finance and staff necessary to undertake any extensive work on its own account.

There is, therefore, no one central organization to which either the student of children's literature at an advanced level or the generally interested teacher or parent can turn in the certainty that he will receive the kind of help which he requires. The Joint Consultative Committee does not remove the need for a national centre for children's literature, a need first expressed in print by John Rowe Townsend in *Growing Point* in 1967, but which had been under discussion by children's librarians for some years before this. Such a national centre would carry out some of the functions already undertaken by the existing associations, co-ordinate others and provide a central information service. It is also usually seen as the guardian of a collection of children's books and books about them.

At the moment the most comprehensive collection of children's books in Great Britain is held by the British Museum, although it is not exploited as such. In December, 1968, a special exhibition of children's books was organized at the British Museum under the title of *Virtue and Delight*. The National Book League maintains, at its headquarters in Albemarle Street, the Reference Library of Children's Books, which provides a comprehensive collection of books published in the preceding twelve months. The Youth Libraries Group is building up a collection of significant twentieth century children's books at the Manchester School of Librarianship.

Special collections of children's books elsewhere in Britain have been built up by public libraries, university libraries (often in the schools or institutes of education) and by college of education libraries. Some of these are intended to be representative of the best books currently available; others are collections of early children's books, usually built up around a donation from a private collector or because of the personal interest of the librarian. So far there has been no successful attempt to make a complete record of all these collections although lists and catalogues have been issued by some of the libraries concerned, such as the Harris Library, Preston, and Hammersmith Public Library.

It is ironical that Britain, which has made a most notable contribution to children's literature, should lag behind other countries in this respect. In the United States, a specialist, Virginia Haviland, was appointed as Head of a newly established Children's Book Section at the Library of Congress in 1963 to exploit the collection there. Her work is complemented by the Children's Book Council in New York, which is comprised of publishers of children's books and which produces publicity material for children's books, by the Center for Children's books at Chicago University and by various research collections such as the Kerlan Collection at the University of Minnesota.

In Canada, interest centres on the Osborne Collection at Toronto Public Library. This Collection was originally made by Edgar Osborne, formerly County Librarian of Derbyshire, and presented to Toronto in 1949. The catalogue of the Collection, which was published in 1958, is now regarded as a standard bibliography of English children's books published before 1911. The Osborne Collection is supplemented by the Lillian H. Smith Collection which contains children's books published since 1911. It was, incidentally, the departure of the Osborne Collection for Canada that seemed to stimulate much of the present interest in early children's books in this country.

In Sweden, the Svenska Barnboksinstitutet in Stockholm was officially inaugurated in 1967 and began work in 1968, financed by the Stockholm Public Library, the Swedish Publishers' Association, the University of Stockholm and the Swedish Society of Authors with additional support from several cultural foundations. This provides an information service and research facilities. In the Netherlands, Bureau Boek en Jeugd at the Hague is supported by the Central Association of Public Libraries and receives help from the state. Its services are geared in particular to the needs of public libraries, but it does also provide a general information service and a centre to which students can come to see Dutch children's books and books about children's literature.

In Germany there is the Internationale Jugendbibliothek, established in Munich in 1949, through the inspiration of Jella Lepman, with financial help from the Rockefeller Foundation. It is now maintained by grants from the city, state and federal authorities and probably constitutes one of the most comprehensive international collections in the world. In addition, West Germany has the Institüt für Jugendbuchforschung at Frankfurt University which specializes in German children's literature, while in East Germany, a Children's Book Section was set up within the German State Library in Berlin in 1951, which thus became the first national library to recognize the importance of children's literature. In Austria Dr Richard Bamberger established the International Institute for Children's Literature in Vienna; this receives official support from the City of Vienna and from the Austrian government.

All these institutions have been established since 1945, many of them in the 1960s, and they carry out a variety of functions though the majority of them act as information and research centres, send out exhibitions, publish booklists and maintain reference collections of books about children's literature as well as of the children's books themselves.

Since children's literature as a clearly separate entity has had a relatively short history, the study of it is a recent development. There were a few, isolated accounts of children's literature published in the early part of this century, but serious, critical interest really developed in the United States in the 1920s, inspired by children's librarians and teachers, under the leadership of Anne Carroll Moore, Head of Work with Children in the New York Public Library; they were concerned about the low standards of many children's books, and their influence helped to counteract the flood of cheap material which was being produced to meet the growing demand. This interest was reflected in such events as the establishment of the Newbery Medal in 1922, and the foundation of *The Horn Book Magazine* in 1924 by Bertha Mahoney and Elinor Whitney, who also set up a special children's bookshop during the same period and compiled carefully annotated lists of recommended books.

In the 1930s this influence was felt abroad, and during the next thirty years there appeared a number of critical works concerned with children's literature, while Great Britain followed the American example with the establishment of the Carnegie Medal and *The Junior Bookshelf* in the 1930s. Some of the critical works which appeared before and shortly after the Second World War are still significant for the student of children's literature.

In 1932 came the publication in France of Paul Hazard's *Books, children and men,* a sound philosophical work, full of quotable quotations, in which Hazard drew attention to the importance of children's literature. In the same year F. J. Harvey Darton's history, *Children's books in England* appeared in this country. The Second World War probably slowed up development, but in the 1940s Dorothy Neal White, a New Zealand children's librarian, published *About books for children* (1946), in which she was very much concerned with general principles, so that the book is still useful today. In 1949, Geoffrey Trease published *Tales out of school,* the first critical survey of contemporary children's fiction to appear in this country.

In 1953 came *The unreluctant years* by Lillian H. Smith, Head of Boys' and Girls' House at Toronto Public Library, and the most authoritative American study of children's literature, *A critical history of children's literature,* edited by Cornelia Meigs, with contributions by leading American critics such as Anne T. Eaton, Elizabeth Nesbitt and Ruth Hill Viguers. In 1954 Batsford published Percy H. Muir's *English children's books,* 1600-1900, a well-illustrated history aimed at the general reader and interpreting, because of the author's own personal interest in children's toys and games, 'books' in the widest possible sense.

The real developments in this field, as far as Great Britain is concerned, came in the 1960s and the growing interest is reflected in the number of books about children's literature which have been published here for the first time, or in new editions, since 1960.

There are now available three useful bibliographies. The first edition of *Books about children's literature,* edited by Marcus Crouch on behalf of the Youth Libraries Group of the Library Association, appeared in 1963. This list was based on a collection of books presented to the Youth Libraries Group in 1959 by Mr H. J. B. Woodfield, but in addition it included other important books on the subject which are reasonably accessible in Britain. The revised edition of 1966 indicates by an

o

asterisk those titles which are to be found in the Youth Libraries Group Collection, housed at the School of Librarianship in Manchester.

In 1966, one of the first productions of the newly formed Children's Book Section at the Library of Congress was an annotated bibliography, prepared under the direction of Virginia Haviland, describing books, articles and pamphlets concerned with the creation of children's books. This guide was prepared on the basis of material held by the Library of Congress, but does include some other items.

Anne Pellowski's *The world of children's literature*, published in 1968, systematically surveys the children's literature of over eighty different countries, grouped in ten sections (one international and nine nationally or linguistically homogeneous groups). It is basically a bibliography, the result of ten years' work, and contains nearly 4,500 entries, but there are so many useful essays and surveys that it provides a most comprehensive outline of the subject generally and, in many cases, the only easily accessible account of children's books in a specific country. Anne Pellowski is the Director-Librarian of the UNICEF Information Centre on Children's Cultures in New York, and has travelled widely in order to collect the material for this work.

During the 1960s there was a new edition of Trease's *Tales out of school* and a reprint of Muir's *English children's books*. In 1946 Roger Lancelyn Green had written a book for children called *Tellers of tales;* in 1965 this appeared in a new edition, extensively rewritten to make it a useful and readable history, for adults, of children's literature from 1800 to 1964. In 1968 there was a welcome reprint of Mrs. E. M. Field's *The child and his book*, first published in 1891 by Wells Gardner, which traces the history of children's books from Anglo-Saxon times and deals with many authors writing before 1850 who have since sunk into obscurity.

The first edition of Margery Fisher's *Intent upon reading* appeared in 1961, a landmark in the critical appreciation of children's literature. Its publication soon led to the establishment of Mrs Fisher as the foremost authority on contemporary children's literature in this country and as a spokesman for

English children's books on the international scene.

The Library Association published Mary Thwaite's *From primer to pleasure* and Marcus Crouch's *Treasure seekers and borrowers;* together these cover the history of children's literature from earliest times up to 1962. Mrs Thwaite's book covers much the same ground as Harvey Darton's but is of rather more practical interest to librarians as she discusses modern editions of stories which have been available to children from the fifteenth century onwards. A more recent history, written on a fairly popular level, is John Rowe Townsend's *Written for children*. Although he covers the earliest beginnings of the literature he gives most attention to the period since 1850 and therefore covers the twentieth century children's authors in more detail than many of the other histories. *Treasure seekers and borrowers* is perhaps more thorough but at times tends to degenerate into a catalogue of authors and titles which are not easily accessible to the general reader because they have long been out of print.

In 1961 Bodley Head launched their series of 'Bodley Head Monographs' which deal with outstanding children's writers. The general editor of the series is Kathleen Lines, and the monographs provide short, critical accounts of the work of children's writers. Although they were originally published singly, in 1968 a new policy of binding up three monographs in the same volume was introduced; this has produced some rather strange bedfellows but has been done in the interests of keeping the costs and therefore the price down.

Two books by Bettina Hürlimann, *Picture-book world* and *Three centuries of children's books in Europe*, have been translated from the German by Brian Alderson, who has added material to make them more relevant to the English reader. In 1966 Longmans Y.B. published here Ruth Hill Viguers' *Margin for surprise*, which had appeared in the United States two years before. This is a collection of stimulating essays; equally stimulating is Sheila Egoff's *The republic of childhood: a critical guide to Canadian children's literature in English* published in 1967 to mark Canada's centennial year. These two books have been written by people with wide and long experience of children's books, who have developed an inspiring philosophy and who are able to communicate their ideas and standards through the printed word.

In 1968 Brian Doyle's *Who's who of children's literature* appeared. This was received somewhat critically, partly because of the rather misleading title, partly because critics seemed unable to resist playing the game of spotting omissions, and partly because of its emphasis on comparatively obscure contributors to nineteenth century boys' magazines, but it nevertheless brought together a lot of useful—and interesting— material not easily available elsewhere.

With growing interest among students, teachers and librarians, there has arisen a need for practical books and so, on this level, *Books and the teacher*, by Antony Kamm and Boswell Taylor, was published in 1966 (since revised) to provide a useful handbook of information about all aspects of books aimed at the practising teacher, while two books by Alec Ellis, *A history of children's reading and literature* and *How to find out about children's literature* were directed particularly at library school students.

The situation with regard to the reviewing of children's books has also changed radically in the last ten years. In 1960 the only journals which included regular reviews of high quality were *The Junior Bookshelf*, which had been established in 1936 by H. J. B. Woodfield inspired by the example of *The Horn Book Magazine*, the *Times Literary Supplement* which published a special *Children's Books* supplement twice a year, and *The School Librarian*, the journal of the School Library Association, which appeared three times a year.

In 1963, following on the success of *Intent upon reading*, Margery Fisher began to publish *Growing Point; Children's Book News*, which appeared first in 1964 as a kind of house journal for the Children's Book Centre (a specialist bookshop in London) later developed under the editorship of, first, Nancy Lockwood Chambers, and subsequently Valerie Alderson, to become by 1969 one of the most useful and comprehensive journals available in the field.

Books for your children, aimed particularly at parents, was started by Anne Wood in 1965, and rapidly developed from a duplicated pamphlet into an attractive printed magazine. In addition to this, *The Times* and *The Guardian* in 1968 both appointed Children's Book Review Editors—Brian Alderson and John Rowe Townsend respectively—and began to include regular features on children's books, while the number of issues of the TLS *Children's Books* and of *The School Librarian* was increased to four a year each.

The first month of 1970 saw the appearance of the first issue of *Signal: approaches to children's books*, edited by Nancy Chambers. This is not a reviewing journal; it concerns itself with serious criticism of children's literature and offers a vehicle for the publication of historical, bibliographical and biographical material relating to the subject, a vehicle which has not previously been available on this scale. Two months later, in March, came the first issue of *Children's literature in education*, edited by Sidney Robbins of Saint Luke's College, Exeter, and, writing in *The Guardian* in April, John Rowe Townsend commented 'In terms of material to be written about, there is plenty of room for both these journals. I hope there is room for them in economic terms.'

The Horn Book Magazine, the main American reviewing periodical, and *Bookbird*, the English language journal published by the International Institute in Vienna, are also useful to the English children's librarian, the first because of its articles and the fact that many of the books reviewed are available in English editions, the second because of its coverage of children's literature on a world-wide basis.

Despite the increased number of journals in which reliable reviews of children's books appear, there are still many British books for children which are not reviewed at all. Many librarians would welcome the provision of the kind of service provided for American books by the Center for Children's Books in Chicago, which issues the *Bulletin of the Center for Children's Books* ten times a year, in which every new book published in America is assessed, whether good, bad or indifferent.

Two factual sources of up-to-date information about children's fiction for librarians are the publishers' catalogues and the lists or cards/slips provided by a number of booksellers who specialize in selling books to libraries. The British National

Bibliography also provides a weekly source of up-to-date information about children's books, and although its use in the field of non-fiction for children is affected by its inclusion of all non-fiction books, whether intended for child or adult, in the same sequence, there is a separate sequence of fiction for children at 823.91J, to which must be added, for complete coverage of the field, the sequences of children's fiction included under language of origin (including a separate sequence for American books). Children's books are included in *British Books in Print*, but at the beginning of 1969 there appeared the first edition of *Children's Books in Print: a reference catalogue*, a useful and convenient tool, listing over 14,000 children's books currently in print.

Selective bibliographies and booklists are produced by the School Library Association, the Library Association and its Groups, and the National Book League, but as these are generally prepared by committees, made up of people who have full-time jobs and therefore have to do the necessary work in their spare time, there tends to be a delay before publication, and most of the lists are dated as soon as they appear. They do, however, provide a useful guide to the librarian engaged in building up basic stock for a new school or branch library. Many public libraries issue their own annotated lists which can be both more up-to-date and geared more precisely to local needs. This is a field in which there is great scope for co-operation and the first attempt to produce nationally the kind of list which is produced individually by many library authorities came at the very close of the decade. This was *Buy, beg or borrow*, edited by Kenneth A. Wood on behalf of the Youth Libraries Group of the Library Association, and advance orders to the tune of 20,000 copies clearly indicates the market for this type of list.

Few bibliographies have been produced commercially, but outstanding in this respect has been the series of *Best children's books of the year*, compiled by Naomi Lewis, very clearly stamped with her personality, which have appeared annually since 1963. There is great emphasis on imaginative literature in these lists, and although the volumes appear too late to be of use as a current selection tool, they are invaluable in providing a review of the best of the year's output and are useful as a guide to replacing books or to building up the stock of new libraries.

In this chapter I have outlined only very briefly the directions in which the student, teacher or librarian might read on from here.

READ ON FROM HERE :

Associations, Societies and Institutions

ALDERSON, B : Notes on the children's book section of the German State Library in East Berlin. *Growing Point*, vol. 8, no. 4, October 1969.

BINDER, L : Two years International Institute for Children's, Juvenile and Popular Literature. *Bookbird*, vol. 5, no. 1, March 1967.

BRITISH MUSEUM : An exhibition of early English children's books. Trustees of the British Museum, 1969. *The catalogue of the Virtue and Delight exhibition.*

CHURCHWARD, S. M : Twenty years of the International Youth Library. *Library Association Record*, vol. 70, no. 11, November 1968.

Collections of early children's books. *Library Association Record*, vol. 68, no. 7, July 1966.

DOWNTON, J. A. and GOOD, D : The Spencer Collection of early children's books and chap-books in the Harris Public Library, Preston. *Y.L.G. News*, vol. 14, no. 1, February 1970.

FOTHERINGHAM, H : The International Youth Library. *Library Journal*, vol. 91, no. 20, November 1966.

HAMMERSMITH PUBLIC LIBRARY : Early children's books : a catalogue of the collection in the London Borough of Hammersmith Public Libraries, 1965.

HAVILAND, V : Serving those who serve children : a national reference library of children's books. *The Quarterly Journal of the Library of Congress*, vol. 22, no. 4, October 1965.

LEPMAN, J : A bridge of children's books. Brockhampton, 1969.

MACRAE, J : Virtue and delight. *Y.L.G. News*, vol. 13, no. 1, February 1969.

NIMMONS, E : The National Book League and the Children's Librarian. *Y.L.G. News*, vol. 13, no. 3, October 1969.

ORVIG, M : Svenska Barnboksinsitutet. *Scandinavian Public Library* Quarterly, no. 2, 1968.

OVENS, W. W : The School Library Association. *Y.L.G. News*, vol. 13, no. 3, October 1969.

PRESTON, HARRIS PUBLIC LIBRARY : Spencer Collection. A catalogue of the Spencer Collection of early children's books and chap-books, 1967.

THWAITE, M : A plea for parity. *Times Literary Supplement*, 26th June 1969.

TORONTO PUBLIC LIBRARY : The Osborne Collection of early children's books, 1566–1910 : a catalogue, 1958.

TOWNSEND, J. A. B. and ALDERSON, B : Services for Children's literature offered by the British Museum *and* A national centre for children's literature. *Library Association. Proceedings of the Public Conference held at Brighton*, 1968. L.A, 1968.

TOWNSEND, J. R : Where do children's books stand? *Growing Point*, vol. 6, no. 6, December 1967 and vol. 7, no. 1, May 1968.

VAN DER MEULEN, A. J. MOERKERCKEN : Bureau Boek en Jeugd. *Bookbird*, vol. 7, no. 1, March 1969.

WEGEHAUPT, H : The section for children's and young adults' books, Deutsche Staatsbibliothek, Berlin. *Unesco Bulletin for Libraries*, vol. 22, no 6, November-December 1968.

WOOD, A : Federation of Books for Children Groups. *Y.L.G. News*, vol. 13, no. 3, October 1969.

YATES, W. E : The Parker Collection of early children's books in Birmingham Public Library. *Y.L.G. News*, vol. 14, no. 1, February 1970.

Bibliographies of Books about Children's Literature

HAVILAND, V. ed : Children's literature : a guide to reference sources. Washington, Library of Congress, 1966.

LIBRARY ASSOCIATION, YOUTH LIBRARIES GROUP : Books about children's literature : a booklist edited by Marcus Crouch. Rev. ed, L.A, 1966.

PELLOWSKI, A : The world of children's literature. New York and London, Bowker, 1968.

Books about Children's Literature

CROUCH, M: Treasure seekers and borrowers: children's books in Britain 1900–1960. L.A, 1962.

DARTON, F. J. H: Children's books in England: five centuries of social life. 2nd ed, C.U.P, 1958.

DOYLE, B. comp: The who's who of children's literature. Evelyn, 1968.

EGOFF, S: The republic of childhood: a critical guide to Canadian children's literature in English. Toronto, O.U.P, 1967.

ELLIS, A: A history of children's reading and literature. Pergamon, 1968.

ELLIS, A: How to find out about children's literature. 2nd ed, Pergamon, 1968.

FIELD, L. F: The child and his book. Wells Gardner, 1891. (Reprinted, Detroit, Singing Tree Press, 1968.)

FISHER, M: Intent upon reading. 2nd ed, Brockhampton Press, 1964.

GREEN, R. L: Tellers of tales: children's books and their authors from 1800–1968. Rev. ed, Kaye and Ward, 1969.

HAZARD, P: Books, children and men. 4th ed, Boston, Horn Book Inc, 1960.

HURLIMAN, B: Picture book world. O.U.P, 1968.

HURLIMAN, B: Three centuries of children's books in Europe. O.U.P, 1967.

KAMM, A. and TAYLOR, B: Books and the teacher. 2nd ed U.L.P, 1968.

LINES, K. ed: Bodley Head Monographs. *Where an author covered by a Monograph is mentioned only or mainly in one chapter, the appropriate Monograph is listed in 'Read on from here' at the end of that chapter. Other Monographs are*:

  AVERY, G: Mrs Ewing. 1961.

  BLISHEN, E, MEEK, M. and GREEN, R. L: Hugh Lofting Geoffrey Trease and J. M. Barrie. 1968.

  BUTTS, D: R. L. Stevenson. 1966.

  COLWELL, E: Eleanor Farjeon. 1961.

  FISHER, M: John Masefield. 1963.

  FISHER, M, GREEN, R. L. and CROUCH, M: Henry Treece, C. S. Lewis and Beatrix Potter. 1969.

  GREEN, R. L, BELL, A. and NESBITT, E: Lewis Carroll, E. Nesbit and Howard Pyle. 1968.

GREEN, R. L : Mrs Molesworth. 1961.

HAVILAND, V : Ruth Sawyer. 1965.

SHELLEY, H, SUTCLIFF, R. and CLARK, L : Arthur Ransome, Rudyard Kipling and Walter de la Mare. 1968.

WILSON, B. K : Noel Streatfeild 1961.

MEIGS, C. ed : A critical history of children's literature : a survey of children's books in English from earliest times to the present. New York, Macmillan, 1953.

MUIR, P. H : English children's books, 1600–1900. Batsford, 1954.

SMITH, L. H : The unreluctant years : a critical approach to children's literature. A.L.A, 1953.

THWAITE, M. F : From primer to pleasure : an introduction to the history of children's books in England, from the invention of printing to 1900, with a chapter on some developments abroad. L.A, 1963.

TOWNSEND, J. R : Written for children. Garnet Miller, 1965.

TREASE, G : Tales out of school. 2nd ed, Heinemann, 1964.

VIGUERS, R. H : Margin for surprise. Longmans Y.B, 1966.

WHITE, D. N : About books for children. O.U.P, 1946.

Periodicals concerned with Children's Literature

Bookbird. International Board on Books for Young People and the International Institute for Children's, Juvenile and Popular Literature, Austria, Vienna. 4 issues a year.

Books for your children. Anne Wood, 100 Church Lane East, Aldershot, Hampshire. 4 issues a year.

Children's Book News. Children's Booknews Ltd, 140 Kensington Church Street, London W.8. 6 issues a year.

Children's Literature in Education. Ward Lock Educational, 116 Baker Street, London W1M 2BB. 3 issues a year.

Growing Point. Margery Fisher, Ashton Manor, Northampton. 9 issues a year.

The Horn Book Magazine. The Horn Book Inc, Boston, U.S.A. 6 issues a year.

The Junior Bookshelf. Marsh Hall, Thurstonland, Huddersfield, Yorkshire. 6 issues a year.

The School Librarian. School Library Association, Premier House, Southampton Row, London W.1. 4 issues a year.

Signal: approaches to children's books. The Thimble Press, Stroud, Gloucestershire. 3 issues a year.
Times Literary Supplement, Children's Books. 4 issues a year.

Bibliographies and lists of Children's Fiction

CLARK, B. ed : Books for primary children : an annotated list. 3rd ed, S.L.A, (*N.B. Includes non-fiction as well.*)

COLWELL, E, PARROTT, F. P. and GREEN, L. E : First choice : a basic book list for children. L.A, 1968. (*Also includes non-fiction.*)

LEWIS, N : Best books for children, 1963 onwards. H. Hamilton, 1964 onwards. (*Predominantly fiction, but some non-fiction included.*)

NATIONAL BOOK LEAGUE : School library fiction. 1 Historical fiction 2 Children and adults 3 Mystery and adventure 4 Children of other lands 5 Animal stories 6 Fantasy 7 Have you read this? N.B.L, 1966, 1967.

PLATT, P : A guide to book lists and bibliographies for the use of schools. 3rd ed, S.L.A, 1969.

WOOD, K. A : Buy, beg or borrow. L.A, Youth Libraries Group, 1969.

List of publishers

Members of the Children's Book Group of the Publishers Association (at July 1st 1970) including distributors from whom information and catalogues can be obtained in Australia, Canada, New Zealand and South Africa. A showroom is available at those addresses in those countries marked with an asterisk.

ABELARD SCHUMAN LTD:
8 King Street, London w.c.2
Australia: *International Textbook Co Ltd, 400 Pacific Highway, Crows Nest, N.S.W.2065
Canada: Abelard-Schuman Canada Ltd, 200 Yorkland Boulevard, Toronto 425
New Zealand: *Oswald-Sealy (N.Z.) Ltd, P.O. Box 1289, 89 Customs Street E, Auckland C.1
South Africa: Hutchinson Group (S.A.) (Pty) Ltd, 701/8 Sandersons Building, President Street, Johannesburg

W. H. ALLEN AND CO LTD:
43 Essex Street, London W.C.2
Australia: Tudor Distributors Pty Ltd, 21 Elliott Street, (P.O. Box 67), Balmain, N.S.W
Canada: Doubleday (Canada) Ltd, 105 Bond Street, Toronto 2
New Zealand: Leonard Fullerton Ltd, 34 City Chambers, Victoria Street West, (P.O. Box 316), Auckland
South Africa: Mr D.H. Tonathy, P.O. Box 9881, Johannesburg

ANGUS AND ROBERTSON LTD:
54/58 Bartholomew Close, London E.C.1
Australia: *221 George Street, Sydney, N.S.W.2000, 107 Elizabeth Street, Melbourne, Victoria 3000 *and* 167 Queen Street, Brisbane, Queensland 4000
Canada: *The Ryerson Press, 299 Queen Street, Toronto, Ontario
New Zealand: *Oswald-Sealy (New Zealand) Ltd, 89 Customs Street East, Auckland
South Africa: *R.H.G. Lamberth, P.O. Box 22, Howard Place, Cape

E.J. ARNOLD AND SON LTD:
Butterley Street, Hunslet Lane, Leeds, Yorkshire
Australia: *Educational Supplies Pty Ltd, P.O. Box 33, 8 Cross Street, Brookvale, N.S.W. 2100
Canada: *J.M. Dent and Sons (Canada) Ltd, 100 Scarsdale Road, Don Mills, Ontario

New Zealand: *Educational Supplies Pty Ltd, P.O. Box 33, 8 Cross Street, Brookvale, N.S.W. 2100
South Africa: *New World Publications (Pty) Ltd, P.O. Box 4429, 5th Floor, S.A. Mutual Building, Darling Street, Capetown

JOHN BAKER LTD:
5 Royal Opera Arcade, Pall Mall, London s.w.1
Australia: John Cochrane Pty Ltd, 373 Bay Street, Port Melbourne, Victoria 3207
Canada: Nelson, Foster and Scott, 299 Yorkland Boulevard, Willowdale, Ontario
New Zealand: D.C. Atkinson, 14 Midland House, 67 Great North Road, Auckland 2
South Africa: Book Promotions (Pty) Ltd, 311 Centre Building, Main Road, Wynberg, Cape Province

THE BANNISDALE PRESS:
46/47 Chancery Lane, London w.c.2

ARTHUR BARKER LTD:
5 Winsley Street, Oxford Circus, London w.1
Australia: Hicks, Smith & Sons Pty Ltd, 301 Kent Street, Sydney, N.S.W.2000
Canada: The Ryerson Press, 299 Queen Street, West, Toronto 2B, Ontario
New Zealand: Hicks Smith & Sons Ltd, P.O. Box 70, Wellington
South Africa: Mr D.H. Tonathy, P.O. Box 9881, Johannesburg

B.T. BATSFORD LTD:
4 Fitzhardinge Street, London w.1

G. BELL AND SONS LTD:
York House, Portugal Street, London w.c.2
Australia: *John Cochrane Pty Ltd, 373 Bay Street, Port Melbourne, Victoria 3207
Canada: *Clarke, Irwin and Co Ltd, 791 St Clair Avenue West, Toronto 10
New Zealand: Mr D.C. Atkinson, P.O. Box 8018, Auckland
South Africa: Book Promotions Pty Ltd, 311 Sanlam Centre, Main Road, Wynberg C.P

ERNEST BENN LTD:
Bouverie House, Fleet Street, London E.C.4
Australia: *T.C. Lothian Pty Ltd, 4/12 Tattersall's Lane, Melbourne, Victoria
Canada: *General Publishing Co Ltd, 30 Lesmill Road, Don Mills, Ontario
New Zealand: Oswald-Sealy (New Zealand) Ltd, P.O. Box 1289, Auckland C.1
South Africa: *Rupert Lamberth (Pty) Ltd, P.O. Box 22, Howard Place, Cape

A & C BLACK LTD:
4, 5 and 6 Soho Square, London WIV 6AD
Australia: *John Cochrane Pty Ltd, 373 Bay Street, Port Melbourne, Victoria 3207
Canada: *Queenswood House Ltd, 17 Prince Arthur Avenue, Toronto 5
New Zealand: *D.C. Atkinson Esq, 14 Midland House, 67 Great North Road, Auckland
South Africa: *Book Promotion (Pty) Ltd, 311 Centre Building, Main Road, Wynberg

BLACKIE AND SON LTD:
5 Fitzhardinge Street, Portman Square, London w.1 and Bishopbriggs, Glasgow
Australia: *T.C. Lothian Pty Ltd, 4/12 Tattersalls Lane, Melbourne, Victoria
Canada: *Queenswood House Ltd, 17 Prince Arthur Avenue, Toronto 5
New Zealand: *T.C. Lothian Pty Ltd, 17 Galatos Street, P.O. Box 3661, Auckland
South Africa: *Cotton and Harkie Pty Ltd, P.O. Box 17, Pinelands, Cape

BASIL BLACKWELL AND MOTT LTD:
48 Broad Street, Oxford
Australia: Australasian Publishing Co Pty Ltd, 55 York Street, Sydney, N.S.W
Canada: Copp Clark Publishing Co, 517 Wellington Street West, Toronto 2B
New Zealand: Antipodes Publishing Co, Empire Building, 17 Willis Street, Wellington c.1
South Africa: New World Publications (Pty) Ltd, P.O. Box 4429, Cape Town

BLANDFORD PRESS LTD:
167 High Holborn, London w.c.1
Australia: *Grenville Publishing Co Pty Ltd, 401 Pitt Street, Sydney 2000, N.S.W
Canada: *The Copp Clark Publishing Co, 517 Wellington Street West, Toronto 2B
New Zealand: *Oswald-Sealy (New Zealand) Ltd, 89 Customs Street East, Auckland c.1
South Africa: H.R. & L. Shapiro, 54 Sturk's Building, 52 Long Street, Cape Town *and* 71 Vanguard House, 176 Market Street, Johannesburg

THE BODLEY HEAD LTD:
9 Bow Street, Covent Garden, London w.c.2
Australia: *William Collins (Australia) Ltd, 36/38 Clarence Street, Sydney, N.S.W. 2000 *and* *4th Floor, A.N.Z. Bank Chambers, 351 Elizabeth Street, Melbourne, Victoria 3000; *CML Building, 41 King William Street, Adelaide, S.A. 5000; *246 Queen Street, Brisbane, Q'ld 4000; *P.O. Box 37, Claremont, Perth, West Australia 6010
Canada: Queenswood House Ltd, 17 Prince Arthur Avenue, Toronto 180

New Zealand: *Hodder and Stoughton Ltd, 52 Cook Street, Auckland c.1
South Africa: H. B. Timmins (Pty) Ltd, Colophon House, 68 Shortmarket Street, Cape Town

BRIMAX BOOKS:
171 Kings Cross Road, London w.c.1

BROCKHAMPTON PRESS LTD:
Arlen House, Salisbury Road, Leicester LEI 7QS
Australia: *Hodder and Stoughton Ltd, 429 Kent Street, Sydney, N.S.W. 2000 *and* 31 Coventry Street, South Melbourne, Victoria 3205
Canada: *Musson Book Co, 30 Lesmill Road, Don Mills, Ontario
New Zealand: *Hodder and Stoughton Ltd, 52 Cook Street, Auckland 1
South Africa: *H. B. Timmins (Pty) Ltd, P.O. Box 94, Cape Town (Showroom: 68 Shortmarket Street)

BURKE PUBLISHING CO LTD:
14 John Street, Theobald's Road, London w.c.1
Australia: Hicks Smith & Sons Pty Ltd, 91 Elizabeth Street, Brisbane, Queensland *and* Box 235 Richmond, 3121 Victoria *and* 301 Kent Street, Sydney 2000, N.S.W
Canada: Ryerson Press Ltd, 299 Queen Street West, Toronto 2B, Ontario
New Zealand: Hicks Smith & Sons Ltd, P.O. Box 70, 238 Wakefield Street, Wellington c.1 *and* 12 Rushkin Street, Auckland
South Africa: D.H. Tonathy Esq, 501/504 Merlen House, 49 Simmonds Street, Johannesburg

JONATHAN CAPE LTD:
30 Bedford Square, London w.c.1
Australia: *Australasian Publishing Co Pty Ltd, Bradbury House, 55 York Street, Sydney, N.S.W.2000; *and* *4th Floor, A.N.Z. Bank Chambers, 351 Elizabeth Street, Melbourne 3000; *303 Adelaide Street, Brisbane, Queensland; *Room 9, 33 Pirie Street, Adelaide
Canada: *Clarke Irwin and Co Ltd, Clarwin House, 791 St Clair Avenue West, Toronto 10
New Zealand: *Antipodes Publishing Co Ltd, Empire Building, 17 Willis Street, P.O. Box 1467, Wellington
South Africa: *Oxford University Press, Thibault House, Thibault Square, Box 1141, Cape Town *and* *69 Walter Wise Building, 50 Joubert Street, P.O. Box 10413, Johannesburg

W & R CHAMBERS LTD:
11 Thistle Street, Edinburgh, Scotland
Australia: *Thomas C. Lothian Pty Ltd, 4/12 Tattersalls Lane, Melbourne, Victoria 3000

Canada: *Smithers and Bonnellie Ltd, 56 Esplanade Street, Toronto 1
New Zealand: *Thomas C. Lothian Pty Ltd, 17 Galatos Street, Auckland c.1
South Africa: *Cotton and Hardie Pty Ltd, Box 17, Pinelands, Cape

GEOFFREY CHAPMAN LTD WITH JOHNSTON AND BACON:
18 High Street, Wimbledon, London s.w.19
Australia: Collier Macmillan International, Bay House, 76/84 Bay Street, Broadway, Sydney, N.S.W.2007
Canada: Collier-Macmillan Canada Ltd, 1125B Leslie Street, Don Mills, Ontario
South Africa: Collier-Macmillan S. Africa (Pty) Ltd, 93 DeKorte Street, Braamfontein, Johannesburg

CHATTO & WINDUS LTD:
39A Welbeck Street, London WIM 8HH
Australia: Hicks, Smith and Sons (Pty) Ltd, 301 Kent Street, Sydney, N.S.W. 2000; 225/227 Swan Street, Richmond, Victoria 3121 *and* 91 Elizabeth Street, Brisbane, Queensland 4000
Canada: Clarke, Irwin and Co Ltd, 791 St Clair Avenue West, Toronto 10
New Zealand: Hicks, Smith and Sons Ltd, P.O. Box 70, Wellington *and* 12 Ruskin Street, Auckland 1
South Africa: Heinemann and Cassell South Africa (Pty) Ltd, P.O. Box 11190, Johannesburg

Wm. COLLINS SONS AND CO LTD:
14 St James's Place, London s.w.1 *and* 144 Cathedral Street, Glasgow c.4
Australia: *Wm. Collins (Australia) Ltd, Box 476, GPO Sydney 2001 *and* 36/38 Clarence Street, Sydney 2000
Canada: *Wm. Collins Sons and Co (Canada) Ltd, 100 Lesmill Road, Don Mills, Ontario
New Zealand: *Collins Bros & Co Ltd, P.O. Box 1, Auckland
South Africa: *Wm. Collins (Africa) (Pty) Ltd, Pall State House, 51 Commissioner Street, Johannesburg *and* P.O. Box 8879, Johannesburg

CONSTABLE AND CO LTD:
10 Orange Street, London w.c.2
South Africa: Hutchinson Group (SA) (Pty) Ltd, P.O. Box 5841, Johannesburg

DELISLE LTD:
Cromwell House, Long Street, Sherborne, Dorset

J. M. DENT AND SONS LTD:
10 Bedford Street, London w.c.2
Australia: *Cambridge University Press (Australia) Pty Ltd, 296 Beaconsfield Parade, Middle Park, Melbourne 3206

Canada: *J.M. Dent & Sons (Canada) Ltd, 100 Scarsdale Road, Don Mills, Ontario
New Zealand: *Cassell & Co Ltd, Box 36013, Northcote Central, Auckland N.9
South Africa: *Macmillan, South Africa (Publishers) (Pty) Ltd, P.O. Box 23134, Joubert Park, Johannesburg

ANDRE DEUTSCH LTD:
105 Great Russell Street, London, w.c.1
Australia: Hutchinson Group (Australia) Pty Ltd, P.O. Box 267, 30/32 Cremorne Street, Richmond, Victoria 3121 *and* Albart House, 89 Stanley Street, East Sydney, N.S.W. 2010
Canada: Andre Deutsch Ltd, c/o Wm. Collins Sons & Co Canada Ltd, 100 Lesmill Road, Don Mills, Ontario
New Zealand: Oswald-Sealy (N.Z.) Ltd, P.O. Box 1289, 89 Customs Street East, Auckland c.1
South Africa: Wm. Collins (Africa) Pty Ltd, P.O. Box 8879, Pallstate House, 51 Commissioner Street, Johannesburg *and* P.O. Box 834, Cape Town

DOBSON BOOKS LTD:
80 Kensington Church Street, London w.8
Australia: *Hicks, Smith & Sons Pty Ltd, P.O. Box 235, Richmond 3121, Victoria *and* *301 Kent Street, Sydney, N.S.W. 2000; *91 Elizabeth Street, Brisbane, Queensland 4000
Canada: *General Publishing Co Ltd, 30 Lesmill Road, Don Mills, Ontario
New Zealand: *Hicks, Smith and Sons Pty Ltd, 238 Wakefield Street, Wellington c.1 *and* *12 Ruskin Street, Parnell, Auckland
South Africa: *Wm. Collins (Africa) (Pty) Ltd, Pallstate House, 51 Commissioner Street, Johannesburg, *540 Grand Parade Centre, Adderley Street, Cape Town *and* *Debmar House, 24 Forbes Avenue, Salisbury

EPWORTH PRESS:
Methodist Book Room, 2 Chester House, Pages Lane, Muswell Hill, London N.10
Australia: Wm. Heinemann Australia Pty Ltd, 33 Lonsdale Street, Melbourne 3000
Canada: G.R. Welch Co Ltd, 222 Evans Avenue, Toronto 18, Ontario
New Zealand: Wm. Heinemann Ltd, P.O. Box 36020, Northcote Central, Northcote, Auckland 9

EVANS BROS LTD:
Montague House, Russell Square, London w.c.1
Australia: *Australasian Publishing Co Pty Ltd, Bradbury House, 55 York Street, Sydney, N.S.W.
Canada: *Methuen Publications, 145 Adelaide Street West, Toronto 1, Ontario

New Zealand: *L. Fullerton Esq, P.O. Box 316, Victoria Street West, Auckland C.1
South Africa: *D.H. Tonathy Esq, P.O. Box 9881, Johannesburg

FABER & FABER LTD,
24 Russell Square, London W.C.1
Australia: *Faber & Faber Ltd, c/o The Macmillan Co of Australia Pty Ltd, 107 Moray Street, South Melbourne, Victoria 3205
New Zealand: *Faber & Faber Ltd, c/o Oxford University Press, Walton House, P.O. Box 185, Wellington
South Africa: *Faber & Faber Ltd, c/o Macmillan South Africa (Publishers) Pty Ltd, P.O. Box 23134, Joubert Park, Johannesburg

VICTOR GOLLANCZ LTD:
14 Henrietta Street, London, W.C.2
Australia: *Hutchinson Group (Australia) Pty Ltd, 30/32 Cremorne Street, Richmond, Victoria 3121 *and* *86 Stanley Street, East Sydney 2010, N.S.W.
Canada: *Doubleday Canada Ltd, 105 Bond Street, Toronto 2
New Zealand: *Hicks, Smith and Sons Ltd, P.O. Box 70, Wellington *and* P.O. Box 2730, 12 Ruskin Street, Parnell, Auckland
South Africa: Meurig Viljoen Esq, 8 Union Avenue, Gardens, Cape Town *and* Hutchinson Group (S.A.) Ltd, 701/8 Sanderson's Building, President Street, Johannesburg

MARY GLASGOW AND BAKER LTD:
140/142 Kensington Church Street, London W.8

GRANADA PUBLISHING LTD:
3 Upper James Street, Golden Square, London WIR 4BP

ROBERT HALE & COMPANY:
63 Old Brompton Road, London S.W.7
Australia: Hicks, Smith & Sons Pty Ltd, 301 Kent Street, Sydney, N.S.W.
Canada: Nelson Foster and Scott Ltd, 299 Yorkland Boulevard, Willowdale, Ontario
New Zealand: Hicks, Smith & Sons Pty Ltd, 238 Wakefield Street, Wellington C.1
South Africa: Denis L. Dorman Esq, P.O. Box 5532, Johannesburg

HAMISH HAMILTON LTD:
90 Great Russell Street, London W.C.1

THE HAMLYN PUBLISHING GROUP LTD:
Hamlyn House, 42 The Centre, Feltham, Middlesex
Australia: Paul Hamlyn Pty Ltd, 176 South Creek Road, Dee Why West, N.S.W. 2099

Canada: The Hamlyn Group (Canada) Ltd, 50 Prince Andrew Place, Don Mills, Ontario
New Zealand: Beckett Sterling Ltd, Midland House, Pollen Street, Auckland
South Africa: International Books Ltd P.O. Box 7896, Johannesburg

GEORGE G. HARRAP & CO LTD:
182 High Holborn, London W.C.1
Australia: *The Australasian Publishing Co Pty Ltd, Bradbury House, 55 York Street, Sydney, N.S.W. 2000
Canada: *Clarke, Irwin and Co Ltd, 791 St Clair Avenue West, Toronto 10
New Zealand: John Hall, Empire Building, 17 Willis Street, Wellington
South Africa: D.L. Dorman Esq, P.O. Box 5532, Johannesburg

WILLIAM HEINEMANN LTD:
15/16 Queen Street, Mayfair, London W.1
Australia: *William Heinemann Ltd, 33 Lonsdale Street, Melbourne, Victoria 3000
Canada: William Heinemann Ltd, 100 Lesmill Road, Don Mills, Ontario
New Zealand: *William Heinemann Ltd, P.O. Box 36020 Northcote, Northcote Central, Auckland 9
South Africa: Heinemann & Cassell South Africa (Pty) Ltd, P.O. Box 11190, Johannesburg

HUTCHINSON AND CO LTD:
178/202 Great Portland Street, London W.1
Australia: Hutchinson Group (Australia) Pty Ltd, P.O. Box 267, 30/32 Cremorne Street, Richmond, Victoria 3121
Canada: Nelson Foster & Scott Ltd, 299 Yorkland Boulevard, Willowdale, Ontario
New Zealand: Hutchinson Publishing Group Ltd, P.O. Box 2281, 1st Floor, 26 Chancery Street, Auckland
South Africa: Hutchinson Group (S.A.) (Pty) Ltd, P.O. Box 5841, Johannesburg

KAYE AND WARD LTD:
194/200 Bishopsgate, London E.C.2
Australia: *Hicks, Smith and Sons Pty Ltd, 301 Kent Street, Sydney, N.S.W. 2000 *and* *P.O. Box 235, Richmond, Victoria 3121; *91 Elizabeth Street, Brisbane, Queensland 4000
Canada: *Queenswood House Ltd, 17 Prince Arthur Avenue, Toronto 5, Ontario
New Zealand: *Hicks, Smith and Sons Ltd, P.O. Box 70, Wellington *and* *12 Ruskin Street, Parnell, Auckland
South Africa: Mr D.H. Tonathy, P.O. Box 9881, Johannesburg

LONGMAN GROUP LTD:
Longman House, Burnt Mill, Harlow, Essex
Australia: *Longman Australia Pty Ltd, Railway Crescent, Croydon, Victoria 3136
Canada: *Longman Canada Ltd, 55 Barber Greene Road, Don Mills 403, Ontario
New Zealand: *Longman Paul Ltd, 5 Milford Road, Auckland 9
South Africa: *Longman Southern Africa Pty Ltd, Vrystaat Street, Paarden Eiland, Cape Town

LONGMANS YOUNG BOOKS LTD:
74 Grosvenor Street, London w.1
Australia, Canada, New Zealand and *South Africa:* As for Longman Group Ltd

LUTTERWORTH PRESS:
4 Bouverie Street, London E.C.4
Australia: *Cambridge University Press (Australia) Pty Ltd, P.O. Box 91, Albert Park, Victoria 3206 *and* 184 Sussex Street, Sydney, N.S.W. 2000
Canada: *G.R. Welch Co Ltd, 222 Evans Avenue, Toronto, Ontario
New Zealand: R.H. Horwood Esq, 75 Kitchener Road, Milford N.2, Auckland
South Africa: J.R. Dorman Esq, P.O. Box 5532, Johannesburg

MACDONALD AND CO (PUBLISHERS) LTD:
St Giles House, 49 Poland Street, London w.1
Australia: *Novalit Pty Ltd, Royal Place, Off 210 Swan Street, Richmond 3121 Victoria
Canada: *Ryerson Press, 299 Queen Street West, Toronto 2B, Ontario
New Zealand: *Whitcombe & Tombs Ltd, 11 Cashel Street, Christchurch
South Africa: *Purnell & Sons (S.A.) (Pty) Ltd, 70 Keerom Street, Cape Town

MACMILLAN & CO LTD:
4 Little Essex Street, London w.c.2
Australia: *The Macmillan Company of Australia Pty Ltd, 107 Moray Street, South Melbourne, Victoria 3205 *and* *155 Miller Street, North Sydney, N.S.W. 2060
Canada: *The Macmillan Company of Canada Ltd, 70 Bond Street, Toronto 2
New Zealand: *Macmillan & Co Ltd, Grand Building, 9 Princes Street, Auckland 1
South Africa: *Macmillan South Africa (Publishers) Pty Ltd, P.O. Box 23134, Joubert Park, Johannesburg

METHODIST BOOK ROOM:
2 Chester House, Pages Lane, Muswell, London N.10

Australia, Canada, New Zealand and *South Africa:* As for Epworth Press

METHUEN & CO LTD:
11 New Fetter Lane, London E.C.4
Australia: *Hicks, Smith & Sons Pty Ltd, 301/305 Kent Street, Sydney, N.S.W. 2000 *and* *225/227 Swan Street, Richmond, Victoria 3121; *91 Elizabeth Street, Brisbane, Queensland 4000
Canada: *Methuen Publications, 145 Adelaide Street West, Toronto 1, Ontario
New Zealand: *Hicks, Smith & Sons Ltd, P.O. Box 70, 238 Wakefield Road, Wellington *and* P.O. Box 2730, 12 Ruskin Street, Parnell, Auckland 1
South Africa: Evans Methuen Pty Ltd, P.O. Box 31478, Braamfontein, Transvaal

A.R. MOWBRAY AND CO LTD:
28 Margaret Street, London w.1
Australia: *Wm. Heinemann Ltd, 33 Lonsdale Street, Melbourne
Canada: *Canterbury House, Anglican Book Society, 242½ Bank Street, Ottawa 4, Ontario
New Zealand: *Wm. Heinemann Ltd, 48 Lake Road, P.O. Box 36029, Northcote, Auckland
South Africa: Cotton & Hardie, Box 17, Pinelands, Cape

FREDERICK MULLER LTD:
Ludgate House, 110 Fleet Street, London E.C.4
Australia: *Hutchinson Group (Australia) Pty Ltd, Hutchinson House, P.O. Box 267, 30/32 Cremorne Street, Richmond, Victoria 3121 *and* *86 Stanley Street, Sydney N.S.W.
Canada: *Saunders of Toronto Ltd, 1885 Leslie Street, Don Mills, Ontario
New Zealand: *Oswald-Sealy (New Zealand) Ltd, P.O. Box 1289, 89 Custom Street East, Auckland C.1
South Africa: *The Hutchinson Group (S.A.) (Pty) Ltd, P.O. Box 5841, Johannesburg

JOHN MURRAY (PUBLISHERS) LTD:
50 Albemarle Street, London w.1
Australia: William Heinemann Ltd, 33 Lonsdale Street, Melbourne 3000
Canada: *Longmans (Canada) Ltd, 55 Barber Greene Road, Don Mills, Ontario
New Zealand: William Heinemann Ltd, 48 Lake Road, Northcote, Auckland
South Africa: Oxford University Press, Thibault House, Thibault Square, Cape Town

NATIONAL CHRISTIAN EDUCATION COUNCIL:
Robert Denholm House, Nutfield, Redhill, Surrey

NATIONAL MAGAZINE CO LTD:
Chestergate House, Vauxhall Bridge Road, London s.w.1

THE OXFORD UNIVERSITY PRESS:
Ely House, 37 Dover Street, London w.1
Australia: Oxford University Press Australian Branch, G.P.O. Box 2784Y, Melbourne c.1, Victoria
Canada: Oxford University Press Canadian Branch, 70 Wynford Drive, Don Mills, Toronto, Ontario
New Zealand: Oxford University Press New Zealand Branch, Empire Building, Willis Street, Wellington c.1
South Africa: Oxford University Press South African Branch, Thibault House, Thibault Square, Cape Town

W. PAXTON & CO LTD:
36/38 Dean Street, London w.1

PENGUIN BOOKS LTD (PUFFIN AND PEACOCK BOOKS):
Bath Road, Harmondsworth, Middlesex
Australia: Penguin Books Australia Limited, 435 Maroondah Highway, Ringwood, Victoria 3134
Canada: Longmans Canada Ltd, 55 Barber Greene Road, Don Mills, Ontario
New Zealand: Hicks, Smith & Sons Ltd, 12 Ruskin Street, Auckland
South Africa: Penguin Overseas Ltd, P.O. Box 155, Cape Town

PERGAMON PRESS LTD:
Headington Hill Hall, Oxford
Australia: *Pergamon Press (Australia) Pty Ltd, Pergamon House, 19A Boundary Street, Rushcutters Bay, n.s.w. 2011
Canada: Burns & MacEachern Ltd, 62 Railside Road, Don Mills, Ontario
South Africa: Rupert Lamberth (Pty) Ltd, P.O. Box 22, Howard Place, Cape

PICKERING & INGLIS LTD:
29 Ludgate Hill, London e.c.4

RAPP & WHITING LTD:
76 New Oxford Street, London w.c.1
Australia, Canada, New Zealand and South Africa: As for Andre Deutsch Ltd

RYLEE LTD:
Daily News Ltd, 161 Queen Victoria Street, London e.c.4
Australia: J.M. McGregor Pty Ltd, Suite 2, 13 Manning Road, Double Bay, n.s.w
Canada: *Mr R. Taylor, Frank Arnott & Co Ltd, 2500 Lawrence Avenue East, Scarborough, Ontario

New Zealand: J.M. McGregor Pty Ltd, P.O. Box 9418, Wellington
South Africa: Denis L. Dorman Esq, P.O. Box 5532, Johannesburg

SCHOLASTIC PUBLICATIONS LTD:
161 Fulham Road, London s.w.3
Australia: *The H.J. Ashton Co Ltd, 14 Cross Street, Brookvale, n.s.w. 2100
Canada: *Scholastic TAB Publications, 123 Newkirk Road, Richmond Hill, Ontario
New Zealand: *The H.J. Ashton Co Ltd, P.O. Box 12–328, 9/11 Fairfax Avenue, Penrose, Auckland 6

SCRIPTURE UNION:
5 Wigmore Street, London w.1
Australia: Jeff B. Hordern, Emu Book Agencies Ltd, 511 Kent Street, Sydney n.s.w. 2000
Canada: Derek R. Patton, Scripture Union, 3 Rowanwood Avenue, Toronto 5, Ontario
New Zealand: G.W. Moore Ltd, 3 Campbell Road, Royal Oak, Auckland
South Africa: Mr S. Fish, Scripture Union Book Agency (Southern Africa), Millard House, 83 Camp Ground Road, Rondebosch, C.P. Cape Town

TRANSWORLD PUBLISHERS LTD:
Cavendish House, 57/59 Uxbridge Road, Ealing, London w.5
Australia: *L.L. Smith Esq, 104 Wellington Parade, East Melbourne, Victoria 3002
Canada: *Wm. Collins Sons & Co Canada Ltd, 100 Lesmill Road, Don Mills, Ontario
New Zealand: *Gordon & Gotch (n.z.) Ltd, 102 Adelaide Road, P.O. Box 1595, Newtown, Wellington
South Africa: *Transworld Publishers Ltd, 63 Sixth Avenue, Orange Grove, Johannesburg

ROBERT J. TYNDALL LTD:
43 Arundel Square, London n.7

UNIVERSITY OF LONDON PRESS LTD:
Saint Paul's House, Warwick Lane, London e.c.4
Australia, Canada, New Zealand and South Africa: As for Brockhampton Press Ltd

WARD LOCK LTD:
Warwick House, 116 Baker Street, London w.1
Australia: *Ward Lock Ltd, P.O. Box 34, Brickfield Hill, n.s.w. 2000
Canada: *Saunders of Toronto Ltd, 1885 Leslie Street, Don Mills, Ontario
New Zealand: R.H. Horwood Esq, 81 Kitchener Road, Milford, Auckland n.2
South Africa: The Hutchinson Group, P.O. Box 5841, Johannesburg

FREDERICK WARNE AND CO LTD:
  1 Bedford Court, Bedford Street, London
  w.c.2
    Australia: *Hicks, Smith and Sons Pty
    Ltd, 225/227 Swan Street, P.O. Box 235,
    Richmond, Victoria 3121, *91 Elizabeth
    Street, Brisbane 4000 *and* *301 Kent
    Street, Sydney 2000
    Canada: *Saunders of Toronto Ltd, 1885
    Leslie Street, Don Mills, Ontario
    New Zealand: *Hicks, Smith & Sons Ltd,
    238 Wakefield Street, P.O. Box 70,
    Wellington c.1 *and* *12 Ruskin Street,
    P.O. Box 2730, Parnell, Auckland
    South Africa: D.L. Dorman Esq, P.O. Box
    5532, 12 Olga Buildings, 121 President
    Street, Johannesburg

WILLS AND HEPWORTH LTD:
  The Angel Press, Loughborough, Leicester-
  shire
    Australia: Gordon & Gotch (Australasia)
    Ltd, Melbourne, Sydney, Brisbane,
    Townsville, Adelaide, Perth, Launceston
    and Hobart

  Canada: Wm. Collins Sons & Co Canada
  Ltd, 100 Lesmill Road, Don Mills,
  Ontario
  New Zealand: Gordon & Gotch (New
  Zealand) Ltd, Wellington, Auckland,
  Christchurch and Dunedin
  South Africa: Wm. Collins (Africa) (Pty)
  Ltd, P.O. Box 8879, Johannesburg *and*
  P.O. Box 834, Cape Town

WORLD'S WORK LTD:
  The Press at Kingswood, Tadworth,
  Surrey
    Australia: William Heinemann Australia
    Pty Ltd, 33 Lonsdale Street, Melbourne
    3000, G.P.O. Box 203C
    Canada: William Heinemann Ltd, 100
    Lesmill Road, Don Mills, Ontario
    New Zealand: William Heinemann Ltd,
    P.O. Box 36020, Northcote Central,
    Northcote, Auckland 9
    South Africa: Heinemann & Cassell S.A.
    Pty Ltd, P.O. Box 11190, Johannesburg

Index

ABBEY BOOKS, 141
About books for children, 201, 210
Abrahams, R, 94
ABRIDGEMENTS, 131
ACORN LIBRARY, 136
Adam Bede, 40
Adamson, Joy, 37
Adcock, J, 100
ADVENTURES IN HISTORY SERIES, 140
Adventures of Sherlock Holmes, The, 177
Adventures of Tom Leigh, The, 107
Aeneid, The, 18
Aiken, Joan, 28, 32, 122, 146
Ainsworth, Ruth, 121
Airlift for Grandee, 170
Alcott, Louisa M, 66, 77, 128, 133
Alderson, Brian W, 22, 112, 203, 205, 207, 208
Alderson, Valerie, 204
ALDINE PAPERBACKS, 144
Alexander, Lloyd, 24
Alice in Wonderland, 25, 127, 128, 132, 162
All Mary, 114
All of a kind family, 67
Allan, M. E, 81, 181
Allen, Eric, 54, 164, 170
Allsorts, 124
Almedingen, E. M, 17, 98
Ambrose, K, 97
Ambrus, Victor, 12, 16, 162, 164, 165
American-Indian tales and legends, 21
AMERICAN LIBRARY ASSOCIATION, 154, 158
Andersen, Hans Christian, 14, 91, 149, 163
Andrew, Prudence, 175
Andrews, J. S, 110
Anne Frank's diary, 187
Anne of Green Gables, 67, 130
ANNUALS, 124
Another home, another country, 175
ANTELOPE BOOKS, 104, 125, 136, 144, 170
Antelope singer, 109
Appiah, Peggy, 20
Arabian nights, The, 19
Arabian nights (Wildsmith), 163
ARBEITSKREIS FÜR JUGENDSCHRIFTUM, 159
Ardizzone, Edward, 132, 143, 164
ARMADA BOOKS, 143
Armstrong, Richard, 46, 85, 170
Arora, S. L, 95
Arthur, Ruth, 30, 182, 183
ARTS COUNCIL AWARD, 160
Arundel, Honor, 170, 180, 182
Asbjørnsen, P. C, 13, 14
Aschenputtel, 13
Ash Road, 57
Ask for King Billy, 54
Atkinson, M. E, 145
Attwell, Mabel Lucie, 132
Atwater, Florence, 115

Atwater, Richard, 115
Austen, Jane, 178
Australia (Folk tales of the world), 21
AUSTRALIAN CHILDREN'S BOOK COUNCIL, 155
Autumn term, 83
Avalanche! 47, 150
Avery, Gillian, 111, 112, 133, 192, 209

BABY PUFFINS, 143
Bagnold, Enid, 39
Bagshaw, Joy, 56
Baker, Margaret, 47, 73
Balderson, Margaret, 93, 158
Ballantyne, Joan, 56
Ballantyne, R. M, 162, 169
Ballet shoes, 85
Balogh, Penelope, 75
Bamberger, Dr Richard, 120, 200
Bambi, 36
BANDIT BOOKS, 168
Bannerman, Helen, 174
BANNERMERE BOOKS, 141
Barbeau, Marcel, 21
Barber, Antonia, 30
Barne, Kitty, 42, 159
Barnes, Margaret Campbell, 112
Barnes, T. R, 142
Barrett, Anne, 55
Barrie, J. M, 25, 132, 191, 209
Bartos-Höppner, B, 98, 104
Bastables, The, 132
Bateman, Robert, 120, 140, 169
Batten, H. Mortimer, 36
Baum, Frank, 25
Bawden, Nina, 51
Bayfield, J, 57
Baynes, Pauline, 19, 163
B.B. (i.e. Denys Watkins-Pitchford), 24, 36, 37, 191
B.B.C, 197
Bear called Paddington, A, 113
Beat of the city, The, 164
Beckley, R, 21
Beehunter, 15
BEGINNER BOOKS, 135, 169
BEGINNING TO READ SERIES, 135
Bell, A, 209
Bells of Nendrum, The, 110
Benary, Margot, 97, 153, 184
Beowulf, 15
Beresford, Elisabeth, 137
Berg, Leila, 12, 72, 121, 136
BERLIN, GERMAN STATE LIBRARY (EAST GERMANY), 200, 207, 208
Berna, Paul, 52, 90, 149, 192
Berries Goodman, 97
Berrisford, Judith M, 41
Best books for children, 211
BEST CHILDREN'S BOOK OF THE YEAR AWARD (NETHERLANDS), 155
Best children's books of the year, 206
Between planets, 60
Bevis, 35, 55

Beware the hunter, 54
Bewick, Thomas, 162
Beyond the jungle, 96
BIENNALE OF ILLUSTRATIONS, BRATIS-
    LAVA, 154, 163
Big drop, The, 168
BIG REINDEER BOOKS, 136
BIGGLES, 48, 141, 142
Bilberry summer, 33
BILLY BUNTER, 80, 145
Billy's monster, 137
Binder, L, 207
Birch, Cyril, 19
Black Beauty, 38
Black cauldron, The, 24
Black Jack, 108
Blish, James, 59
Blishen, E, 88, 112, 134, 209
Bloch, Marie H, 98
Blue fairy book, 12
Blue Peter, 124
Blyton, Enid, 33, 49, 81, 85, 140, 142, 144, 145
BODLEY HEAD MONOGRAPHS, 193, 203,
    209
Bond, Michael, 113, 146, 162, 193
Bonzon, Paul-Jacques, 150, 152
Book of dragons, A, 13
Book of ghosts and goblins, A, 163
Book of riddles, The, 169
BOOK OF THE YEAR PRIZE (AUSTRALIA),
    155
Bookbird, 37, 57, 77, 120, 149, 187, 205, 207,
    208, 210
Books and Bookmen, 142
Books about children's literature, 201
Books and the teacher, 204, 209
Books, children and men, 201, 209
Bookseller, The, 196
BOOKSELLERS ASSOCIATION, 197
BOOKS FOR NEW ADULTS, 193
Books for your children, 32, 134, 187, 204, 210
Books for primary children, 211
BOOKS, SELLING OF, 147
Born free, 37
Borrowers, The, 23, 24, 129
Borton de Treviño, Elizabeth, 92
Boston, Lucy M, 29, 144, 191
Bott, G, 57
Boucher, Alan, 93
Bowen, Elizabeth, 123
Bows against the barons, 103
Box for Benny, A, 72
Boy and the monkey, The, 104
Boy who sprouted antlers, The, 115
Boy who was afraid, The, 171
Bradbury, Bianca, 96
Brand, Christianna, 116, 164
Brand, Max, 133
Brazil, Angela, 79, 144
Breck, V, 193
Brent-Dyer, Elinor M, 80, 141, 144
Bridesmaids, The, 139
Bridge of children's books, A, 193, 207
BRIGGS BOOKS, 170, 171
BRIGHT ARROW SERIES, 169
Brinsmead, H.F, 90, 164, 176, 184, 185, 187,
    193

British Books in Print, 206
BRITISH MUSEUM, 198, 207, 208
British National Bibliography, 205
BROCK BOOKS, 136, 170
Brontë, Charlotte, 182
Bronze bow, The, 158
Brown, Pamela, 139
Brown, Roy, 52
Bruce, Dorita Fairlie, 80
Bruckner, Karl, 97, 104, 149, 152, 155
Buchan, John, 164, 177
Buckeridge, Anthony, 81, 118
Buddee, Paul, 53, 170
Bull, Angela, 74
Bull beneath the walnut tree, The, 122
Bulletin of the Center for Children's Books,
    205
BUREAU BOEK EN JEUGD, 199, 208
Burnett, Frances Hodgson, 69, 133
Burnford, Sheila, 37
Burning candle, The, 98
Burroughs, Edgar Rice, 146
Burston, Geoffrey, 152
Burton, Hester, 47, 101, 104, 107, 112, 184,
    185, 193
Burton, Virginia Lee, 144
Bus girls, The, 83
Butts, D, 112, 209
Buy, beg or borrow, 206, 211
Byron, May, 132

Cameron, E, 77
Candle in her room, A, 30, 182
CAORLE EUROPEAN PRIZE, 154
Cape, Jonathan, 189
CAREER BOOKS SERIES, 139
CAREER STORIES, 178
Carey, M.C, 12
Carnegie, Andrew, 155
CARNEGIE MEDAL, 57, 71, 85, 104, 105, 106,
    108, 119, 155, 156, 160, 190, 191, 200
Carrington, Noel, 143
Carroll, Lewis, 25, 128, 162, 209
Carter, Bruce, 51
Case of the silver egg, The, 53
Castaway camp, 145
Castaway Christmas, 47
Castle Blair, 133
Castors away! 107
Catcher in the rye, The, 184
Catherall, Arthur, 48
Catseye, 62
Cavanna, Betty, 176
CENTRE FOR CHILDREN'S LITERATURE,
    198
Cerf, Bennett, 169
CHALET SCHOOL SERIES, 141
Challenge of the Green Knight, The, 16
Chambers, Aidan, 172, 179, 187
Chambers, Nancy Lockwood, 204, 205
Charity at home, 184
Charley, 76
Charlotte sometimes, 30
Charlton, K, 112
Charmouth Grange, 102
Chauncy, Nan, 104, 109, 112, 155, 184

CHICAGO, CENTER FOR CHILDREN'S
BOOKS, 199, 205
Chief's daughter, The, 105, 125, 169
Child and his book, The, 202, 209
Child of the swamps, 97, 152, 155
Children of Green Knowe, The, 29, 32
Children of the Mayflower, 104
Children of the New Forest, The, 102
CHILDREN'S BOOK CENTRE, 204
CHILDREN'S BOOK CIRCLE, 155, 188, 196,
197
CHILDREN'S BOOK COUNCIL, 199
CHILDREN'S BOOK GROUP, 188, 196, 197
Children's Book News, 112, 165, 204, 210
Children's books in England, 201, 209
Children's books in print, 195, 206
CHILDREN'S EDITORS, 188
CHILDREN'S ILLUSTRATED CLASSICS,
131, 162, 177
*Children's literature: a guide to reference
sources,* 208
Children's literature in education, 205, 210
CHILDREN'S SERVICES DIVISION,
AMERICAN LIBRARY ASSOCIATION,
154
Chilton, Irma, 180
Chinese myths and fantasies, 19
CHIP CLUB, 147
Chivers, Cedric, 139
CHOSEN BOOKS, 131, 162
CHOSEN BOOKS FROM ABROAD, 131
Christie, Agatha, 178
Christopher, John, 60, 61, 64
Chronicles of Robin Hood, 17
Churchward, S.M, 207
Cinderella, 13
Circus is coming, The, 85
City of gold and lead, The, 64
CITY OF VIENNA PRIZE (AUSTRIA), 155
Clark, B, 211
Clark, L, 210
Clarke, Pauline, 28
Clashing rocks, The, 18
Cleary, Beverly, 181
Clever car, The, 137
Clewes, Dorothy, 183, 184
Cloud with the silver lining, The, 94
Coatsworth, Elizabeth, 94
Cockett, Mary, 175
Collected stories for children, 121
COLLEGES, INSTITUTES AND SCHOOLS
OF EDUCATION GROUP, 197
COLLIE BOOKS, 144
Columbus sails, 108, 164, 190
Colwell, Eileen, 12, 22, 121, 209, 211
Complete fairy tales (Perrault), 14
Complete Greek stories, 18
CONGRESS, LIBRARY OF, 14
Contender, The, 180
Cook, E, 22
Coolidge, Susan, 67, 76
Cox, Palmer, 145
Cresswell, Helen, 23, 138
Critical history of children's literature, A,
201, 210
Crompton, Richmal, 145

Crossley-Holland, Kevin, 13, 16, 160
Crouch, Marcus, 112, 120, 165, 187, 201, 203,
208, 209
Crown, A.W, 20
CROWN BOOKS, 170
Cruikshank, George, 162
Cry of the peacock, The, 182
Cue for treason, 103, 106
Cumming, Primrose, 42
Cunningham, Julia, 180
Curle, Jock, 189

Daddy-long-legs, 133, 177
Dalenoord, Jenny, 161
Dalton, Clive, 170
Damian and the dragon, 173
Daphne sets a fashion, 87
Dark danger, 182
Darton, F.J. Harvey, 201, 209
David Copperfield, 169
David in silence, 75
Day of the cats, The, 93
Death of metal, 62
Defoe, Daniel, 46
DeJong, Meindert, 91, 154, 160
Destry rides again, 133
Devil-in-the-fog, 155
Devil's dump, 168
Dickens, Charles, 123, 138
Dickinson, Peter, 64, 193
Diekmann, Miep, 155
Disney, Walt, 130
DISPLAYS, 195
Divine, David, 56
Do, look and listen, 122
Dodge, Mary Mapes, 89
Dog Crusoe, The, 162
Dog so small, A, 34, 37
Dohn, Janice, 142
Doll's day for Yoshiko, The, 91
Dolphin crossing, The, 101
Dorp dead, 180
Douglas, O, 133
DOVER BOOKS, 145
Down the bright stream, 191
Down to earth, 63
Downing, Charles, 18
Downton, J.A, 207
Doyle, Arthur Conan, 58, 177
Doyle, Brian, 142, 204, 209
Dr Doolittle, The story of, 31, 147, 176
Drabble, Margaret, 178, 181
DRAGON BOOKS, 145
Dragon Slayer, 15
Drdek, Richard, 184, 186
Dream of Sadlers Wells, A, 141
Dream watcher, The, 184
Dream-time, The, 104, 107
Dreamtime, The: Australian aboriginal myths,
21
Drought, 95
Drum, The, 180
Drumbeats, 145
Duke, Madelaine, 183
Durrell, Gerald, 36
Durstine, Virginia, 94

Duvoisin, Roger, 14

Eager, Edward, 27, 192
Eagle of the Ninth, The, 105
EARLY BIRD SERIES, 125, 136, (paperbacks), 144
Earthfasts, 30
Earthquake, 95
Eaton, Anne T, 201
Edge of the cloud, The, 191
Editha's burglar, 133
EDUCATIONAL PUBLISHERS COUNCIL, 188
Education Libraries Bulletin, 153
Edwards, Dorothy, 121, 174, 175
Edwards, Monica, 43, 139, 141, 181, 192
Edwin, Maribel, 33
Egoff, Sheila, 203, 209
Eight cousins, 133
Eleanor, 151
ELEANOR FARJEON AWARD, 155, 188
Elidor, 26, 164
Elizabethan, The, 124
Elliott, Roberta, 93
Ellis, Alec, 32, 37, 204, 209
Ellis, A.W, 77
Emil and the detectives, 53
End of term, 83
Endless steppe, The, 187
English children's books, 1600–1900, 201, 202, 210
English fables and fairy stories, 15
English fairy tales, 15
ENGLISH PICTURE READERS, 169, 171
Enright, Elizabeth, 68, 77, 192
Eric: or little by little, 78
Estes, Eleanor, 192
EVERGREEN LIBRARY, 138
Ewing, Mrs, 66, 133, 209
EXHIBITIONS, 196

FABER PAPERBACKS, 144
Fables from Aesop, 18
FAIRY TALES, 11
Fairy tales (Perrault), 14
Fairy tales and legends (Andersen), 14, 163
Fairy tales from the Pacific Islands, 21
Fairy tales of long ago (Carey), 12
FAIRY TALES OF THE WORLD, 14
Faithful parrot and other Indian folk stories, The, 20
Falkner, J. Meade, 48
Family from One End Street, The, 71, 159
Family story in the 1960s, The, 77
FAMOUS FIVE SERIES, 140
Faralla, D, 34
Far-distant Oxus, The, 39
Farjeon, Eleanor, 121, 124, 125, 154, 155, 209
Farmer, Penelope, 30
Farmer's boy, 67
Far out the long canal, 92
Farrar, Dean, 78
FAVOURITE FAIRY TALES TOLD IN .., 14
FEDERATION OF CHILDREN'S BOOK GROUPS, 197, 208

Ferguson, Ruby, 40
Feustel, G, 97
Fidler, Kathleen, 140
Field, C, 32
Field, L.F. (*Mrs*. E.M.), 202, 209
Fifteen, 181
Fifth Chinese daughter, 176
Fifth form at St. Dominic's, The, 78
Fifty favourite fairy tales, 12, 132
FIND-OUTERS SERIES, 140
Finlay, Winifred, 182
Finn family Moomintroll, 116
Finn's folly, 185
Fireweed, 186
First choice, 211
First job, 87
First men in the moon, The, 58
FIRST STEPS IN READING, 136
Fisher, Margery, 37, 65, 77, 125, 139, 155, 193, 202, 204, 209, 210
Fisk, Nicholas, 62, 174
Five children and it, 27
Five of us—and Madeleine, 139
Five spinning tops of Naples, 97
Flambards in summer, 185
Fleming, Ian, 182
Fletcher, D, 126
Fly-by-night, 41
FLYING FOAL BOOKS, 136
Flying horseman, The, 42
FOLIO SOCIETY, 132
Folk literature, 22
FOLK TALES, 11, 173
Folk tales for reading and telling, 12
FOLK TALES OF THE WORLD, 20
Ford, B, 142
FOREIGN AWARD WINNERS, 150, 192
Forest, Antonia, 69, 73, 81, 83, 84, 141, 181
Forgotten door, The, 64
Fortnum, Peggy, 162
Fortunes of Philippa, The, 79
Fotheringham, H, 207
Four rode home, 42
Frank, Anne, 187
FRANKFURT, JUGENDBUCHFORSCHUNG, 200
French, Alan, 17
Friday miracle, The, 125
Friends and enemies, 98
Friends of Croix-Rousse, The, 152
FRIENDS OF THE OSBORNE COLLECTION, 197
Frog in a coconut shell, The, 93
From primer to pleasure, 203, 210
From the earth to the moon, 58
Full fathom five, 54

Gag, Wanda, 14
Game, The, 186
Garfield, Leon, 104, 108, 112, 123, 146, 155, 160, 163
Garner, Alan, 13, 26, 32, 146, 155, 184, 186, 193
Garnett, Eve, 71, 164
Garthwaite, M, 16
Gates of Bannerdale, 181

Gauntlet, The, 110
Gayler, Marjorie, 87
GAZELLE BOOKS, 136
Geordie foresters, The, 170
George, Jean, 35
Geraghty, A, 196
GERMAN YOUTH BOOK AWARD, 155, 158
Ghosts, The, 30
GHOST STORIES, 30
Gift from Winklesea, A, 138
Gill, Margery, 12, 162, 165
Ginger and no 10, 175
Girl like Cathy, A, 183
Girls of St Cyprian's, The, 79
Goalkeeper's revenge and other stories, The, 122
Gobbling Billy, The, 118
Golden Gorse, 38
Golden phoenix, The, 21
Golding, William, 46, 185
Gollancz, Victor, 193
GOLLANCZ REVIVALS, 133
Good, D, 207
Good Master, The, 92
Good wives, 180
Goodbye my shadow, 181
Gordon, J.A, 172
Gorgon's head, The, 18
Goudge, Elizabeth, 191
Graham, Eleanor, 32, 132, 143
Grahame, Kenneth, 32, 144, 162, 192
Grange at High Force, The, 56
Grass rope, A, 28
Gray, J.E.B, 20
Great big enormous turnip, The, 12
Great emergency, A, 133
Great expectations, 169
Great fire, The, 105
Great gale, The, 47
Great northern?, 56
Green children, The, 160
Green, L.E, 211
Green, Roger Lancelyn, 13, 16, 17, 22, 202, 209
Gretel of St. Bride's, 83
Grettir the strong, 17
Grey, Elizabeth, 87
Greyhound, The, 34
Grice, Frederick, 74, 111, 139, 164
Griffiths, G.D, 37
Griffiths, Helen, 34
Grimm, Jakob and Wilhelm, 13, 15, 149
Gripe, M, 152
Groves, J. Percy, 102
Growing Point, 198, 204, 207, 208, 210
Guardian, The, 125, 205
GUARDIAN AWARD, 104, 155
Gudmundson, S, 94
Guide dog, 184
Guide to book lists and bibliographies for the use of schools, A, 211
Guillot, René, 35, 104, 149, 154, 155
Gulliver's travels, 127, 131, 162
Gumble's Yard, 71

Hadfield, Alice M, 15

Hag calls for help, The, 27
Haggard, Rider, 49, 177
Half a world away, 109
Half magic, 27
Hamish Hamilton book of magical beasts, The, 13
HAMMERSMITH PUBLIC LIBRARY, 198, 207
Hampden, John, 173
Hamre, Leif, 54, 150
HANS ANDERSEN AWARD, 91
HANS ANDERSEN MEDAL, 154, 157
Hans Brinker, 89
Hardcastle, M, 168
Harnett, Cynthia, 104, 105, 161, 164
Harris, Joel Chandler, 20
Harris, Mary, 81, 83, 88, 144
Harris, Rosemary, 119, 120, 157, 191
Haugaard, K, 176
Hautzig, Esther, 184, 187
Havelok the Dane, 16
Haviland, Virginia, 14, 199, 202, 207, 208, 210
Hawthorne, Nathaniel, 17
Hazard, Paul, 201, 209
Heartsease, 64
Heidi, 89, 149
Heinlein, Robert A, 60, 193
Hendon fungus, The, 62
Henry, Marguerite, 34
Henty, G.A, 102, 145
Herald, Kathleen, 41
Hereward the Wake, 108
HERO TALES, 11
Hero tales from the British Isles, 15
Heroes, The, 18
Heron ride, The, 42
Hewett, Anita, 12, 122
Heyer, Georgette, 112
Higgins, J.E, 100
High and haunted island, The, 184
High house, The, 170
High king, The, 24
Hilbert, Peter Paul, 118
Hilder, Rowland, 131
Hildick, E.W, 55, 81, 180
Hill, Denise, 137
Hill, Lorna, 141
Hill of the Red Fox, The, 54
Hills End, 46, 47
History of children's reading and literature, A, 204, 209
Hobbit, The, 23, 159
Hobstones, The, 56
Hodges, C. Walter, 104, 107, 108, 112, 131, 164, 190
Hodgkin, M.R, 165
Hogarth, G, 165
Holbrook, D, 187
Holden, A, 176
Holiday trench, 56
Holm, Anne, 50, 152, 192
Holt, Victoria, 182
Home from the hill, 73
Homeless Katie, 73, 170
Hope, Antony, 49
Hope-Simpson, Jacynth, 105

Horn Book Magazine, The, 22, 37, 77, 100, 112, 200, 204, 205, 210
Hornstranders, The, 93
Hough, Charlotte, 122
Hound of Ulster, The, 15
House at Pooh Corner, The, 31
House in Cornwall, The, 145
House of cats, The, 173
House of sixty fathers, The, 92
House of the nightmare and other eerie tales, The, 122
How a picture book is made, 195
How to find out about children's literature, 204, 209
Huddy, Delia, 70, 85
Hughes, Fielden, 81
Hughes, Shirley, 162
Hughes, Ted, 65
Hughes, Thomas, 78
Hull, Katharine, 39
Hulpach, V, 21
Humphrey's ride, 94
Hundred million francs, A, 52, 53
Hunter, Norman, 116
Hunters of Siberia, 98
Hürlimann, Bettina, 203, 209
Hurricane, 95
Hurricane, The, 94
Huston, A, 176
Hutton, M, 22, 32, 160

I am David, 50, 51, 152
I CAN READ BOOKS, 135, 169
I own the race-course, 76
Iliad, The, 18
In his little black waistcoat, 163
In spite of all terror, 101
In-between Miya, 91
Incredible adventures of Professor Branestawm, The, 116
Incredible journey, The, 37
India (Folk tales of the world), 20
Indian tales, 20
Indian tales and legends, 20
Inglelow, Jean, 128
INNER RING BOOKS, 167, 171
Intent upon reading, 139, 155, 193, 202, 204, 209
INTERNATIONAL BOARD ON BOOKS FOR YOUNG PEOPLE, 149, 154
INTERNATIONAL INSTITUTE FOR CHILDREN'S LITERATURE, VIENNA, 149
INTERNATIONAL YOUTH LIBRARY see MUNICH, INTERNATIONAL YOUTH LIBRARY
Intruder, The, 186
Iron man, The, 65
Irwin, Margaret, 112, 123
Ishii, Momoko, 91
Island of the blue dolphins, 46
Island of the great yellow ox, 56
It's like this, cat, 184
Ivory horn, The, 17

Jackals of the sea, 49

Jack and the beanstalk (Lines), 12
Jack and the beanstalk (Stobbs), 12
Jackanory, 21
JACKANORY BOOKS, 144
Jackie's pony camp summer, 41
Jacobs, Joseph, 15
Jacobs, W. W, 123
Jacques, Robin, 163
Jamberoo Road, 110
James, M. R, 123
Jane Eyre, 28, 127, 130, 169, 182
Jane plays hockey, 85
Jansson, Tove, 116
Japanese tales and legends, 19
Jean behind the counter, 86
Jefferies, Richard, 35, 55
Jenkins, A. C, 95
Jenkins, Alan, 164
JENNINGS BOOKS, 140
Jennings goes to school, 81
Jenny Kimura, 176
JETS, 169, 171
Jill's gymkhana, 40
JOAN TATE BOOKS, 168
Johns, W. E, 48, 142
JOINT CONSULTATIVE COMMITTEE ON CHILDREN'S BOOKS, 197
Jonah Simpson, 95
Jones, Howard, 54
Jonsson, Runer, 114, 155
José, 97
Joseph, J. R, 174
Journey from Peppermint Street, The, 92, 160
Journey with a secret, 51
Joy Street, 124, 125, 126, 138
Judy and Jasmin, 174
Junior Bookshelf, The, 22, 37, 57, 88, 112, 120, 126, 165, 200, 204, 210
JUNIOR PORTWAY REPRINTS, 141
Just a street, 155
Just like Jennings, 118
Just so stories, 121

Kamm, Antony, 187, 190, 194, 196, 204, 209
Kamm, Josephine, 87, 175, 178, 183, 193
Kamm, Margaret, 169
Kästner, Erich, 53, 75, 154, 158, 189
Kate and the family tree, 74
KATE GREENAWAY MEDAL, 155
Kay, Mara, 98
Kaye, Geraldine, 170
Keats, Ezra Jack, 174
Keeping, Charles, 162, 163, 164, 165
KEEPSAKE LIBRARY, THE, 133
Kelly, E. P, 156
Kendall, Carol, 24
Kerlan Collection, 199
Key, Alexander, 64
Key system for indicating reading ability and interest age, 195
Kiddell-Monroe, Joan, 19, 162, 163
Kidnapped, 102
Kim, 174
King Arthur and his knights of the round table, 16
King Arthur and his round table, 16
King, Clive, 111, 115

King of the wind, 34
King Solomon's mines, 49, 177
Kingdom of the elephants, 95
Kingsley, Charles, 17, 25, 108
Kipling, Rudyard, 79, 111, 121, 174, 210
KNIGHT BOOKS, 145
Knight crusader, 108
Knight, Frank, 104
Knights of the cardboard castle, 137
Knights of the golden table, The, 17
Krüss, James, 154

de Ladebat, M. P, 47
Lägerlof, Selma, 89
Lampel, R, 151
Lamplugh, Lois, 56
Land is bright, The, 97
Landsborough, Gordon, 143, 145
Lang, Andrew, 12, 17, 18, 19, 22, 132, 145
Lantern bearers, The, 105, 157, 185
Lark in the morn, The, 84
Lark on the wing, The, 85, 190
Last battle, The, 157
Latchkey children, The, 54, 164
Lawrence, D. H, 178
LEGENDS, 11
Leitch, Patricia, 42
L'Engle, Madeleine, 64
Lepman, Jella, 89, 149, 193, 199, 207
Lepus: the brown hare, 36
Let the balloon go, 75
Lewis, C. Day, 52, 164
Lewis, C. S, 25, 31, 32, 157, 209
Lewis, Hilda, 27, 29
Lewis, Naomi, 125, 206, 211
LIBRARY ASSOCIATION, 155, 160, 187, 197, 206, 208
Library Association Record, 207
Library Journal, 207
LIBRARY OF CONGRESS, 14, 199
Lights in a dark town, 106
LILLIAN H. SMITH COLLECTION, 199
Lindgren, Astrid, 90, 114, 120, 149, 154
Lindsay, Norman, 119
Lines, 142
Lines, Kathleen, 12, 122, 132, 203, 209
Lion, the witch and the wardrobe, The, 25
Lipsyte, Robert, 180
Lisa goes to Russia, 99
Little Black Sambo, 174
Little bookroom, The, 121
Little grey men, The, 24, 191
Little house in the big woods, The, 67
Little Katia, 98
Little Lord Fauntleroy, 134
Little man, The, 158
Little Peter stories, 121
Little women, 66, 71, 128, 131, 133, 159, 162, 177
Lively, P, 32
Liz, 184
Load of unicorn, The, 106
Locked crowns, The, 16
Lofting, Hugh, 31, 164, 189, 209
Lomas, D, 57
LONDON WEEKEND TELEVISION, 197

Lonely Maria, 94
LONE PINE SERIES, 140
LONG AGO CHILDREN, 104
Long way home, The (Stephan), 51
Long winter, The, 67
Longest weekend, The, 182
LONGMANS YOUNG BOOKS, 193, 195
Lord Mayor's show, The, 43, 193
Lord of the flies, 46, 185
Lord of the rings, The, 23
Lottie and Lisa, 75
Lotus caves, The, 60
Louie's lot, 180
Lucinda, 96
Lucinda's year of Jubilo, 68
LUCKY CLUB, 147

McAlpine, Helen *and* William, 19
MacGibbon, Jean, 184
Macken, Walter, 56
Mackenzie, Compton, 138
McLean, Allan Campbell, 54, 57
McNeill, Janet, 55, 122
Macpherson, Margaret, 70, 192
MacRae, Julia, 196, 207
MacVicar, Angus, 59
Maggie, 193
Magic fishbone, The, 123, 138
Magic pudding, The, 119, 120
Magician's nephew, The, 25
Magnolia Buildings, 71
Mahoney, Bertha, 200
Maitland, Antony, 163
Malay cruise, 170
Malory, *Sir* Thomas, 15, 106
MANCHESTER SCHOOL OF LIBRARIAN-SHIP, 198
Mandrake: a pony, The, 41
Manning-Sanders, Ruth, 13, 21, 104, 163, 173
Man with a sword, 108
Maplin, Bird, The, 107
Marder, J. V, 112
de la Mare, Walter, 121, 124, 144, 191, 210
Margin for surprise, 203, 210
Mark of the horse lord, The, 185
Marryat, *Captain*, 102
Marsh king, The, 108, 190
Martin, J. P, 31
Martin, Nancy, 86, 170
Martin rides the moor, 43
Mary Jane, 96
Mary Poppins, 27, 147
Masefield, John, 209
Masha, 98
Masters, R. E, 170
Mathinna's people, 109
Mattie, 37
du Maurier, Daphne, 182
Mayne, William, 8, 13, 28, 30, 70, 81, 88, 117, 118, 146
Meek, M, 112, 209
Mehta, R, 95
Meigs, Cornelia, 77, 201, 210
Melcher, Frederick G, 154
MERLIN BOOKS, 145
Meynell, *Sir* Francis, 132

Michaelson, Vera, 172
Middle Moffat, The, 68
Mike Mulligan and his steam shovel, 144
MILDRED L. BATCHELDOR AWARD, 158
Milne, A. A, 31, 144, 162, 192
MINNESOTA, UNIVERSITY OF, 199
Minnipins, The, 24
Miriam, 97
Miscellany, 124, 125
Mitchison, Naomi, 98
Moby Dick, 127, 130
Moe, J, 13, 14
Molesworth, Mrs, 66, 133, 210
Montgomery, L. M, 67, 130
Monty of Montego, 94
Moomin-sagas, 120
Moon in the cloud, The, 119, 120, 157, 191
Moonball, The, 63
Moonfleet, 48
Moore, Anne Carroll, 200
Moore, Patrick, 59
Moorland Mousie, 38
Mopsa the fairy, 128
More tales from Grimm, 14
Morris, Ruth, 51
Morte d'Arthur, 106
Mould, G. H, 32
Mountford, C. P, 21
Mr Corbett's ghost and other stories, 123
Mr Galliano's circus, 33, 85
Mr Garden, 125
Mr Popper's penguins, 115
Muir, L, 88
Muir, Percy H, 201, 202, 210
MUNICH, INTERNATIONAL YOUTH
    LIBRARY, 89, 149, 160, 199, 207
Murdoch, Iris, 181
Mutineers, The, 46
Myeko's gift, 176
My family and other animals, 37
My friend Flicka, 145
My name is Pablo, 97
My naughty little sister, 121
My new home, 133
My side of the mountain, 35, 36
MYTHS, 11
Myths of the Norsemen, 17

Namesake, The, 108, 190
Narni of the desert, 90
NATIONAL ASSOCIATION OF TEACHERS OF
    ENGLISH, 197
NATIONAL BOOK AWARD OF AMERICA, 160
NATIONAL BOOK LEAGUE, 197, 198, 206,
    208, 211
National Velvet, 39
Naughtiest girl in the school, The, 81
Naughton, Bill, 122
Neal, Philip, 23
Nesbit, Edith, 27, 29, 68, 110, 132, 133, 139,
    209
Nesbitt, Elizabeth, 201
Neville, Emily, 97, 184
NEW ADVENTURE LIBRARY, 138
New tales of Robin Hood, 17
New Tenants, The, 70

NEW YORK PUBLIC LIBRARY, 200
Newbery, John, 154, 193
NEWBERY MEDAL, 34, 46, 68, 109, 154, 155,
    156, 184, 200
Night the rain came in, The, 70
Nimmons, E, 208
NIPPER BOOKS, 72, 136
No boats on Bannermere, 81
No more school, 117
No place like Trickett's Green, 70
No strangers here, 183
NONESUCH CYGNETS, 131
Nordy Bank, 57
North for adventure, 170
Norton, André, 62, 64, 65, 193
Norton, Mary, 32, 129, 144
Norwegian fairy tales, 14
NORWEGIAN STATE PRIZE, 155
Nourse, Alan, 61
Nurse Matilda, 116, 164
Nye, Robert, 13, 15

O'Dell, Scott, 46
Odyssey, The, 18
Off the shelf, 194
O'Hara, Mary, 145
Old Peter's Russian tales, 14
Oliver, M, 97
Oliver Twist, 28
Oman, Carola, 16
On the run, 51
One is one, 101
One rupee and a bundle of rice, 95
Open the door, 125
Orczy, *Baroness*, 133
Ordinary and the fabulous, The, 22
Orphans of Simitra, 150
Orvig, M, 208
OSBORNE COLLECTION, 199, 208
Otter three two calling, 54
Otterbury incident, The, 52, 53, 164
OUT AND ABOUT BOOKS, 140
Out of step, 175, 182
Out of the sun, 175
Out of this world, 65
Ovens, W. W, 208
Overloaded ark, The, 36
Owen, Mably, 65
Owl service, The, 155, 186
Oxenbury, Helen, 12
Oxenham, Elsie J, 80, 88, 141
OXFORD CHILDREN'S LIBRARY, 138
OXFORD ILLUSTRATED CLASSICS, 131
OXFORD JUVENILE LIBRARY, 193
OXFORD MYTHS AND LEGENDS, 14, 19, 163

PAGEANT OF HISTORY SERIES, 140
Painted garden, The, 69
Pair of Jesus-boots, A, 72
Palmer, C. E, 94
Papas, William, 18, 164
PAPERBACKS, 132
PAPERMACS, 144
Pappa Pellerin's daughter, 152
Parcel of trees, A, 70

Park, Ruth, 170
PARKER COLLECTION, BIRMINGHAM, 208
Parker, Richard, 62, 70, 74, 139, 193
Parkinson, C. Northcote, 43
Parrott, F. P, 211
Pastures of the blue crane, 176
Paton, Jane, 125
Paul, the hero of the fire, 143
Pauline becomes a hairdresser, 87
Pavilion, The, 77
PEACOCK BOOKS, 146, 179
Pearce, Philippa, 29, 34, 37
Pearsall, R, 142
Pellowski, Anne, 202, 208
PENNANT BOOKS, 138
Penny plain, 133
Penny pony, The, 42
Penny's way, 82
Perrault, Charles, 13, 15, 149
Persson, L.-C, 153
Peter Pan, 25, 128, 130, 132, 162
Peyton, K. M, 41, 43, 107, 184, 185, 187, 190, 193
Phipson, Joan, 90, 155
Picard, Barbara Leonie, 13, 15, 17, 18, 20, 101, 104
Picture-book world, 203, 209
PICTURE PUFFINS, 143
PIED PIPER BOOKS, 136
Piemakers, The, 23
Pigeon Post, 57
Pigeons and princesses, 121
Pigman, The, 184, 186
Pilgrim's progress, The, 127
Pineapple child and other tales from Ashanti, The, 20
Pippi Longstocking, 114
Plaidy, Jean, 112
Planet of fire, 59
Platt, P, 211
Play to the festival, A, 181
PLOWDEN REPORT, 173
Pollard, Michael, 172
Ponies plot, 43
Pony raffle, The, 170
Pool of fire, The, 64
Pope, Ray, 180
PORPOISE BOOKS, 143
Porter, Sheena, 57, 74
Portrait of Margarita, 182
PORTWAY JUNIOR REPRINTS, 139
Potter, Beatrix, 209
PRESTON, HARRIS LIBRARY, 198, 207, 208
Pretty little pocket book, A, 193
Price, Willard, 48
Prisoner of Zenda, The, 49
Private beach, 70
PRIX JEUNESSE (FRANCE), 155
Professor Challenger stories, The, 58
PUBLISHERS ASSOCIATION, 188, 196, 197
PUBLISHERS' CATALOGUES, 194
Puck of Pook's Hill, 111
PUFFIN CLUB, 146
PUFFIN PICTURE BOOKS, 143
PUFFIN POST, 146
PUFFIN STORY BOOKS, 143
Pullein-Thompson, Christine, 42, 73, 139, 170

Pullein-Thompson, Diana, 42
Pullen, Alan, 167
Purple valley, The, 182, 183
Pyle, Howard, 209
PYRAMID BOOKS, 179, 193

Quarterly Journal of the Library of Congress, The, 207

Rackham, Arthur, 123, 162, 165
Rae, Gwynedd, 113
Railway children, The, 68, 147
Ramu, 95
Ransome, Arthur, 14, 39, 55, 57, 164, 189, 210
Rata, 176
Rathnamal, Sita, 96
Ray, Mary, 104
READ ALOUD BOOKS, 136
REAL LIFE ADVENTURE, 140
Red Biddy, 122
RED BISON BOOKS, 136
Red elephant blanket, The, 90
Red Indian folk and fairy tales, 21
Red pony, The, 179
Reed, A. W, 21
Reed, Talbot Baines, 78
Reeves, James, 13, 15, 18, 22, 121
REINDEER BOOKS, 104, 136, 170
Reluctant dragon, The, 138
Reluctant readers, 172, 187
Republic of childhood, The, 203, 209
Requiem for a princess, 183
Return to the Heron, 42
Rich man and the shoemaker, The, 12
Rider of the white horse, The, 185
Riot, 95
Road to Agra, The, 95, 155
Robbins, Sidney, 205
Roberts, A, 21
Robin Hood, 16
Robin in the greenwood, 17
Robinson Crusoe, 46, 127, 131, 132
    influence of, 51, 60, 61
Robinson, Joan G, 76, 192
Robinson, Veronica, 75
Rockets in the dunes, 56
Rodman, Maia, 94
Roe, M, 120
Roller skates, 68
Rose in bloom, 133
Rose, J, 32
Rosina and son, 42
Rosina Copper, 42
Rudge, K, 148
Rufus, 73
Runaway, The, 51
Rust, Doris, 21
Ryder, J, 165

SALAMANDER BOOKS, 136, 170
Salinger, J. D, 184
Salkey, Andrew, 95
Salten, Felix, 36

Sam and me, 180
Sama, 155
Sanchez-Silva, José Maria, 154
Sand, 82
Sapphire for September, A, 185
Saturday in Pudney, A, 52, 53
Saturdays, The, 68
Saville, Malcolm, 140, 145, 170, 182, 183
Sawyer, Ruth, 12, 68, 210
Scandinavian Public Library Quarterly, 208
Scapegoat, The, 74
Scarlet Pimpernel, The, 133
SCHOLASTIC PUBLICATIONS, 147
School Librarian, The, 22, 32, 57, 65, 77, 112, 120, 160, 204, 205, 210
SCHOOL LIBRARY ASSOCIATION, 197, 204, 206, 208
School library fiction, 211
School paperback bookshop, The, 147
SCOOP CLUB, 147
Sea change, 85, 86
Second-hand family, 74
Secret garden, The, 69, 134
Secret mountain, The, 49
SECRET SEVEN SERIES, 140
SEE-SAW CLUB, 147
Seraphina, 83
Seredy, Kate, 92, 100
Serraillier, Ian, 13, 15, 16, 17, 18, 22, 50, 139, 152, 169
Seton, Ernest Thompson, 35, 36, 55
Seuss, Dr, 135
Severn, David, 145
Severnside story, A, 74, 164
Sewell, Anna, 38
Shadow of a bull, 94
Shanta, 96, 174
Shaw, F. L, 133
Shelley, H, 210
Shepard, E. H, 162
Sherlock, Philip, 20
Sherry, Sylvia, 72, 93
Shilling a mile, 168
Ship that flew, The, 27
SHORT STORIES, 122
Shute, Nevil, 49, 178
Signal, 205, 211
SIGNAL BOOKS, 138
Silver sword, The, 50, 51, 147, 153
Simon, 105
SIMON BLACK BOOKS, 57
Sirga, 35
Skid pan, 169
Skirrow, Desmond, 53
Sleigh, Barbara, 138
Šmahelová, Helena, 99
Small pinch of weather, A, 122
Smith, 160
Smith, Lillian H, 201, 210
Smith, Vian, 43, 193
Smitty and the plural of cactus, 170
Snow White, 130
Snowball, The, 138
Snowy day, The, 174
SOCIETY OF AUTHORS, 197
Sommerfelt, Aimée, 95, 97, 149, 155
Song of Hiawatha, 162

Songberd's Grove, 55
Southall, Ivan, 46, 47, 75, 184, 185, 192
Space hostages, 62, 174
Spaniards are coming, The, 104
Speare, Elizabeth, 104, 109, 158
Spence, Eleanor, 57, 90, 104, 109, 110
SPENCER COLLECTION, 207, 208
Sperry, Armstrong, 171
SPHERE BOOKS, 144
SPORTS FICTION, 84
SPORTS FICTION SERIES, 140
Spring of the year, The, 84
Spyri, Johanna, 89, 149
Stairs that kept going down, The, 138
Stalky and Co, 79
STAR CLASSICS, 146
Steffos and his Easter lamb, 91, 161
Steinbeck, John, 179
Stephan, Hanna, 51
Sterling, Dorothy, 96
Stevenson, Robert Louis, 48, 107, 123, 209
Stewart, Angus, 172
Stewart, C. D, 112
Stewart, Mary, 178, 182
Stig of the dump, 111
Stobbs, William, 164, 170
STOCKHOLM PUBLIC LIBRARY, 199
Stolen seasons, The, 56
Stolz, Mary, 181
Storey, Margaret, 74
Story of Peter Cronheim, The, 97
Story of the Pandavas, The, 20
Story of the three little pigs, The, 12
Story of the treasure seekers, The, 68
Story-teller's choice, A, 12
STORY-TELLING, 11, 12
Stories of King Arthur and his knights, 15
Storm over the blue hills, 95
Storr, Catherine, 73
Streatfeild, Noel, 69, 85, 99, 139, 145, 192, 210
String of time, 180
Stucley, Elizabeth, 71
Styles, Showell, 51
Suddaby, Donald, 17, 62
Sue Barton, 87
Sugar cube trap, The, 183
Summer in between, The, 57
Sunday Times, 23
SUPER HAMPTON LIBRARY, 139
Super Nova and the rogue satellite, 59
Sutcliff, Rosemary, 8, 13, 15, 17, 104, 105, 112, 125, 157, 164, 169, 184, 185, 210
SVENSKA BARNBOKSINSTITUTET, 199, 208
Swanhilda of the swans, 34
Swarm in May, A, 82
Swiss fairy tales, 14
Swiss family Robinson, The, 131, 149
Switherby pilgrims, The, 110
Sword at sunset, 185
Sword of Ganelon, The, 139
Sykes, Pamela, 137
Symons, Geraldine, 111

Takao and grandfather's sword, 91
Tale of Ancient Israel, The, 162

Tale of the turnip, The, 12
Tale of two cities, The, 127
Tales from Grimm, 14
Tales from the Australian bush, 21
Tales from the Pacific, 21
Tales of Joe and Timothy, 174
Tales of the British people, 15
Tales of the Hodja, 18
Tales of the Norse gods and heroes, 17
Tales of Troy and Greece, 18
Tales out of school, 201, 202, 210
Tangara, 109
Tanglewood tales, 18
Target island, 51
Tarka the otter, 36
Tate, Joan, 168, 175, 180
Tatham, C. S, 88
Taylor, Boswell, 204, 209
Taylor, J, 165, 196
Taylor, J. K. G, 77
Taylor, N. B, 18
Taylor, Sidney, 67
Teachers World, 100, 148, 172, 187
Tell me a story, 121
Tell me another story, 121
Tellers of tales, 202, 209
TEMPO BOOKS, 168
Tenniel, *Sir* John, 128, 162
Terror by night, 123
Terror by satellite, 58
Thapar, R, 20
That summer with Ora, 151
These happy golden years, 67
Thirty-nine steps, The, 164, 177
Thøger, M, 96, 174
Three centuries of children's books in Europe, 203, 209
Three poor tailors, The, 12
Three towers in Tuscany, 182
Thunder in the sky, 107
Thursday kidnapping, The, 69
Thwaite, Ann, 124
Thwaite, Mary F, 203, 208, 210
Tim and Terry, 174
Time of trial, 107, 112, 185
TIME, PLACE AND ACTION SERIES, 140
Time to love, A, 97, 184
TIME-TRAVEL STORIES, 110
Timely reading, 194
Times, The, 205
Times Literary Supplement, 88, 204, 205, 208, 211
To the wild sky, 46, 185
Todd, Barbara Euphan, 117, 143
Tolkien, J. R. R, 23, 32, 159
Tom Brown's schooldays, 78
Tom's midnight garden, 29
TOPLINERS, 145, 179, 180
Toppling Towers, The, 77
TORONTO PUBLIC LIBRARY, 199, 208
Town that went south, The, 115
Townsend, J. A. B, 208
Townsend, John Rowe, 71, 125, 184, 186, 198, 203, 208, 210
Travers, P. L, 27
Treadgold, Mary, 39, 42, 139, 159, 170

Trease, Geoffrey, 16, 81, 102, 112, 141, 181, 201, 202, 209, 210
Treasure of Siegfried, The, 17
Treasure Island, 47, 48, 49, 55, 124, 128, 129, 131, 132
Treasure seekers and borrowers, 203, 209
Tree and leaf, 32
Treece, Henry, 54, 104, 107, 144, 164, 170, 209
Trevor, Meriol, 106
Tring, A. Stephen, 81
Trnka, Jiri, 154
Trumpeter of Krakow, The, 156
Trust a city kid, 176
Tucker, M, 172
Tunnel in the sky, 60
Turi's papa, 92
Turner, Philip, 56
Turtle net, The, 94
Twelve and the genii, The, 28
TWENTIETH CENTURY CLASSICS 133
Two little savages, 35, 55
Two sisters, The, 180
Two worlds of Damian, The, 98

Uchida, Yoshiko, 91
Uncle, 31
Underhill, Ruth M, 109
Underwater adventure, 48
Unesco Bulletin for Libraries, 208
Universe between, The, 61
Unnerstad, Edith, 90
Unreluctant years, The, 201, 210
Unwilling adventurers, The, 53, 170
Up with the Joneses, 75
Use of English, The, 32, 88, 112, 142, 172
Uttley, Alison, 191

Van Der Loeff, A. Rutgers, 47, 90, 91, 149, 150, 161
Van der Meulen, A. Moerkercken, 208
Various specs, 122
Verne, Jules, 58
Vicke the Viking, 114, 155
VIENNA, INTERNATIONAL INSTITUTE FOR CHILDREN'S LITERATURE, 149, 200, 205, 207
Viguers, Ruth Hill, 201, 203, 210
Viking's dawn, 107
Village that slept, The, 47
Vipont, Elfrida, 76, 83, 84, 85, 104, 123, 190
Virtue and delight, 198, 207
Visitors from London, 159
Voyage of the Dawn Treader, The, 26
De Vries, Leonard, 97

Walsh, Jill Paton, 101, 184
Walters, Hugh, 58
War dog, 170
Ward, R, 57
Warden's niece, The, 111
Water babies, The, 25
Watkins, T, 32
Way of danger, The, 18

Way of the story-teller, The, 12
Wayland's Keep, 74
Wayne, Jenifer, 70
We couldn't leave Dinah, 39, 159
Wear, W. H, 153
Weathermonger, The, 64
Web of Caesar, The, 54
Webb, Kaye, 125, 143
Webster, Jean, 133, 177
Wegehaupt, H, 208
Weirdstone of Brisingamen, The, 26, 32
Welch, Ronald, 104, 107, 108, 110, 164
Welcome to Mars, 59
Wells, H. G, 58
Wershba, Barbara, 184
West Indian folk tales, 20
Westwood, Gwen, 90
What Katy did, 67, 76, 131, 162
Wheel on the school, The 92
When jays fly to Barbmo, 93, 158
Where, 112
Whisper of Glocken, The, 24
Whistler, Rex, 14, 162
White, Dorothy Neal, 201, 210
White, Edward Lucas, 123
White horses and black bulls, 164
White mountains, The, 64
White Shirt, 95
Whitlock, Pamela, 39
Whitney, Elinor, 200
Who's who of children's literature, 204, 209
Widdershins Crescent, 71
Wild horse of Santander, The, 34
Wildcat under glass, 153
Wilder, Laura Ingalls, 67, 77
Wildsmith, Brian, 12, 163
Willard, Barbara, 42, 74, 77, 184
WILLIAM BOOKS, 140, 142
Williams, Ursula, Moray, 63
Williams-Ellis, Amabel, 13, 19, 65
Williamson, Henry, 36
Wilner, I, 77
Wilson, Barbara Ker, 192, 210
Wind in the willows, The, 32, 128, 144, 162
Windfall, 107

Windsor-Richards, A, 36
Wingate, John, 54
Winnie the Pooh, 31, 128, 130
Winter holiday, 55
Winter's tales for children, 124, 125
Witch of Blackbird Pond, The, 109, 158
Wolves of Willoughby Chase, The, 28
Wonder Book, A, 18
Wonderful adventure of Nils, The, 89
Wonderful wizard of Oz, The, 25
Wong, Jade Snow, 176
Wood, Anne, 204, 208, 210
Wood, Kenneth A, 206, 211
Wood, Lorna, 27
Woodfield, H. J. B, 201, 204
Woolpack, The, 105
Workhouse child, The, 111
World of animals, A, 37
World of children's literature, The, 202, 208
Worzel Gummidge, 117, 143
WREN BOOKS, 136
Wren, P. C, 145
Wrightson, Patricia, 63, 76, 77, 90, 155
Wrinkle in time, A, 64
Written for children, 203, 210
Wyndham, John, 49, 65, 178
Wyss, Johann, 149

Yates, W. E, 208
Yeoman, John, 114
Y. L. G. News, 187, 196, 208
Yolen, J, 176
Yonge, Charlotte, 66, 177
Young folks, 124
Young mother, 178, 182, 193
YOUNG PUFFINS, 146
YOUTH LIBRARIES GROUP, 197
Youth on the wing, 99

ZEBRA BOOKS, 144
Zei, Alki, 153
Zindel, Paul, 184
Zinkin, Taya, 20
Zoo on the first floor, 118